The Streets Of Gorbals Past

Danny Gill

Copyright © 2020 Danny Gill

All rights reserved, including the right to reproduce this book, or portions thereof in any form. No part of this text may be reproduced, transmitted, downloaded, decompiled, reverse engineered, or stored, in any form or introduced into any information storage and retrieval system, in any form or by any means, whether electronic or mechanical without the express written permission of the author.

The views expressed in this work are solely those of the author and do not necessarily reflect the views of the publisher, and the publisher hereby disclaims any responsibility for them.

Front cover photo:
St Francis Pipe band marching along
Cumberland St. circa 1959
Thanks to Charlie Molloy and family

ISBN: 9798647644671

PublishNation
www.publishnation.co.uk

Other books by Danny Gill which can be bought on Lulu.com and Amazon, either as a paperback or a Kindle e-book.

All proceeds from this book will be shared equally between:

The upkeep of the Southern Necropolis Graveyard on Caledonia Road in the Gorbals area of Glasgow; and

The Benny Lynch statue campaign.

My sincerest thanks to everyone who purchases this book.

Danny Gill
2020

- - - -

This book is dedicated to the memory of Gorbals lassie and my pal Cathy Byrne

R.I.E.P Cathy xx

Contents

Chapter 1 – Poems	1
Chapter 2 - Section 1 Gorbals street map	13
Chapter 3 – Bits and Pieces	38
Chapter 4 - Section 2 Gorbals street map	44
Chapter 5 - Gorbals People's Stories	83
Chapter 6 - Section 3 Gorbals street map	99
Chapter 7 – Topics	132
Chapter 8 - Section 4 Gorbals street map	143
Chapter 9 – People's snippets	178
Chapter 10 - Section 5 Gorbals street map	189
Chapter 11 – Gorbals People's Stories	235
Chapter 12 - Miscellaneous	246
Chapter 13 – Gorbals Bonus Story	256
Epilogue	283

Foreword

The Gorbals of today is so much different when it was just a cluster of huts centuries ago at "Brigend", Where is/was the Gorbals ? well it all depends what year or what decade or even what century you are talking about. For all intents and purposes the area of the Gorbals that I will be talking about in this book will be from 1900 - 1975.

The reason that I state these years are [1] from 1900 onwards the Gorbals with its two adjoining wings of Laurieston and Hutchesontown became widely accepted as the greater Gorbals area or just the Gorbals, so when someone mentioned the Gorbals it encompassed those three areas.

Easiest way for me to explain it is to compare it to the three leafed shamrock, three separate units but at the same time all the one unit. [2] As the year reached 1975 the "new builds" had outnumbered the old tenements, of course there were still lots of tenements about in 1975 but the majority were in a state of disrepair and awaiting to be demolished.

My book "The streets of Gorbals past" will be the afore mentioned area of Laurieston/Gorbals /Hutchesontown = the greater Gorbals area.

Meanwhile Oatlands is actually an appendage/off-shoot/connection of Hutchesontown and today officially is part of the Gorbals historical area. Easiest way to explain this is compare it to the map of the U.S.A. where you have the state of Florida which is connected to the mainland but yet is on its own "dangling in the water" with the Atlantic ocean one side of it and the Gulf of Mexico waters on the other side. Oatlands is the same, an off-shoot part of Hutchesontown but yet on its own.

So I always class Laurieston /Gorbals/Hutchesontown as the greater Gorbals area and Oatlands as the outer Gorbals area [well its not Springburn is it, lol]. Its up to or down to each person where they want the Gorbals area to be, I am just stating mine.

I have already had a book published about Oatlands called "Once upon a time in Glasgow's Oatlands" so this book "The streets of Gorbals past" deals with the greater Gorbals area.

As I previously stated the years that I will cover in this book will be from 1900 to 1975 but mainly the 1940's/50's and early 60's. I mean no disrespect at all to the good Gorbals people who were born or brought up in the "new builds" of Q.E.sq, Norfolk court, the Dampies etc, etc but it's that era of the old tenements that I wanted to capture in this book and maybe someday I or another author will write a book about the Gorbals "new builds" and that era that took the place of the old tenements.

I want to take you all on a walk down the streets of Gorbals of the old tenements, when we still had open coal fires, over 130 pubs and over a thousand shops and we shopped daily as we had no fridges in our tenement houses back then.

How can I take you on a walk down every street of Gorbals without trying to confuse you [and me !!], what I have done is divided my Gorbals street map into 5 sections, each section is in a different chapter and I start with a perimeter edge of that section be it 3 sided/4 sided or even 5 sided and once I have covered that perimeter edge I will then go into the perimeter edge and discuss first all the vertical streets form south to north and then the horizontal streets west to east.

No matter where you lived in the Gorbals your street will get a mention and hopefully [you may be named ?] you will recognize peoples names etc.

To go down every street just naming numbers from 1 to 299 etc could be a wee bit on the "tedious side" so what I have done is to try to bring the streets "to life" with peoples comments who lived on the streets, the names of shops, pubs names, schools, Churches, and every now and then I have inserted street map images to help us remember where the streets actually were.

I have also inserted other chapters including Gorbals people's story's, a few of my poems at the beginning of the book with photos. Chapters of topics, news - bits, peoples snippets, a miscellaneous chapter and a bonus chapter by a good friend of mine Alexander Neil at the end to encompass what life was like growing up in the Gorbals of the 1930's/40's for him.

Of course it was a near impossible job to try and place all the shops in their proper order and get them on the correct side of their streets, same with the pubs etc. So please forgive me if I have made any mistakes. I did try my utmost to get all the info correct but the Gorbals is such a vast area that I fear I have made the occasional error.

I do hope you enjoy the trip back down memory lane as much as I did when composing it, back to a time of "The streets of Gorbals past".

    When we had nothing but we had everything.

Acknowledgements

I owe a great debt of gratitude to all the great Gorbals people who came to my aid and sent me info of shops, pubs Church's etc, I remembered a fair bit but others I didn't and I could not have compiled this book with your great help. Some gave me more info than others and for that I am so grateful but everyone of you who went out of their way to assist me was a star and every piece of information was filed away, so many many thanks all my pals. There are really too many to mention but a big thanks to you one and all.

Also many thanks to the people who sent me in their personal photos to be included in my book, starting off in alphabetical order are = Tony Brannan, Cathy Byrne, Barbara Carroll, City of Glasgow archives, Helen Ann [nee Mortimer] Congalton, Carol Connelly, Daily Record, Cath Dorran, Betty Gillan/Gordon Smith, Glasgow district council, Eddie Graham, Frances Hogan, Duncan McCallum, Norrie McNamee, Charlie Molloy, Ann McLaughlin, Peter Mortimer, Allan Robertson, Brian O'Rourke, Urban Glasgow, Len Vine and Ann [nee Clark] Ward. Not forgetting Maggie McKay and Lorraine White who appear on the blurb on the back cover of my book.

A big thanks once again to Norrie McNamee who has helped me unstintingly with the collection of his photos for all of my books, he has never let me down once, many thanks Norrie.

Last but not least I have to thank David and Gwen at PublishNation for giving me another book to be proud of with answering all my questions and prompt replies. It does make a big difference when you get a publisher who cares about your book.

Chapter 1

Poems

Poem 1

The Auld Tin Bath

Who remembers getting washed in the sink or the old tin bath
At the time I felt like greetin but as I look back now I can laugh

I wid dread Sunday nights and the sound of that whistlin kettle
Because wae it's boiling watter Ma wid fill up that bath a metal

The auldest wean went in first, like thay were King o the Castle
Us younger weans had to wait oor turn, hating all o this Hassle

Well your Ma scrubbed you that hard that yer skin wid turn rid
People o my generation know this is the truth, I really dont kid

Drying yourself in front of the open fire, feelin good and sleek
Listenin to your siblings saying, Ma I had a bath only last week

But as you grew older, your life changed to being a bit dreamy
Cos yer Ma gave you money for a hoat bath in the old Steamie

Now I have a bathroom so enormous, it would give ye a Fright
But I'll never forget that auld tin bath, and every Sunday Night.

Who can ever forget that auld tin bath of zinc, whether it was a Friday night , Saturday or Sunday night that we used to dread coming along.

See it wasn't too bad if you were an only child but if you had brothers and sisters and you were the youngest then you would be last to go in and the water was clatty by that time.

Oh thank the Lord that when I got older [about 11 years old] my Ma used to give me the money to go to the nearby Steamie and I would have the magic experience of having a hot bath and it was in a proper bath.

No more tin baths for me on a Sunday night, it was great going to the Steamie and I really looked forward to it every Friday when I came home from school. I would pay for my hot bath at the window on the ground floor of the Steamie, get my carbolic soap and a very thin towel and away upstairs to sit on a wooden bench until the attended shouted out my turn.

Of course we don't go through all that rigmarole nowadays as we have our own indoor bath or shower and yes we take it all for granted now, but just think back of how it used to be living in the old tenements [although some tenements were lucky to have an inside bath].

I tell my grandweans here in London what their Granda had to used to do to have a hot bath and they look on in sheer amazement.

Although I will never forget that auld tin bath on a Sunday night.

Poem 2

Benny Lynch

Glasgow has given us Famous People, names too many to repeat.
I'll mention one called Benny Lynch, born in 17 Florence-Street.

Born in the Gorbals, when the auld tenements were still a standing.
Benny entered the Boxing with his daily training oh so demanding.

As a Flyweight Benny was Brilliant, he'd never let the fans down.
Going to Manchester, beating Jackie Brown for the World Crown.

Glasgow and Scotland sang his praise, yes Benny he was our King.
Watching him with pride, beating his opponents in the boxing ring.

So when Benny's career was over, he abdicated his Boxing Throne.
With his biggest fight out of the ring, he faced Demons of his own.

And Benny's Fans all over this Planet, hold him with terrific Pride.
His name now lives on forever, in the Gorbals area of the Soo-Side.

In Benny's memory we want a statue of him Erected and Unfurled.
Benny Lynch fae the Gorbals was Boxing Champion of the Wurld.

Like other fine champions, Benjamin John Lynch was born impoverished, on April 2, 1913 in an area of Glasgow known as the Gorbals. It was built to house the hordes of immigrants, mainly Irish but also Eastern Europeans, working in the industrial areas of Glasgow. The Gorbals was chronically overcrowded, with many families living in just the one room with a kitchen off to the side. Some of these families had up to ten children. The room would be part of a tenement block where several families would co-exist on one crowded block. Benny's block was home to fourteen families. His family life, like the lives of many in the area, was dysfunctional. His father John took heavily to the drink and Benny's mum, Lizzie, succumbed to the attentions of another man. When she left to set up home with another fellow, Benny and his brother were packed off to live with an uncle and aunt and their seven children in another one room, one kitchen dwelling. Benny loved his time with his new family. His auntie was a dab hand in the kitchen and the home, if it could be called a home, was always filled with joy and laughter despite the privations.

Benny's great fortune was finding a manager who was like a brother, father and mother rolled into one. Sammy Wilson was not your typical avaricious manager who manipulated and fleeced his charge. He was a successful street bookmaker and held in high esteem by the men of the area. Being a former boxer of some standing himself, he understood what it took to make a mark in the sport. Sammy knew that nothing could build stamina like running, not your flat-track running but hill running to build up the legs so that when the fifteenth bell rings you can jump up off the stool still full of energy. Of the fight game. It was better to hit than be hit.

And Benny sure knew how to hit and hit hard for a small man he could hit his weight 3 times over so it was said.
Benny's boxing record spoke for itself and also he became Scotland's first ever world champion boxer which lay the door open for others later.

Poem 3

Twomax

In this knitwear factory in the soo-side women toiled with cotton and flax.
'Twas founded by 2 Macs, Mr McLure+McIntosh, shortening it to Twomax.

From every street in the Gorbals oor women worked hard every single day.
Others came from Kinning park or Oatlands , which wasn't all that far away.

We all knew someone who worked there, a relation or maybe a neighbour.
And those wummin diddny half earn their pay with all of their daily labour.

Workers all headed for Rutherglen Rd, to get into work by the factory horn.
Some of them came from Florence street, where oor Benny Lynch wiz born.

Makin fashion knitwear for Marks n Spencer, C+A and shops over the Toon.
Until the demand for it's clothing collapsed, and sadly Twomax closed doon.

No more a knitwear factory, it changed to housing allocation to get folk cosy.
Women hoping to get new housing opposite weans were playin in the Rosie.

Another part of Glasgow/Gorbals history ends Twomax is now sadly forlorn.
Hoping my Gorbals poem keeps alive this memory to a generation yet unborn.

Who will ever forget Twomax's knitwear factory on Rutherglen rd it was a place of employment for thousands of women over the years and my own big sister worked in there as her first job after leaving school.

This old mill survived the wholesale clearance of the 50's and 60's and is now a "B" listed building.

It was built as a cotton spinning mill between 1816-21 and is the oldest surviving iron framed mill in the city and possibly in Scotland.

Its first proprietor was Robert Humphreys who was succeeded by Robert Thomson. The mill probably ceased spinning some time in the 1860s
And was subsequently used by various clothing manufactures for almost a century.

It has been used as converted offices and some studio accommodation and later as a housing accommodation to try and get people housed.

All the women who worked in it when it was Twomax's worked long hard shifts and then went home to make dinner for their husbands and children.

It was also common for a "menage" sounds like "minaudge" which was a money club, where a certain amount of women chipped in with money every pay-day and every 3 months or so each one got the amount of money paid in by all as their "turn" which really helped.

The person who ran the "minaudge" got a "free week".

Poem 4

Cumberland Street

The Toon had Argyle and Sauchiehall street, to buy yourself a treat
But nothing could compare with all the shops in Cumberland street.

Having Saint Francis Chapel + the Paragon picture hoose next door.
A flea ridden cinema whose hard benches made your bum very sore.

Butchers, bakers and linen shops canny name a shop that wasn't there.
Quinn the barbers where a bowl got put oer ma heid as he cut my hair.

Passing by Lawmoor police station, and the Polis were all tough cops.
But I never gave it a second glance, I was too busy lookin in the shops.

A Pub was on every corner, fur a man to swally a pint and a wee dram.
Women were oot for the messages, while pushin their wean in a pram.

I'll never forget all those shops, walking wae my Ma and wee Granny.
As they tried to spot a bargain, us soo-siders were known to be canny.

Those Gorbals shops were better than Sauchiehall st, in my estimation.
Now they're a thing of the past just like Cumberland st railway station.

Cumberland street circa mid-1950's.

What a wonderful place Cumberland street was, just look at all the shops on either side of the street, and always so busy. Plenty of people going for their messages, remember in those days people never had fridges in their tenement houses, so meat and perishables had to be bought on a daily basis otherwise they would go "off" and it was common to see people leave their milk on the window ledge overnight to keep it from turning sour. I absolutely loved walking along Cumberland st and looking in all the many many shop windows, I would go with my Ma and wee Granny but as I grew older I was allowed to go there on my own. People although busy doing their daily shop would always bump into neighbours and exchange local news [gossip ha ha] in fact this is how we got the saying "going for the messages" we would go to get shopping but exchange "messages" with neighbours when we met them. Everybody else in Scotland goes for groceries but we Glaswegians go "for the Messages". Remember in the 1950's when the photo above was taken we had no television sets [only the very odd person would have one] or mobile phones or lap tops to get the news, so we had to rely on the local news by word of mouth from friends we met in the street, or get back home and turn the radio on to hear what was happening in the World. My best memories of the Gorbals was walking along Cumberland st back then.

Chapter 2

Section 1 of my Gorbals street map

From Eglinton toll - going down Eglinton st then reaching Cumberland st, going along it then coming to Pollokshaws rd and going along it and back up to Eglinton toll with all streets in between.

Let me take you back to the time when the auld tenements were still standing, back to a time when we had that close knit community spirit we all shared, we might not have had much money but what we had we shared. Back to a time when life seemed so less stressful than today's rushing about, back to a time when us weans would play our street games under the watchful guidance of our parents and neighbours who done their "windae hingin" and kept an eye on us weans.

Back to a time when we still lit the old coal fire every morning and dumped last nights ashes in the back court midden, then our growing up attending school then leaving school getting a job, having a drink in the many pubs that were in the Gorbals back then in the day or going to the dancing but always coming back to our tenement building which was our home be it a room and kitchen or a single end, this is that era that I am taking you back to when people seemed to have more time for each other.

Unfortunately with the demolition of the tenements and as we moved out to the housing schemes and maybe further afield we lost that close knit community spirit but our memories still burn bright as we remember those days when "We had nothing but we had everything".

So lets take a walk and rekindle those days of the streets of Gorbals past.

We will always travel in the south to north direction, that's Eglinton toll to the river Clyde and west to east, Eglinton st to Shawfield stadium direction.

Eglinton st, West side.

We will start with the west side of Eglinton st and the Maxwell arms pub, which was number 679 at the corner of Maxwell rd/Eglinton st, I clearly remember it but sadly I never popped into it to have a beer [it was usually the Star bar for me] there was a Dentist above here and his name was Mr Gummer, yes honestly, what a name for a Dentist eh!!!. You had a small number of shops beside the Maxwell arms about six in total and one of these was a barbers shop and a wee guy called Frank used to cut my hair in there, he was under five feet tall and used to have a wee kind of platform to stand on as he worked but he was a good barber, there was also a newsagents shop in this small parade of shops and a bakers called McKechnies at the back.

Margaret Herd,
"I came from Cavendish st and went to get freshly baked rolls in the mornings. Where these shops ended you had a Pend/lane which led you through to this bakery shop".

Then on walking along a wee bit we came to Cardwell st [formerly Lillybank st] which had tenements there numbering 3 to 21 on the south side and only number 24 to 28 on the north side.

Just past here you had a piece of "spare grun" and here Arnold Clark the car firm had cars on display and for sale with the prices on their windows.

Many a time I looked at these cars for sale as I was travelling on the bus into the Toon for work but I never ever saw anybody looking at the cars or talking to a salesman.

Then after this we come to Gourock st [formerly Lillybank rd] which only had one tenement there with close numbers 26 and 20.

Then we continue along Eglinton st and at the corner of 614 Eglinton st we had Arnold Clark's car showroom, actually part of the tenements from number 614 to 590 were the last standing tenements designed by the architect Alexander "Greek" Thomson there was another short tenement building abutting to number 590 but it was designed by another architect and did not look a patch on Thomson's tenements.

These tenements ended at what was called Lauder st and at this gable end junction we also had another car space belonging to McKenzie's motors and this is where Lauder st stood, he had cars of his placed at the "spare grun" adjacent to the gable end of the tenement.

In between Arnold Clark's and McKenzie's car shops/spaces you had about eight shops, one being McLaughlin's licensed betting office, Conroys shop, a saw service shop, a shop called Cryptos and a few others with a newsagents shop right at the gable end.

There were only 3 numbered tenements in Lauder st south side which were 3, 5 and 7.

With only 2 numbers on the opposite side at the corner of Lauder st and Eglinton st which was number 2 Lauder st and the return elevation of the tenement standing at 450 Eglinton st.

There were no more tenements at this point in Eglinton st as we had the Caledonian railway line leading into the Central station in the Toon.

At one time we had an Eglinton st railway station at 580 Eglinton st but this has long been closed now [closed 1965.] As we progress down the West side of Eglinton st we come to Kilbirnie st [once Crawford st] which could took us into the areas of Plantation/Tradeston and Kinning park.

Then we travel onwards down the West side of Eglinton st and we come to Cumberland st on the opposite side. Now then we travel back up Eglinton st till we come to the Star bar and then we work our way back down Eglinton st but this time on the east side until we come to Cumberland st.

Eglinton st, east side.

The photo above is of the Star bar. [note St Andrews cross inscribed in the stone work just above the first floor window at the gushet.]

The Star bar has many memories for me as I used to get the bus there at the weekend, have a drink or two, [Dougie was the manager back then in the late 60's] and then over to McNees pub for a few more and off to the Plaza dance hall to tread on the toes of all the poor lassies.

Above the Star bar we had another Dentist and his name was Mr Leighton. If you look closely above the gushet [V shaped junction] at the Star bar you will see the name "St Andrews cross" engraved into the stonework as this is the official name of the crossing although most people including myself always called it Eglinton toll.

Cecilia Murray,
"My Name is Cecilia Murray and I remember one occasion when I went to the Star Bar with a friend.

We both had very young children and nights out were usually visiting each other's flats and having a few drinks. This was 1967 and the usual routine was that the men went for a pint and brought back a "cairry oot". Well we got a bit fed up with this and told them that we were going out and would bring back the booze.

We went to the Star and had such a good time blethering that we didn't notice the time.

Pubs closed about 9.30 I think. Totally panicking we begged them to sell us the alcohol but to no avail. That was the last time we did that"!!!!

Above the Star bar tenement building on the roof you had a "drying green area" for women to dry their clothes and what a view there must have been from so high up.

Next to the Star bar tenement building and moving along we had this large Garage and I believe there was tyre vulcanising work done in there [?], we pass by Gourock st and come to the tenements numbered 491 to 433 in Eglinton st east side.

Now at 491 we had the usual 4 storey high tenement [I say 4 high as we had low doon, 1 up, 2 up and 3 up landings] but next to it we only had ground floor and one floor above with tenement dwellings and that was owned by the Caledonian railway company.

The ground floor consisted of a parade of shops including a doctors surgery, carpet retailer shop, a fine art gallery shop and a licensed grocer's called Sproule's at the junction of Eglinton st and Turriff st.

Then passing by Turriff st we come to numbers 429 to 355 which was a fine row of tenements known as "Queens park terrace" and was the work of architect Alexander "Greek" Thomson. It has been said it was his finest work by many people. It was a beautiful looking row of tenements and there was great anger when this row of tenements was demolished in the early 80's with many people protesting against its demolition but the demolisher's sadly won.

At number 429 we had the Gordon bar which **Peter Thomson** used, saying it was a tiny wee pub but sold hot Scotch pies and peas and had a great pint of beer. Now at the other end of the tenement at number 355 we had the Devon bar, and in between the Gordon bar and Devon bar on the ground floor we had lots of shops including Cymon's textiles, Dollar Rae the shop-fitting outfit, a newsagents a dairy and many other regular shops.

Now The Devon bar was situated at the corner of Devon st and Eglinton st, crossing over Devon st to the opposite corner of it we had the Eglinton Congregational Church [later becoming the Christian science Church] and beside this we had another wee row of shops including a dairy, grocers and a used car shop called "City car company" which abutted onto the "Errigal View" public house previously known as "The Cathkin bar" and "The Rendezvous bar". I remember having a few drinks in it when it was the Rendezvous, it had a great games room with three dartboards and a couple of tables for domino players oh and a great pint of Guinness. !!!.

Moving on we pass by Cavendish st where the Errigal bar stood at its corner with Eglinton st and now come to a row of tenements stretching from Cavendish st to Wellcroft place numbered 307 to 241. With **Isabella Eileen Henriques** being born in number 287 Eglinton st.

At the corner of Cavendish st/Eglinton st we had a very large shop frontage for Premier shop fitter's designs and it went on for a good length down Eglinton st with other shops alongside including Johnstone's Bakery shop, Mrs Kelties grocery shop [you got "tic"in there] John Kelly's newsagents then a glass merchants, then "the puzzle pend" and another lane next to the pend, then an engineering company shop and another shop [?] which then took us to a Wholesale warehouseman stationery shop at the very corner where Wellcroft place stood at the corner with Eglinton st .- [Its worth noting that in the middle of this row of tenements there was an open space leading to workshops in the back courts].

Then at the other side of Wellcroft place we had the Office public house [formerly McAllisters] which had a good darts team in the 1960's and 70's.

David Craig,
"Tells me that he, Tam Baird, Jim Marshall, Tam Robertson, Billy Baird, George McGinley etc were all part of that darts team".

While **Les Docherty** from Caledonia rd worked as a barman in the Office bar at this time of the darts team, he was also a grocer for the Co-op in Norfolk st, sadly he has passed away now.

One of the things that stuck in my mind was that in the Office pub it had a sign outside the toilets, Fox's for men and Vixien's for the ladies and of course at the gents [Fox's] there was a bit of a step down, which you tended to forget after a good few swally's. My pal **Pat Holland** can verify that !!

The photo shows the Office bar and the entrance into Wellcroft place.

Danny Goodwin
"Has told me that he remembers Peter O'Keefe running the Office pub at the time he drank in there. Then just along from the Office bar you had the Kiloran bar which was a great wee cosy pub and you always got a friendly greeting. Of course in between the Office and Kiloran pubs there stood a Health shop".

I have to say that when I finished work for the day I would sometimes go to the Granite city pub to have a drink with my work mate Jimmy Currie who lived across the streets in the new build houses at the start of Pollokshaws rd. [which I believe were originally planned for police officers+families].

Anyway I would have a couple of pints with Jimmy and then make my way along to Eglinton st to catch the 48 bus back to South Nitshill [where we moved to after the back of our tenement had collapsed in 1961].

I would stand at the bus stop outside the Kiloran and say to myself, right I'll have another pint before my bus comes, but back in those days we had no smart phones with bus time alerts to tell us when the next bus was coming, so I had to have a drink of my pint and keep "keeking" out the door to see if my 48 bus was in sight.

If I saw it coming then I would try and quickly finish my pint but sometimes I wasn't quick enough and the bus went passing by and had to wait till the next bus came along and I had no more money to buy another pint !!!. Not like today when we have bank cards and just swipe them on the pubs card reader, back then hardly anyone had a bank account.

Cumberland st, south side.

Now we come to Bulloch's Licensed grocer shop at the corner of 215 Eglinton st/Cumberland st and as we move along Cumberland st, next to Bullochs we had a few shops including The Highland school of motoring, a French polishers, Miss Muffets bakery shop, an Orange hall and farther along I believe we had a bookmakers shop.

Then Masons groceries shop and a Teachers public house at number 90 Cumberland st/Salisbury st.

Eddie Graham tells me,
"Mrs Mason and her family lived up our close at 84 Cumberland Street next door to my Uncle Archie and Auntie Phyllis Graham.

Above is a photo of a great Gorbals man and friend of mine, Eddie Graham, who has a tremendous amount of knowledge of the Gorbals area.

My mother just like all the other Mothers around that area of Cumberland Street got their messages from Mrs Mason's shop and she gave us tic for our groceries. She was a great women and well liked by everyone in our family.

She owned both shops in either side of out close between Salisbury Street at Teachers Pub and Abbotsford lane.

The close numbers on this section of Cumberland st were numbers 4 next to Bullochs to number 128, then we turned right into Pollokshaws rd and go heading back up towards Eglinton toll.

Pollokshaws rd, west side.

Pollokshaws rd started at number 2 west side and ended at the Star bar which was number 302.

Going along Pollokshaws rd as I say we had tenements starting at number 2 and finishing at 30 where it met with Surrey st. Going past Surrey st we pass Surrey lane.

Then we came to 60 and 72 Pollokshaws rd which was the Cavendish bar at number 72 and opposite the Cavendish bar we had the Abbotsford Chalmers Church on the opposite corner of Cavendish st situated at 98/100/102 Pollokshaws rd, then more or less "spare grun" then we had the frontage of the Abbotsford primary school.

Then we come to Devon st and at number 134 on the corner of Pollokshaws rd and Devon st we had the Mill Inn pub and a row of tenement dwellings till we came to the Glen bar at number 190 Pollokshaws rd and the junction of Turriff st, this was **Jim Todd's** local pub as he lived right next to it.

I would like to add that in between the Mill Inn and Glen bar we had an opening that allowed access to workshops at the back of this row of tenements.

It was quite common back in the day of the old tenement back courts to have workshops/outhouses which brought in more rent revenue to the "greedy factors" whom were more concerned in gathering extra capital than carrying out repair works to tenements and workhouses alike and this added to the rundown of the tenements in general.

Authors note,
If only the factors had carried out proper maintenance work on the tenements, we could have had tenement dwellings that could quite easily been refurbished rather than been left to

"fester" with raw sewage rife and rats running around. [I'm not saying all the tenements mind you].

The photo underneath shows the Mill Inn on Pollokshaws rd/Devon st. On the opposite side of Pollokshaws rd we have the printing works which was once part of the massive St Andrews cross electrical works.

Going past Turriff st we had the unemployment office right on the corner and then numbers 202 to 250 Pollokshaws rd took us to Gourock st.

Of course at number 220 Pollokshaws rd we had the Cockatoo public house where **Charlie Savage** a bus driver at Larkfield bus garage drank, one time owners of the Cockatoo were "**Big Eamon** and **John Mack**".

Ann Rawden Quinn's Da drank in there too. Of course now at Gourock st we had that large tyre vulcanising garage at 292 and the Star bar at number 302.

Pollokshaws rd, east side.

Going back down to the other side of Pollokshaws rd to the east side we go back down to the bottom and at the corner of Cathcart rd /Pollokshaws rd we had a public lavatory, actually back in those days we had quite a lot of public street lavatories which were a God send to bus drivers and pedestrians if we ever needed the urge.

So leaving the lavatory and heading up Pollokshaws rd again we have a mass of railway sidings/workings and we don't have any tenement buildings till about opposite Devon st, where we have numbers 159 to number 191 and it was here that 191 abutted to the printing works at 197 In the middle of these tenements we had a passageway allowing access for horses and carts to the small workshops at the back of the tenements.

We also had a few shops in between 159 - 191 a newsagents and a grocers as far as I can make out.

Danny MacKay,
"I was born at 180 Pollokshaws Rd. Just opposite Glasgow Corporation Print Works - during WW-2 there was an underground air raid shelter where all the neighbours gathered during the blitz - it would be interesting to know if this shelter still exists ?

Alex Horsley owned the car showroom, Peter Keenan did not own any pub in the area - his pub was in Broomielaw and he was a personal friend of mine - another famous boxer lived opposite - Jackie Patterson.

The pub on the corner of Turriff St was The Glen owned by Chas Douglas.

The pub on the corner of Devon St was the Mill Inn and The Cockatoo bar was just up from Turriff St. There was a lane between Turriff St & Devon St where there was a cooperage & a tyre vulcaniser garage.

Of course at Eglinton Toll there was The Star Bar where we all met on a Tuesday before going to The Plaza Dance Hall - happy days".

Then when these tenements ended we had the printing works which was a part of what was that mighty St Andrews works, built and completed in 1900 for the Glasgow Corporation Electricity company but in the late 1930's part of it was converted into the print works for the Corporation.

We will now deal with all the [vertical] streets heading south to north as in the Star bar to Cumberland st direction whilst keeping in mind some of these streets will not terminate at Cumberland st but continue as I move onto section 2 of my Gorbals street map

MacKinlay st, west side/east side

MacKinlay st is the first street we come to and on the west hand side, we had a run of tenement dwellings numbers 70 to 4.

On the opposite side of MacKinlay st we had numbers 51 to 11 with the small Elgin st U.P Church [junction with Turriff st] so at number 51 Mackinlay st stood this Church and tenements in between it until we came to number 11 which had a large hall abutting to it and this then brought us to Devon st.

Katy McHaghney,
"I lived in MacKinlay st and said I remember nearby we had Leonard's shop with Mick Keatings shop next to it. One day my Ma sent me to Mr Keating's shop to ask for "tic" and she told her Ma that he had said sorry "no tic", young Katy was actually too embarrassed to ask for the "tic". Katy's Ma pulled up Mick Keating in the street only to be told that Katy was lying" !!!

Cavendish place.

Next we come to Cavendish place which as far as I can make out was an open passageway which abutted against the back of Johnston's bakery building [which had its entrance via Wellcroft place and Cumberland lane.]

Cumberland lane, west side/east side.

Actually Cumberland lane was a cul-de-sac, it had a couple of dwellings there and was accessible from Wellcroft place, you had Johnston's bakery building on the west side [with 1 dwelling] and on the east side you had numbers 41 and 33 but it came to a dead end.

It has been said that World champion boxer Benny Lynch lived here for a while.

Abbotsford place, west side.

Then we come to Abbotsford place west side starting at numer134 to 46.
Now the Four ways public house stood at number 134 and travelling down to the junction with Cavendish st at number 100, we cross over Cavendish st and carry on along Abbotsford place starting again at at number 92.

Then at number 86 Abbotsford place we had the Rising sun/Hole in the wall public house ran by Mr Clancy senior, [his two sons John and James Clancy have ran a few pubs themselves and to this present day as I write they run the Laurieston bar in Bridge st in the Gorbals.]

There were more tenements after Mr Clancy's pub and they ended at number 46 which then became the corner of Cumberland st.
At the junction of Abbotsford place/Cumberland st at number 46 Abbotsford place we had offices belonging to John

Crawford & Co [Plumbers] Ltd on the ground floor and directly beneath it in the basement was Taylor's Laboratories.

Abbotsford place, east side.

As we travel back up Abbotsford place and on the opposite side the east side we had Abbotsford place primary school at 131 with the Janitors house next to it at and at 129 an additional building next to the janitors which I believe was the infants school.

Then we cross over Cavendish st and carry on down Abbotsford place tenements until we come to the junction with Cumberland st at number 49.

George MacNamara lived with his family at number 79 Abbotsford place, and says "most of his brothers worked at the Barras" over the Clyde in the Gallowgate.

Catherine Orozco
"I also lived in Abbotsford place and used to go to Mary Perry's sweetie shop [I think it was off of Cavendish st ?] and I loved the penny tray.

My Ma used to use Masons dairy every day for her messages, she would write everything in a little book with the date on the top of the page and Mr or Mrs Mason would write the prices down beside each item and total it at the bottom of each page.

Come a Friday my Ma would go to the shop and pay her weekly "tic" Mr and Mrs Mason were such nice people".

Abbotsford lane west side/east side.

Then next we come to Abbotsford lane which ran from Cavendish st to Cumberland st [**before it continued on after we cross Cumberland st which is my next section of the Gorbals street map**].

In this section of Abbotsford lane west side we had a few dwellings numbers 128 to 96.

On the opposite side the east side of Abbotsford lane we had the return elevation of tenements from Cavendish st showing at the beginning of the lane and as we go along we pass by the back end of a garage/workshop with its entrance in Salisbury st, **[see it in the street map]** and one tenement dwelling number 91 until we reach the end of Abbotsford lane showing the return elevation of tenements that stood in Cumberland st and at that point we find ourselves in Cumberland st.

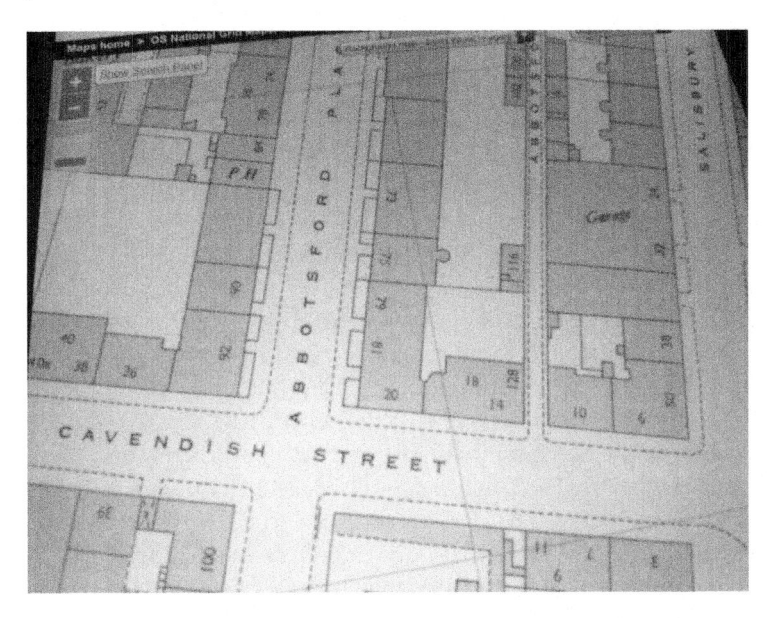

The photo above shows the back of the garage in Abbotsford lane.

Salisbury st, west side/east side.

Next we had Salisbury st starting at number 50 west side and running down to number 2, at number 32 to 24 you had a large garage/workshop with all the other buildings as tenement dwellings.

On the opposite side you had the Cavendish bar at number 71 east side and then a row of tenement dwellings leading us down to number 1 and then Salisbury st ended at Cumberland st but continued in the same line after crossing over Cumberland st but it then became Nicholson st.

Surrey lane, west side/ east side

Then moving on next we have Surrey lane with numbers 172 to 158 west side, after 158 it was just all open ground down to Cumberland st.

Then on the opposite side east side, we had numbers 129 to 119 with open space again, there may have been another dwelling after that but the line of the railway bridge hides that [if any] on the digital street map that I use.

Surrey st, west side/east side.

Then next we had Surrey st with numbers 74 to 52 tenement dwellings west side [once again the railway line on my digital map obscures any other dwelling if any] and dwellings 141 to 129 on the opposite side east side, where I believe A. Ritchie had a workshop/garage, then next a bootmakers and then Andrew Renfrew a building demolisher had an office.

Which brings us now to Cumberland st but Surrey st does continue over Cumberland st in the next section of my Gorbals street map.

Mae Munro,
"I lived at number 56 Surrey st with brother Johnny and sister Peggy, we all went to Abbotsford school. I have great memories of V.E. day, I also remember Masons shop".

Alan Yates Lived at number 50 Surrey st.

So now we have finished with the [vertical streets] running south to north we come to the [horizontal streets] running west to east in my first Gorbals map section.

Gourock st, south side/north side.

We first of all have Gourock st [formerly Lillybank st] with that large garage abutting onto the Star bar on the south side, on the opposite side north side we had only a tiny row of tenement dwellings with a furniture shop at the corner of Gourock st/Eglinton st.

This part of Gourock street ran between Eglinton st and Pollokshaws rd. [a very short distance.]

Turrif st, south side.

Moving down we next come to Turriff st which was formerly called Elgin st.

We had numbers 2 to 12 south side and number 12 was the Castle bar [formerly the Balmoral bar] and above the old Balmoral bar once was a pawn shop named the "Elgin street loan co", [and over the years what a blessing the pawn shop was to our Ma's if they ran out of money to put a dinner on the kitchen table for her family.]

Next to that we had Hutchesontown's grammar school for girls until it was taken over in 1912 and became a Jewish school. Right beside this you had the Labour exchange office or the "Bru" as we used to call it and operated as such from 1918 until the 1970's when it was demolished.

Turrif st, north side.

On the opposite side of Turriff st the north side you had the Glen bar at the corner with Pollokshaws rd, a hall next to the Glen bar and then the Elgin st U.P Church at the corner of Turriff st/MacKinlay st then crossing over MacKinlay st you had tenement dwellings numbered 15 to number 1 which was the Gordon bar at the junction with Eglinton st.

Devon st, south side.

Moving on we next come to Devon st with numbers 41 to 5 at the south side, we had the Devon bar at the corner with Eglinton st /Devon st and as we moved along in between numbers 33 to 39 we had a Pend allowing access into work shops in the back courts.

Remembering that there was a stable for horses in Devon st in one of the Pends. Crossing over MacKinlay st we came to number 9 and 7 Devon st where there stood a large hall, then passing number 3 dwelling we come to the Mill inn public house at the junction of Devon st /Pollokshaws rd.

Shelia McGee,
"Eddie Benson newsagent in Eglinton St... Eddie was so nice... Beside the fruit shop owned by a lovely lady whose name I can't remember.. Beside it the chippie... I worked there for years when I was a student.

Frank and Mcael Vettraino and their granny who always gave me into a row for giving out too many chips and she was always fighting in Italian with the two sons... Happy days there.

Then in Devon Street was it Mr Toward's dairy... Remember going in for pint milk.. Quarter of spam etc... Always a big queue... He was a wee fat man with red face and wore a white coat... Again I remember the friendliness of everyone...

Beside him was Leonard's newsagents it was a real dark shop and I remember Leonard as a old wizened man... I lived in Devon street... I've a few other stories if you want them... And good luck with the book".

Devon st, north side.

On the opposite side the north side we had at Devon st/Abbotsford place - Abbotsford primary school which could be classed as number 4 Devon st and then we had the four-ways pub at the corner of Abbotsford place and Devon st.

The Fourways pub was number 6 Devon st and we had tenement dwellings along until number 34 and next to that we had a Pend leading to buildings in the back and next to this Pend we had the Congregational Church which later became the Christian Science Church and stood at the corner of Devon st/Eglinton st.

Linda Duncan,
"I remember Leonard's newsagents in Devon st he used to put his L initial on his bottle of Irn Bru bottles, when I went in to buy them and he knew if the initial was forged on any other returns, I can a remember that initial very well because he always done it a certain way, I tried it a couple of times myself but never got away with it Lol. I stayed at 5 Cavendish place".

Cavendish st, south side.

Next street running west to east was Cavendish st, at the corner at Cavendish st /Eglinton st we had the Errigal view pub at number 57 Cavendish st south side with "spare grun" next to it then we come to numbers 41 and 39 and there was a Pend there allowing access to workshops in the back.

We cross over Abbotsford place and continuing along Cavendish st we now pass by the infant section of Abbotsford school and we have tenement numbers 11, 9, 7 and 3 . Actually number 3 was the Abbotsford Chalmers Parish Church. [Pollokshaws rd]

Cavendish st,north side.

While on the opposite side of Cavendish st north side we had a row of tenements whose numbers were 60 to number 2. [Cavendish bar]

From number 60 we had tenements 60,58,56, and 54 with a big open space [crossing Cavendish place] then numbers 48 to 36 and here we had tenements ending at Abbotsford place.

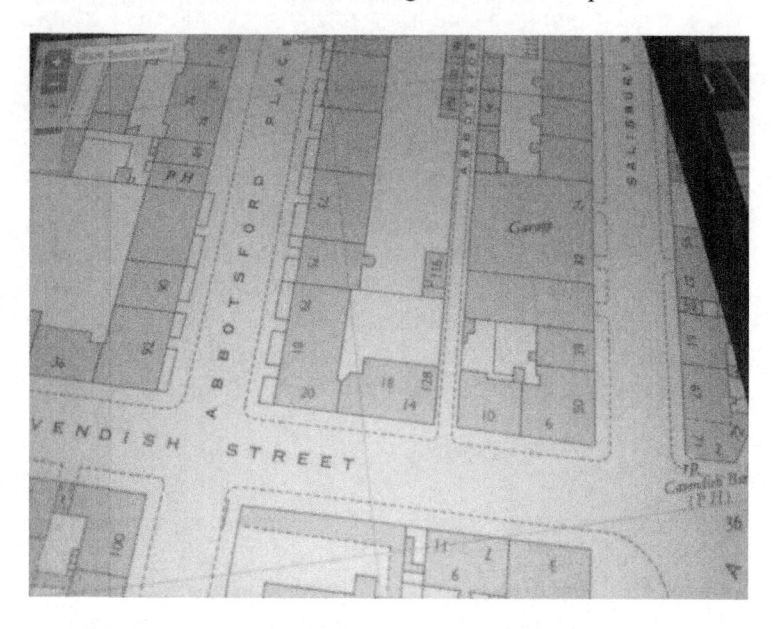

Photo above shows Cavendish street left to right numbers, 60 - 2 and Cavendish bar extreme right at number 2.

So crossing over Abbotsford place we continue along Cavendish st with number 20, 18 and 14 tenement dwellings [crossing Abbotsford lane] numbers 10 and 6 [crossing Salisbury st] and finally number 2 Cavendish st which was the Cavendish bar.

Wellcroft place.

Then the last [horizontal] street we have in this first section of my Gorbals street map was Wellcroft place which I actually discussed earlier in my streets running south to north, this is where we had Ritchie's haulage yard/office and Johnston's bakery and near to it was Johnston's paint-works and not forgetting Cumberland lane which ran down the side of the Bakery. The famous cyclist **Robert Miller** [came 4th in the tour de France race in 1984] **Margaret Sanderson** and **Rosie Sleigh** were all born here in Wellcroft place.

This is the end of section 1 of my Gorbals street map.

- - - -

Author's summing up of section 1

Well folks that is section 1 of my map of "The streets of Gorbals past" finished, I hope you have followed the way I tried to lay the streets out, it wasn't an easy job but its the only way I could have done it.

You will probably have noticed that some pub names have changed over the years that's why I tried to keep it in the decades of the 1940's/ 1950's and early 1960's. Street names have also changed so once again I tried to keep them as the most updated ones [that I knew in the 50's and 60's.]

Oh how the face of the Gorbals area has changed over the years, people of my generation [I'm 72 now] will remember it the way I have laid it out, whilst people of a younger generation born in the Gorbals in the 1970's + and later will be more in tune with all the new build houses rather than the old tenements that my generation was brought up in.

Its good that people now living in the greater Gorbals areas all have inside toilets, bathrooms etc and some with back gardens too but to me the auld tenements with all their wrongs was our hame.

My belief was and is that lots of the tenement buildings and those fine Churches/Chapels/Synagogues/Schools etc etc, could have been saved and refurbished but the "order " from the authorities above was flatten the Gorbals and when they did that they took away that wonderful close knit community spirit that we all shared and loved, plus the lack of repair work "not carried" out by greedy "factors" led to some of our tenements to become completely run down.

Some people will say you are looking through "rose-tinted glasses" when you describe the tenements as good places to live but that's exactly what they were - they were great places to live, you only had to look at the pristine net curtains hanging from the tenement windows, the pride that women took of washing the stairs every week [taking weekly turns] the friendliness of all the people.
Sure there were a few "bampots" but you get them in every area of every large city.

No, overall our upbringing in the greater Gorbals area was one of being happy and the vast majority of people were hard working and honest people. We might not have had much money but what we had we shared. What a wonderful childhood us as weans had while growing up, playing all our street games and as I say we had that close knit community spirit which sadly disappeared as we moved out to the new housing schemes and only people who actually lived through that era of our generation will know what I mean and this is what I have tried to re-live with us all as I take us all on a trip back to "The streets of Gorbals past".

Not that I'm saying there isn't a community spirit in the "new builds" area of the Gorbals today but it will never ever be as that way it was in my generation.

The photo above shows Alexander "Greek" Thomson's iconic Church at the top of Hospital st/Cathcart rd. [very bottom of the photo to the left an inch in] and you can also make out old Gorbals cross at the very top right hand side of the photo.

This photo is the personification of the Gorbals area that people of my generation will readily remember and identify with.

Chapter 3

Bits and Pieces

The Star bar

This pub used to be called "The Quadrivium Bar" in later Latin translated to "as where the four roads meet". It used to be a great place to have a quick drink before heading over to the Plaza dance hall and for years had a great 3 course dinner menu and very reasonable priced.

The hoat peanut man

Who remembers leaving the Gorbals swimming baths or maybe the Palace picture hoose and walking along Cleland st to under the railway bridge where Mr Checkman had his wee shop, selling hoat peanuts, toffee apples, home made tablet and lots of other sweeties that us weans loved oh man it diddny half make your mouth water.

White washed Sannies/ Transisterised Trannies.

Do you recall the long hot summer months when we played in the streets as weans with our sannies on, they were nice and white when your Ma bought them but they got dirty, so your Ma whitewashed them with a mixture of lime/chalk and water and left them on the tenement windae sill overnight to dry. You couldn't wait till the next morning until they were dry and you ran down the stair to play with your wee pals with your Ma's word of warning ringing in your ears "don't you dare get any taur on them" as the tar on the pavements often melted underneath the strong sunshine back in those days.

In the early to mid 1960's we had a new craze it was a small transistorised radio that could fit in your jacket pocket but we all called it a "Tranny" you could listen to a new Pirate radio station called Radio Caroline as you walked along the street and wasn't it great taking it with you when you went to Saltcoats and lay on the beach listening to it.

The Coliseum.

The Coliseum fist opened as a Theatre in 1905. Variety was staged twice nightly, with musical plays and pantomimes also being performed. During the break time actors would cross over Eglinton st and have a drink in the Coliseum bar. Then when "Talking movies" came on the scene the Coliseum became a "Picture hoose" which myself and many thousands of others enjoyed over the years. In the 60's it became the first Cinerama cinema in Scotland with a huge convex screen. It closed as a cinema in 1980 but reopened as a Bingo hall in 1987 but after that ceased to operate in 2003. It was unoccupied for years until a large fire broke out in it in 2009 on May 25th and was so badly damaged it was demolished the next month. One of the nicest Gorbals picture hoose's had bit the dust and with it many of our happy memories of a night out.

Dixon's Blazes.

The Gorbals sky at night time was lit up with Dixons Blazes for years until it was closed down in 1958. It was the soo-sides Aurora Borealis and we always though that it would be there forever. Sadly a work place that had employed so many workers from the Gorbals area closed due to a recession but what a sight at night time with the sky lit up. Again another piece of Gorbals history was demolished.

The Hula Hoop craze.

In the late 1950's and/or early 60's we had a craze that took over not only the soo-side but it seemed all of Glasgow. It was a big plastic ring which was very light in weight and you stood in the middle of it and you would sway your hips like a Hula Hula dancer.

You had to try and keep the hula hoop sliding up and down your body, it seemed the faster you spun it around your body then the better chance you had of stopping it falling down to your ankles. It sure did make you sweat and your head would spin sometimes but you kept at it !!!. then as soon as this craze started it finished, If I remember correctly it only lasted a couple of months in the summertime.

Bridge st Subway. [underground]

It has always amazed me all of my life why Bridge st subway station was thus named. I mean it's actually in Eglinton st, so why wasn't it called Eglinton st Subway station ?.

The only thing I can think of is it was because of its proximity to the old Bridge street railway station which was the rail terminus before the Central station was built, and people wanting to get to Bridge st railways station knew if they alighted at Bridge st subway station they were close to the rail station. A mystery eh.

Eglinton st.

Eglinton street was originally named Marlborough st, it was named after John Churchill the Duke of Marlborough. It was later renamed in recognition of the Earl of Eglinton who had been a major investor in the Glasgow, Paisley and Johnstone canal which terminated at Port Eglinton.

Taylor the Dentist.

Of all the Dentist's that operated in the greater Gorbals area Mr Taylor had a terrible reputation, his Dentist's surgery was in Crown st and many a wean and even adult still has nightmares of going to visit him and his wee receptionist called Margaret.

The Pawn shop.

"Uncle's" was a saviour for many a Ma or Granny in the Gorbals, come a Monday morning and no money left they would pawn their husbands suit [which he usually only wore on a Saturday night] and this would help put a dinner on the table for a few days.

Of course oor Ma's would have a wee cleaning job to help get another few shillings for the other days. There always seemed to be a bit of a "stigma" when a person went to visit the pawn shop, they would look over their shoulder to see if anyone recognized them or that they recognized and if the coast was clear then race up the pawn shop's stair as fast as they could run.

Of course if they saw someone who recognized then they would go look in another shop window until all was clear. When pawning their item it would be redeemed come the Friday night when their husband got paid but the whole rigmarole would start all over come Monday morning again.

Yes many thanks to "Uncle" for helping us out over the years gone by.

Langbank st.

Was reputed to be Glasgow's shortest street at around 30 feet long, with no close entrance it was actually just the return end of the tenement at 198 Eglinton st and it had a wee scrap metal shop at the end of this cul de sac. [previously named William st.]

Devon st.

This street was named after Sir Hugh Cortney, the English Earl of Devon.

The Menage.
[sounds like Menodge or Minawdge.]

The Menage was a group of about 13 women who each week paid in say 2/6 d and every Friday one of these women would get their chance of having the whole 30/- in the one lump sum. And I know nowadays 30/- or £1-50 pence is hardly anything but back then it was a lot of money.

Do you remember your Ma being in a Menage. Getting that 30/- was a God send as there was so much that they could do with it, back in those days 30/- could get you an awful lot. Of course the person who ran the Menage and collected the weekly money from everyone got a "free week". They never paid into it because of all the responsibility they had of making sure the money was paid by everyone.

Washin the stair.

Three families living on the same tenement landing and the woman of the house each took "their turn" of washin the stair and it was done with pride by our Ma's, they would be down on their hands and knees scrubbing the stair with a pail of hot water beside them and Oh you daren't try and pass them by as they carried out their chore, otherwise you would get a "skite" of a wet cloth over your legs.

When the stair was washed then it was chalk-whitened at either side and some Ma's chalk-whitened designs were very artistic. In fact some women would go and wash other peoples stair's for them for a small amount of money. But you daren't miss your turn of washin the stair, if you did then your door was soon chapped and your were told in no certain manner you had "missed your turn".

Of course if a person wasn't well then one of the other women would gladly do their turn of the stairs for them as neighbours always stuck together when one of them wasn't keeping well.

Daily Record.

I always remember at night times just after 11 pm you would hear the paper man shouting out "Record" at the top of his voice and as young lad of about 9 or 10, I always wondered how could you get tomorrows newspaper today but of course you did and you read the paper from cover to cover. Mostly men would read it from the back cover backwards as the football news was paramount for the male population. Then you would read about what "Pat Roller" was up to in catching any crooks.

Nicholson street.

This street was named after Scottish architect Peter Nicholson who carried out much design work for Buildings in the Gorbals area [especially in Carlton place.]

Allan Henderson,
I must mention Allan a pal of mine, he actually lives in Wick but his Mother was a Gorbals girl and he was no stranger to Thistle st, we are on opposite sides of the "Old Firm" but are both mature enough to respect each others views and share a laugh sending each other PM's.

Andrew Ewing,
"Uncle"Andrew lived in a single end [the landing above me] back in 1960 when he was unemployed he won the football pools. His win was a couple of hundred pounds which was an awful lot of money back then, he got my Uncle Hughie [my Ma's brother] to wallpaper and paint his single end and was over the moon. He took all his pals to the pub after the decorating was all done and after a few drinks said "knowing my luck the hoose will fall doon". Unfortunately "Uncle" Andrew was right as the next morning the back elevation of our tenement collapsed, within a few weeks were all moved to the new housing schemes. Poor "Uncle" Andrew I never saw him again.

Chapter 4

Section 2 of my Gorbals street map

Continuing down Eglinton st/Bridge st then along Carlton place then up Gorbals st until we come back to Cumberland st north side, and all the streets in between running south to north and west to east.

Eglinton st west side. [continued]

Now we continue down Eglinton st on the west side [opposite Cumberland st] and we had an open air gents toilet and just along from there you had Ian Fair's car showroom and he had a sign outside his place saying "A Fair exchange" then past this you had an old disused Church hall and **Dennis Doogan** told me it became the LMS boxing club. A well known location in its day, it saw some noted boxers pass through its portals.

Beside this we had a petrol station with a large Esso sign and then we come to Langbank st [William st] which was reputed to be the shortest street in all of Glasgow, it was actually only the return elevation of number 198 Eglinton st and this cul-de sac was only 30 feet long with a scrap dealers at the end of it. We had numbers 198 to 146 in this row of tenement dwellings that took us from Langbank st to the corner of Cook st and on the ground floor we had the usual shop fronts including a Remnants warehouse shop, a photo artist shop and a wee grocers shop among others and at the end of this row of tenements we had the Clydesdale public house abutting onto number 146 Eglinton st.

Crossing over Cook st and continuing moving north down Eglinton st we have numbers 122 to 68 until we come to

Wallace st, we had a varied selection of shops again on the ground floor including a plumbing shop, a surgical store, an opticians, the Coliseum pub, a Pet shop and finally the Tradeston tool store.

I have to tell a story about this tool store, way back in 1964 when I was a 16 year old 2nd year apprentice bricklayer I went in there to buy an American brick trowel for my work called a "Marshaltown" trowel as it was the best trowel of the day.

Anyway the shop assistant told me that because of the Vietnam war going on, America was holding on to all its steel to make guns for the US army so no more steel for trowels etc, and me being young and taking people at their word I believed him and bought another trowel [but not an American one].

Can you imagine how I felt when later on that day I found myself over at Glasgow cross and Bells tool shop had loads of these "Marshaltown" trowels in their shop window. How could a shop assistant tell a blatant lie to a young lad just to get a sale but he did didn't he !!. It wouldn't have happened a few years later as I would have went back and created "murder polis" ach well we all live and learn, eh.

On the opposite side of Wallace st stood the Cottage bar [which had once been called the Eglinton arms and also the Southern bar public house] and we had tenement dwellings from 56 on to number 2.

Next to the Cottage bar we had Bothwell's electrical suppliers shop, a piece of "spare grun" then The Eglinton stores shop then the "Wee Red shop", Myers tables, chairs and stools shop, Leah's hair stylists, a Polo Signs shop and the Southern cafe. Actually this Southern Cafe was also called "Hells Kitchen" and was run by an ex policeman called Bill McColl and his wife Agnes, it had downstairs and upstairs seating and was loved by the "younger generation" who would buy a bottle of coke and listen to the juke box playing all the hits of the day.

Jim McClafferty,
I used go for records for the juke box along with **Shug McCabe** for Hells kitchen café. Bill and Agnes gave us the money to buy them.

Next to "Hells Kitchen" you had newsagents and another shop beside it and this brought us to Nelson st.. Remembering that between numbers 28 and 24 we had an open passageway allowing access into the back courts to workshops and/or tenement door entrances which could be reached by stairs.

Bridge st west side

We now come to Nelson st and the beginning of Bridge st and we have the Laurieston bar right on the corner, this pub is run by the Clancy family and is a terrific pub where you still can get "hoat pie and peas" a great family run pub with brothers John and James and John's son Joseph and John and James' sister Ann all helping out.

I have been in the Laurieston bar a few good times when I have been up to Glasgow on my holidays and its a great wee pub, well ran by the Clancy family and a great pint. First sign of trouble and you are barred immediately and rightly so.

So from the Laurieston bar number 58 at one corner of Bridge st we had the Sou Wester pub [which had a brilliant darts team, winning so many Trophy's, cups etc] standing at the other corner numbered 24 Bridge st.

We had a few shops in between the Laurieston and Sou Wester pubs, there was a Hatters/Hosiery shop next to the Laurieston then a along a bit we had a cafe/restaurant, then a newsagents ran by a wee woman named Nellie, a few more shops then a large fronted shop called Masons TV shop [which later became a cash and carry shop] and next to that stood the Sou Wester pub.

Then next we move along Bridge st and cross over Kingston st [formerly King st] starting at number 22 which used to be the Commercial Bank and onto number 4 which is the junction of Bridge st/Clyde place.

Among the shops on the ground floor level were the Commercial bank on the corner at number 22, then we had a large carpet shop plus "The TEC" which had 2 large shop windows, selling a variety of goods from prams, cycles, radios and toys. Above the "TEC" and carpet shops once stood the facade of the original Bridge st railway station and it was here that the main entrance to Bridge st railway station once stood. The last shop at the end of this parade of shops was the Clydesdale supply company selling TV sets and this was the end of Bridge st as we came to the junction with Clyde place.

Now having travelled down the west side of Eglinton/Bridge st we will double back up to Cumberland st and travel down the east side of Eglinton st/Bridge st until we land at Carlton place.

Eglinton st, east side.

At the corner of Eglinton st and at the corner with Cumberland st we had number 203 Eglinton st to number 155 Eglinton st which is the corner of Peebles st [Formerly Margaret st]. There was a car showroom right at number 203, then Clark's shoe shop, Douglas' newsagents, a Chemist's, and Mitchell's jewellery shop,

Irene Bremner. [Ritchie]
Said there was a jewellers called Mitchell's just before Eglinton Lane, where my brother lived. I know it wasn't on the corner, so it must have been next to the Lord Nelson, It also sold toys, china and gifts, so was not a typical jeweller. We used to put money into a Christmas club every year with them and next to that stood the Lord Nelson public house right on the corner of Eglinton Lane.

Jean Wright lived up close number 179 Eglinton st, also up the same close of 179 Eglinton st we had a money lender called Munro.

Crossing Over Eglinton lane we then had Johnny's dairy shop a Chippy and then Georges "wet" Fish shop, Rita's fruit shop, Blackwoods tobacconist, and another car showroom at the corner of Peebles st [formerly Margaret st].

Then we have numbers 153 to 129 Eglinton st, at 153 we had a bank on the corner a shop next to it and then The George public house, I believe we had a run of more shops including a Bakers shop, Rae's chippy, a denture repair shop, , Dr Verrico's surgery, and the Eglinton st post office with the Stags head pub on the corner of Kelty st [formerly Buchanan court].

Crossing over Kelty st we come to the Beford picture hoose which stood in between Kelty st and Beford st at number 125 to 117 Eglinton st.

How many stories do we all have of going to the Bedford on the Saturday morning matinee to cheer on the goodies and boo the baddies and coming out and then pretending to be the Lone Ranger riding on your imaginary horse while slapping your backside to make your "Horse" go faster or pretending to be Robin Hood and aiming your "imaginary bow and arrow" at your wee pals etc, it was great entertainment for us weans and then later as we grew up it was the back seats for winching, when you paid to get it to the Bedford with your girlfriend but never saw the blooming picture but you never complained eh lol.

The New Bedford History.

The building was originally erected as the Eglinton Street United Secession Church in 1825. The church closed in 1920 and the building was converted into a cinema in 1921.

The original Bedford Cinema was destroyed by a fire in March 1932. The cinema's owner, a Mr Bernard Frutin, immediately commissioned a replacement.

The New Bedford was designed by Lennox and McMath and was built by Mr A.B. King. The newly built cinema was opened on 26 December (Boxing Day) 1932.

It is a notable example of Art Deco architecture in the city.

Bernard Frutin sold the cinema to George Green in 1936.

The New Bedford Cinema screened its final film, a double bill of Dirty Harry and Klute, on 8 July 1973 and reopened on 12 October 1973 as a Mecca bingo hall.

Moving on down Eglinton st we had the Mally arms pub on the corner of Bedord st with a couple of tenement dwellings numbered 105 to 79, who remembers going to the "Mally fur a Swally" said **Jim Todd,** the top twenty music lounge too and I always enjoyed a great pint of Guinness in there, we had a few shops then the Coliseum picture hoose numbered 97 to 85. what a fine building was the Coliseum, which started off in life as a theatre, then with the advent of "talking pictures" it became a Picture hoose in 1925 and many a time I went there to see a film. [of course "silent movies" were in vogue until the late 1920's when the "talkies" took over, I do believe it was 1927 that the "Jazz singer" with Al Jolson created film history with the first "talkie".]

Marina Raffan's Mammy **Bella Raffan** was a cleaner in the Coliseum and also cleaned the Bedford Picture hoose.

Right beside the Coliseum Picture hoose we had two shops,one belonging to Birrell's the jewellers and next to that was Tomkinsons shop which sold umbrellas and leather goods and this stood at number 79 at the corner with Herbertson st. [of course these shops changed names over the years].

Then we come to number 75 Eglinton st and this row of tenements took us to number 1 Eglinton st.

We start with number 75 which I believe was Skinners the bakers, then a sweetie shop, then we had the Station bar public house and a newsagents shop, then Bridge st subway station [underground] and do you all remember that "smell" when you walked down into the Subway stations, I loved it.

Next to the subway we had a Bata shoe shop then a run of other shops, then at number 23-19 we had the old Eglinton Electreum Picture hoose [actually this Picture hoose had its screen down in the basement, you entered at street level but the floor had such a very sharp incline that the screen was almost at basement level and while watching a film sometimes you clearly heard the rumble of the underground /subway trains passing by.]

Then next to that stood the old Black Bull inn public house and next to that we had an access lane leading into the back courts [with a Pend leading to the back of the Eglinton Electreum for a back door fire escape]. Then we came to Ockrims clothes shop [I believe Ockrims was a clothes shop, although a friend of mine said it might have been a stationers shop. ?] and next to that stood the British Linen bank at number 1 Eglinton st.

There was a Dentist's surgery ran by a Mr Devine above this bank.

We now come to Bridge street east side.

In this next row of Tenements numbered 69 to 29 Bridge st,we start with Stevenson Taylor's public house which stood at number 69 Bridge st and the savings bank of Glasgow building next door to it. Then we had Allen's carpet shop and then that massive warehouse and drapery store belonging to the Kinning Park Co-operative society, next to that stood the India buildings which were originally built as a wholesale stationers then we had a bank of Scotland premises as we now reach Oxford st and as we cross over Oxford st we come to numbers 27 to 17 Bridge st. We had Pfaff's a German company sewing machine shop right on the corner at number 27 Bridge st and a few other shops including a shop front belonging to a John Bach and next to it was the Del Rio's fish and chip restaurant where you could sit down to eat and also we had a chippy called Pepe's but I think that took the place of John Bach's shop at a later date. [?]

Then of course at number 17 we had the Army and Navy shop [which was once a post office.] which stood right on the corner of Bridge st and Carlton court.

Then crossing over Carlton court we come to numbers 15 to number 1 Bridge st, so on the corner of Carlton court and Bridge st we had numbers 15 to 5 belonging to a large premises belonging to Alexander Sloan and Co. [built on the old site of Dewar's hotel.] a cafe /restaurant where I remember going into with my Ma on several occasions and lastly we had at number 1 to 3 that large Bank of Scotland building with its return elevation turning into Carlton place. [inclusive of what used to be Clyde terrace.]

We now come to Carlton place. [inclusive of Clyde terrace]

Next we will go along Carlton place and next to the Bank of Scotland we had the Carlton Zoo or if not next then the next number after that. We have numbers starting at 87 Carlton place and going along to number 2 which was the start of Gorbals st. We have to look in amazement at those fine buildings all along Carlton place with its Church's and terraced houses built originally for prosperous business folk.

In Carlton place you had the T.U.C club there, the Stella Maris and Communist club, all worthy watering holes and deeply appreciated. The Communist party owned the whole building from the basement right up the stairs to the Star club bar and lounge as well as all the offices above. This was the Communist party's headquarters.

The photo above is of Carlton place with the Gorbals Parish Church in view [later to be called John Knox Church.]

Of course Carlton place takes its name after the London residence of the Prince of Wales but he never took up residence !!! then we come to a bank on the corner of South Portland st and opposite is that Iconic South Portland st suspension bridge of which Gorbals people have used since its opening way back in the mid 19th century, easy access to St Enoch's sq and the Toon.

At number 84 on one of the floors we had Mozart Allens music publishers and **Mick Lynch** tells me he worked there from 1966-68.

Getting back to Carlton place, from Bridge st all along to Gorbals st Carlton place had the finest of terrace houses and Church buildings including Buchan st school, Gorbals Parish Church [later became known as John Knox Church] and a large training centre building in between South Portland st and Nicholson st.

I must say that I never remember shops in Carlton place until we came to just after Buchan school where I think we had a car repair shop, a shop with D and N lettering above the top of its large window, another shop beside it and the Clydesdale bank on the corner with Carlton place and Gorbals st.

The auto/car repair place was number 14 and went along till we came to the Clydesdale bank at number 2. there was a Pend in between number 11 and 8 Carlton place to allow access to the back court which could be used to take merchandise into these aforementioned shops.

We now come to Gorbals st west side

So starting with the Clydesdale bank at the corner of Gorbals st we move south along Gorbals st from number 8, next to the Clydesdale bank was a shop named Marly's, there were two other shops and then a pubic house at number 20 which I believe was called McCabes [?] , next to that was a Fairway products premises, and right on the corner at Oxford st/Gorbals st was Harry Crowns woolen/trimmings shop. Then crossing over to Oxford st we had a bank of Scotland building at number 32 Gorbals street.

David Winestone
Was born and lived at 40 Gorbals st until 1964, he tells me "that across the road was Maxwell electrician, Leon's Jewish deli, Gorbals Post Office, great times so sad the old Gorbals is gone".

Now moving along Gorbals st there was a large wholesale warehouse belonging to Lewis Greenberg, then a hairdressers, Huddlestons fabric people shop, Tropp's furrier, Ralstons newsagents and next door was Bennys bar at number 62, and a wholesalers shop after that then we had the junction with with Norfolk st.

The photo above is of Frances Hogan standing outside a shop in Norfolk st Gorbals in the day before the supermarkets took over.

Years ago we had an ornate cast iron clock and pubic drinking fountain in the middle of the street which was the centre of Gorbals cross, I don't remember that as it had been replaced with a simple clock on a pole when I was young lad. Although I remember the downstairs public toilet nearby, which I had used back in the day.

Now crossing over Norfolk st and continuing along Gorbals st [right at Gorbals cross] where we had Arthur Black's tailor/shirts shop then next to that we had a Restaurant, then a florists shop, next was Doyles bar and a premises called Textile house at number 84 to 90 which was a drapery shop, passing Textiles shop we come into Gorbals st proper and quite a few shops including a Chemists, Frank Hallsides sweetie shop etc and then we arrive at number 104 Gorbals st at the junction with Dunmore st.

Then crossing over Dunmore st we come to numbers 106 to 154 Gorbals st where we had quite a few shops including a ladies hairdressers called Pearls, **Laurence Edwards** said My Aunt had a hairdressers shop called "Pearls" opposite the Palace picture hoose in Gorbals st.

Susan Rigmond said I got my hair dyed purple in that [Pearls] hairdressers and didn't have enough money to get it set so had to do it myself that was in 1961 and I worked in Littlewood's in Argyle St, I thought I was going to get my books when my supervisor said I had to report to managers office lol but instead I got promotion on to make up counter and became agent for Gala make-up.

Then we come to the Gorbals swimming baths, and what great memories do we all have of here.

I remember when I was about 8 years old and couldn't swim at that time. I just stayed down the shallow end and was "scooshing" out from the side to try and get the confidence to try and learn to swim. Well I was walking past the middle of the swimming pool when this other boy came running along and pushed me into the water !!!.

I was struggling for breathe and trying to keep my head above the water line but was going under until the swimming hall attendant saw what had happened and dived in to haul me out.

I was coughing and spluttering and in shock. The attendant said to me, son get back in the water now or you will never learn to swim, so I walked down to the shallow end and jumped in. Do you know what, within two weeks I was swimming up and down the length of the Gorbals swimming bath, I think it was the fear of being thrown in again and drowning that spurred me on to learn to swim !!.

Then of course after swimming my wee pals and me would walk round into Cleland st, along to Mr Checkman's peanut shop [under the bridge] to buy some hot peanuts or a bit of tablet etc.

How many weans done this eh, or maybe after coming out of the Palace Picture hoose after seeing a good film we headed for the hot peanut man.

Now after leaving Gorbals swimming hall we cross over Bedford lane and continue along Gorbals st west side, with numbers 162 along to 266,

We had a cobbler shop, then the British Linen bank with tenement dwellings above [this building today in 2020 has been lovingly restored/refurbished], then an outfitters shop, Logan & Morton's garage, Co-op bakery shop, Minnie De Marco's newsagents, a launderette ran by a polish man [named Ken?], Rosse's building yard behind the advertisement billboards, McPartland's pub, the dog & cat home, Davemore Springs a small engineering enterprise, the Pend, Singers sewing machine shop, Mrs Olivers fruit shop, Smellie the glaziers, Feds the removers office then the bridge with Motherwell's grain store right at the corner with Gorbals st and Cumberland st.

Susan Rigmond.
The grain store [Motherwells] used to charge batteries for old radios obviously when people only had gas light. The Connelly brothers were our doctors all the time we lived there and there was also a rag store under the bridge where we took our rags to get money for going to the pictures

I have to remind you the reader that over the years the shop names have changed so what a younger generation will remember could well be different from my generation. This applies to all the shops, etc covering the greater Gorbals area.

We now come back to Cumberland st but <u>North</u> side this time.

We will go along Cumberland st from numbers 268 to number 3, which takes us to the junction at Eglinton st.

We had the Grain shop [Motherwell's] at number 268 and Bob Nimmo's shop at the corner with Surrey st.

Hugh Cassidy
Said I remember Nimmo's newsagent at the corner of Cumberland st and Surrey st, I got my first school bag from that shop then went onto Abbotsford primary school in 1961.

Also **Alan Yates** and **Edward Flannagan** remember using Bob Nimmo's shop.

Then crossing over Surrey st we had tenement dwellings numbered 111 to 89 which took us to the junction with Nicholson st.

Then crossing over Nicholson st we had numbers 85 to 75 Cumberland st and we had a few shops including the Marigold cafe [and in the middle of 85/55 we had Abbotsford lane] which take us to the corner of Abbotsford place.

At the corner of Abbotsford lane on Cumberland st at numbers 71 to 55 we had a small row of shops, there was a dispensing Chemists, a shop called "Jimmies", Browns store, a Launderette and Caldwell & Co wholesalers then crossing over we had number 51 onwards to number 3.

We had the Argyll halls at number 35 and next to that we had the Laurieston Renwick U.F.Church which stood at 19 Cumberland st. This fine Church dates from 1870, most Churches stand on their own but this one was actually flush in line with the tenements either side of it.

Jock Kerr
said "I used to go to the Lauriston Renwick church BB's Lifeboys youth club".

Then next to this Church we had tenement dwellings from number 17 to number 3 which takes us back to the corner of Cumberland st and Eglinton st.

That is the outside perimeter of Eglinton st east side, Carlton place, Gorbals st west side and Cumberland st north side finished. So we now will go down all the vertical streets [south to north] within this perimeter area.

Kilbarchan st, west side/east side.

We will start going along these streets working south to north and the first street we come to is Kilbarchan st [formerly South Stirling st] which stood at a right angle to Peebles st and it went on passing the back of the Bedord Picture hoose and crossed over Bedford st but then became Coburg st.

In Kilbarchan st we had numbers 24&12 west side which were dwellings then on the opposite side we had a warehouse at number 17 Kilbarchan st east side and then an empty space then numbers 9 &7 which took us to the back of the Bedford Picture hoose and the junction with Bedford st

Then as I said the line of Kilbarchan st carried on but now became Coburg st.

Coburg st, west side.

With the numbers starting at 146 Coburg st west side and ending at number 6 Coburg st. [crossing over Herbertson st, Norfolk st and finishing at Oxford st.]

After 146 Coburg st we had a wide alleyway [the collie brae ?] and the Coliseum Picture hoose which was a really huge building and the side/end of the Coliseum picture hoose stood on Herbertson st.

Crosssing over Herbertson st we had number 112 Coburg st to number 60 which were tenement dwellings, in between we had open access to the back of Bridge street subway station [underground] and "spare grun" between number 62 and number 60.

This now took us to the junction with Norfolk st and as we cross over Coburg st it has numbers 38 to number 6 with number 34 being the Locheil public house.

Numbers 20 to 12 was the back of the Co-op warehouse where all our Ma's went to get their twice yearly "Divvy pay-out", a friend of mine **May Bishop-Sweeney** told me she had her first job here after leaving school, May also told me there was a pawn shop here in Coburg st at the junction with Oxford st and it was run by Mr and Mrs Crossan [whose son **Alan Crossan** now owns the Clutha pub as I write in 2020]

Coburg st, east side.

We now go back to the east side of Coburg st and start with the odd numbers from 145 to 3, actually the tenement numbered 145 was the return elevation of the tenements in Bedford st.

After this there was a large open space until we came to numbers 79 to 71, on the ground floor of number 71 we had a large hall then open space with number 67 set back from the main line of Coburg st then after this more open space.

Then we had tenement number 57 and next door to it we had Websters public house right on the corner of Coburg st /Norfolk st.

I'm **Geraldine Jones**, I lived at 19 Coburg st facing the Co Op building, a cobblers on one corner, Massey's grocers on the other a pawn shop up a close in another.

Then crossing over Norfolk st we continue along Coburg st at number 41 where we had a run of tenement dwellings until we reach the junction with Oxford st and this was where Coburg st ended.

On this side of Coburg st and opposite the Lochiel bar we had Dr Berkleys surgery and next door to that we had a Bookmakers shop.

The continuation of Abbotsford place [from Cumberland st] - leading onto - South Portland st.

Abbotsford place, west side/east side.

Abbotsford place starts here at number 44 and travels to number 2 which is at the junction with Bedord st. This was a wide and handsome street of Georgian style terraces and were splendid looking buildings in their day. On this the west side of Abbotsford place and at number 20 stood Geneen's Kosher hotel, ran by family matriarch Sophie Geneen, this was a popular venue for all sorts of celebration for the Jewish community. It opened in 1930 and lasted for over 30 years.

The photo above is of a young Lenny Vine [Leonard Vine] taken outside of his home at number 10 Abbotsford place, you can read Len's story in Chapter 5 of my book [Gorbals peoples story's].

In the close-mouth entrances along Abbotsford place we had many tiled close entrances [wally closes] there stood stone upright columns [portico style] at the close entrances and was a much desired residence back in the day.

On the opposite side of Abbotsford place we had the uneven numbers starting at number 45 and ending at number 1.

We had Caldwells wholesalers shop at the start on the corner of Abbotsford place/Cumberland st and once again we had stone upright columns at each close entrance.

This street was laid out in the 1830's and was once described as Glasgow's Harley st, with lots of medical and professional people residing here. The upper floors consisted of only one apartment per landing and to the back of these fine buildings we had brick built curved stair towers which allowed more floor space in the apartments. So we now reach number 1 Abbotsford place and are at the junction with Bedford st.

Michael Quigley

I'm a Gorbals boy who came from Coventry new city at 11 years old and I got quite a culture shock when I arrived with my older brother to Glasgow central railway station, it was a dark wet miserable smoggy day the Tram's had stopped running but trolley buses were all over the streets.

We walked up Eglinton street to our new address at number 79 Abbotsford place. My Granny and two uncles and aunties lived in tenements above the railway bridge at the top end of Abbotsford place both were named Lynch including Granny Lynch.

Then I found out that the Irish family's were the best in the world to live beside, Duffy's, O'Donnell's, McGlees, all made our family very welcome, these were some of the best days of my life playing in back courts we were a family of 10 children and were one of the last to move to one of the housing schemes we ended up in Castlemilk, no way the same as Gorbals people.

We cross over Bedford st and find that Abbotsford place has now became South Portland st.

South Portland st, west side

Now starting at the west hand side [even numbers] we have the Morven bar public house and we have number 136 leading down to number 4, which was where the South Portland st suspension bridge started.

From number 136 to number 86 South Portland st we had a straight line of tenement dwellings with a few shops on the ground floor which then took us to Norfolk st.

Then crossing over Norfolk st and continuing along South Portland st we restart with the Portland arms public house on the corner with Norfolk st and next to that we had number 80 to number 32, in between these numbers we had a few shops and **Frank Ford**, tells me that George Chisholm the trumpeter lived there in South Portland st in our tenement for a while, we had Sadie and Joe Hamilton's fish and Chip shop at number 30, across the street we had Tannahill's fruit and veg shop and the Ayrshire Farmers dairy, which then took us to Oxford st.

Crossing over Oxford st and continuing along South Portland st we come to "spare grun" and pass over the lane that was Carlton court and come to number 12 and finish at number 4 with a large Bank building that stood on the corner at the end of South Portland st and the junction with Carlton place.

South Portland st, east side.

We now double back to the odd numbered side of South Portland st starting at number 115 to number 51, I believe that we had an ice cream shop owned by the Tamberinie family at one of the corners.

At numbers 95 to 93 we had an Institute building [but I'm not sure who attended this building] and next door to this we had a Jewish Synagogue numbers 89 to 85, [this later became an Irish dance hall] then as we travel along this part of South Portland st we come to number 15 with the Gordon bar right at the corner with Norfolk st.

Crossing over Norfolk st we come to numbers 45 to 33 South Portland st and at number 45 we had The Gorbals Library building right on the corner and right beside this we had a Church building, then number 39 until we reach 33 and Oxford st. [Right opposite the Library there was a crisp factory that all the weans loved.] I believe there was a ladies hairdressers shop ran by Mrs Green near to the end of the street here.

Mary Ellen McAuley
Says,Thanks for the memories, I remember the crisp factory in South Portland st most vividly, It was the highlight of the week

as Shealagh Duffy and I would deliberately wait to the last minute on a Friday after school to go into the factory in order to get big bags of the crumbs leftover from the big crisps.
I can still taste them. Magic moments.!!

Crossing over Oxford st we have a pub right at the corner of South Portland st/Oxford st at number 31 called the Kings arms.

Then we have dwelling numbers 29 to 15, a wide passageway beside number 15 which gained access to the training college [occupational] which had its buildings Facade on Carlton place, then we come to number 3 and arrive at Carlton place and the South Portland suspension bridge which took us over to St Enoch's square and the Toon. There was a Mr and Mrs Bowmans dairy shop but I'm not sure exactly of its position. ?

PS.
There was also a factory where Chickens were "slaughtered" in South Portland st but I don't know its precise location. As with some of the information I gather it can be spot on but on others I don't know exactly although I try my very best to find out.

We now will travel down Abbotsford lane which becomes Norfolk court and then ending up as Oxford lane.

Abbotsford lane, west side/east side.

Actually Abbotsford lane only has four dwellings west side at numbers 28/26/24/ grouped together, then loads of open space until we come to number 2 which is at the junction with Bedford st.

Now the east side had dwelling number 33 at the start and travelling all the way down among open space until it comes to the Clock bar at the junction with Bedford st. So there are no factory's or workshops there to describe or talk about.

Norfolk court, west side/east side.

Reaching the end of Abbotsford lane we now cross over Bedford st and we have the start of Norfolk court, we have number 80 on the west side which was actually a Day Nursery then open space until we come to the back of the Institute building with the Jewish Synagogue next to it which had a back entrance to it from Norfolk court then nothing but open space until we travel along and come to Norfolk st.

Doubling back to the east side of Norfolk court we have numbers 77 to number 5 which were dwellings and now we arrive at Norfolk st.. All in all Norfolk court was more or less a lane-way with a few dwellings and loads of open space on view.

Oxford lane, west side/east side.

Crossing over Norfolk st and more or less in line with Norfolk court we come to Oxford lane west side which had the side elevation of Norfolk st library on show.

The district where the city's first public lending library had opened in Main Street [Gorbals st] in November 11th, 1901. But that rented accommodation had its limitations, and it was replaced by this new Gorbals Library in Norfolk Street in 1933.

Then after going past the side of Norfolk st library it was just open space and dwellings at number 8 and 6 west side and the return elevation of tenement dwellings from the front of Oxford st, which abutted next to number 8 and 6.

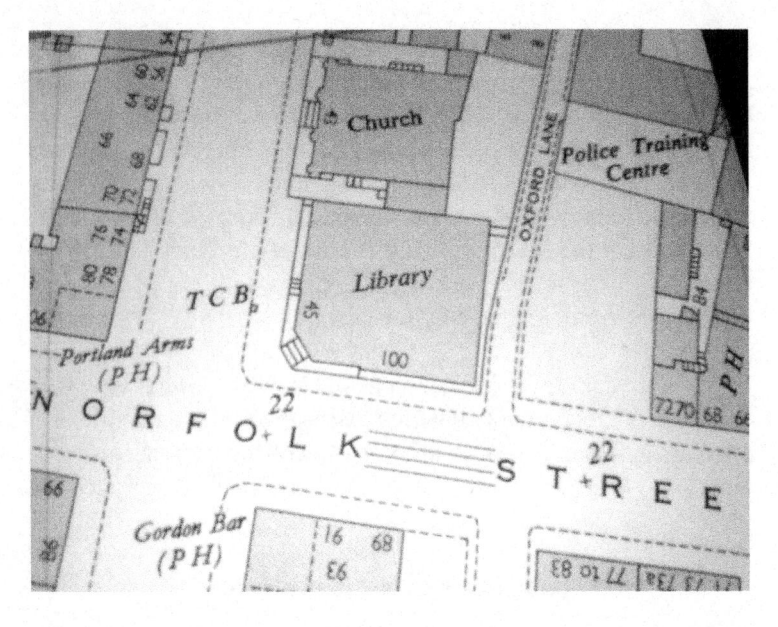

We go back to the other side of Oxford lane east side and its all a big open space until the first and only building we come to which is the Police training centre, then we have a few dwellings number 15 and number 3 which were actually sleeping accommodation for visiting police officers attending training courses and now at the end of number 3 we arrive at Oxford st.

We now come to Nicholson st [which at one time had sections of it called Apsley place and Warwick st] but it was eventually all called Nicholson st.

Nicholson st, west side.

We start on the west side at number 240 and travel down this line of fine tenement dwellings until we reach number 168 then cross over Bedford st, once more a fine example of well built tenements in this street and we must think if only they could have been refurbished but as I have said before that the powers that be had only one plan and that was to flatten the tenements in the greater Gorbals area.

There were shops on either side of Nicholson st with the usual grocers, dairy's and newsagents but I'm afraid I have searched and asked but can only find a few [as opposed to Eglinton st and Gorblas st etc where I had plenty of photos of shops with names and plenty of people remembering their names. Although I am sure that the reader will get the general lay out of Nicholson st, I am sorry for failing to provide more info about shops here.]

I'm Bobby Smith,
I was born 1952 at 94 Nicholson St .... attended Gorbals primary school in Buchan St. went to the Glasgow medical mission Sunday school in Oxford St. left the Gorbals when I was 11 to go to Househillwood but still went to Sunday school for years after I left.

After crossing over Bedford st we continue down the west side of Nicholson st from number 162 to 92, with a Pend between numbers 128 [b] - 128 [a] which gained you access to the back court and you could walk through to Norfolk court saving a long walk down/up to the intersecting streets.

Liz Holland,
Told me, "my Granny ran a Shebeen don't know if it was Nicholson St then or Warwick St as it used to be called, it was before I was born so would have to ask older relatives for you Danny. My Grannies name was Annie Gannon. I do remember my mum telling stories about the police warning her when they were gonna raid her place so she could get rid of whatever she had in the house, she emigrated to Australia in the 50's". Xx.

On leaving number 92 Nicholson st we come to Norfolk st and cross over and we come to number 86 Nicholson st and we have the the Norfolk Arms public house on the corner of Nicholson st /Norfolk st.

After that we have numbers 82 and 80 tenement dwellings in Nicholson st and right next to that we had the large Police training Centre building [which returned into Oxford st and and then returned into Oxford lane and returned again. [this police training centre was actually 4 sided with a courtyard in the centre of it, which could have been used for "unarmed combat lessons for police officers] ?? " or other activities.

There were two gated "Pends" to allow access into this courtyard, one in Nicholson st and the other on the big open space to the right of Oxford lane [looking north to the river Clyde direction.]

We now come to Oxford st and we carry on over to Nicholson st and numbers 36 to 16 tenement dwellings. In between number 24 and 16 we had an open passageway which gave access to the the Training Centre After number 16 Nicholson st we had the return elevation of dwellings from Carlton place which abutted against number 16 and that takes us to Carlton place facing the River Clyde.

Nicholson st, east side.

We now double back to the east side of Nicholson st starting at the corner with Cumberland st and we have number 259 to number 177 tenement dwellings.

Crossing over Bedford st we continue along Nicholson st and we had the Double Eagle pub on this corner and number 157 abutting up to it until we reach number 145. Then between 141 to 131 we had St Johns R.C. School.

There was Forey's wee Dairy shop just three closes down from Bedford st on Nicholson st but I don't know the number or whether it West or East side but it was there. Also there was Babbin's a Jewish Bakers shop but again I couldn't find its position.

Then tenement dwellings at numbers 129 to 115 until number 111 to 95 was where a large Bonded Warehouse stood and next door to that was William Robin's public house at the corner with Norfolk st.

Then crossing over Norfolk st we continue along Nicholson st east side at number 87 to 61 and the Reformed Presbyterian Church that stood at number 61 and the return elevation of Oxford st tenements abutted against the R.P. Church.
Just at the side of the Church we had a Pend that allowed access to dwelling number 63.

Crossing over Oxford st we come to number 31 at the corner of Nicholson st east side which had tenement dwellings along to number 15, we had a few shops here including a drapers, a newsagents and premises owned by Thomson&Co [which would all at a later date become cash and carry shops as lots of shops did in the Gorbals in the 70's / 80's +].

At the end of dwelling number 15 in Nicholson st we had an open passageway which gave access to a few small business's in the back court including a Plumbers workshop a sugar merchant and bakers sundries, and tradesmen met and traded from here. After this open passageway we had a Church hall standing at the corner of Nicholson st and Carlton place and this indeed took us to Carlton place proper.

We now come to Surrey Lane which continues in the same line to become Portugal lane.

Surrey lane, west side/east side.

Starting once again at Cumberland st and working our way North [towards the River Clyde] we start with the return tenement dwellings from Cumberland st at the entrance to Surrey lane West side, and continue down past "spare grun" until we reach the Bohreen bar and this is us now at Bedford st.

Owney Pringle
had a garage up Surrey lane just along from The Bohreen bar and he kept fruit in it for his store.

So we double back to the East side of Surrey lane and once again start at Cumberland st,we have once again the return tenement dwelling elevation from Cumberland st at the start of Surrey lane and number 101 abutting to it.

We then have a vast open space until we come to the back of the Starch and Gum Woks factory/building with number 27 next to it and going on to number 9 and once again the return elevation of the tenement dwellings from Bedford st, this taking us to Bedford st proper.

Portugal lane, west side/east side.

We now come to Portugal lane and have to enter it through a Pend with tenement buildings above [in Bedford st] we travel along **both** sides of Potugal lane and pass in between St Johns R.C. School to the west side and St John's R.C Church to the east side of the lane.

We have no tenement dwelling numbers on the West side and we pass by the back elevation of the Bonded Warehouse [facade in Nicholson st] and we go through another Pend with tenement dwellings above and enter into Norfolk st.

We go back to the East side of Portugal lane and just after the back elevation of St John's R. C. Church we have numbers 27 to number 3 and once again we come to the Pend with tenement dwellings above taking us through to Norfolk st.

We now come to Surrey st which later continues as Portugal st.

Surrey st, west side/east side

We will start with the return elevation of tenement dwellings from Cumberland st which is the first building on the West side of Surrey st and our first number West side in Surrey st is number 50 then a vast open space until we come to the Starch and Gas Works Factory/building then passing that we have dwelling numbers 28 to number 18 and once again to a vast open space and which takes us to Bedford st.

Doubling back to the East side of Surrey st we start at the corner of Cumberland st/Surrey st and we had Bob Nimmo's corner shop and then we had numbers 105 to 35.

Now in between numbers 99 and 97 we had a Pend allowing access into the back for an Electric Sub Station.

Then numbers 97 to 83 were occupied by the large Grain Mill building then next to that we had a Bakery and next to that we had numbers 75 to 29 tenement dwellings, next to that a bit of open ground and then the Surrey bar public house stood, which then took us to a Church on the corner with Bedford lane [this Church was demolished and later became Lipton's monumental sculptures yard].

Portugal st, west side/east side.

I'm Betty Gillan,
I lived in 32 Portugal street right beside St John's Chapel me and my late brother Tommy Smith (later know as the Gorbals Artist) both loved all the weddings as children when they threw the money out the cars to all the children in the street. There was a wee shop in Portugal st and they sold penny or twopenny drinks of ginger which I loved. We moved in 1957, after leaving the Gorbals one of my first jobs was back in the Gorbals in 1965 working in Montgomery & Son Cork factory think it was near Hospital St or Ballater Street.

In Portugal st we had numbers west side from 124 to number 2, on the corner with Bedford st/Portugal st you had Fred the Barbers then from number 124 to 96 we had tenement dwellings then the Presbytery for St John's R.C.Church, then next to that stood the Church itself, you had Fitzpatrick the newsagents where you could also buy religious items like holy statues etc, and the owner was a grade one football Referee.

Then you had Rosses bar at number 24 Portugal st and at the very end of Portugal st you had McGovern's Central bar which also stood at 47 Norfolk st.

Doubling back to the East side of Portugal st we had spare ground on the corner of Bedford lane /Portugal st then number 77 and next to that was the lodging house [model] which had the numbers 69 to 55 and next to the Model we had another R.C School at the corner with Dunmore st. Which was the infants school for St John's.

Then crossing over Dunmore st but still on Portugal st we had dwellings numbered 29 to number 1 and number 1 was Ropers public house.

Bedford Row, west side/east side

Standing with our back against Bedford lane we enter Bedford row west side and we had a large Hall which took in numbers 52 to 32, then the back of the Lodging house was next and then we had the R.C.School for infants attending St John's, which took us to Dunmore st. Now doubling back to the start of Bedford row East side we had the back elevation of the Gorbals swimming hall [and Steamie and hot baths] then next we had tenement dwellings numbered 27 going to number 1 on the corner which was Dunmore st.

Photo above is of between Bedford lane - Dunmore st.

Next we have Dunmore lane, west side/east side.

Crossing over Dunmore st we start going along Dunmore lane [which was the continuation of Bedford row] west side and at the corner we had the return elevation of dwellings from Dunmore st and then we had numbers 12 and 8 Dunmore lane with the return elevation of tenement dwellings from Norfolk st. at the other end of Dunmore lane.

Then doubling back to the East side of Dunmore lane we had once again the return elevation of tenement dwellings from Dunmore st and then we had number 19 Dunmore lane which was the old Cattle food mill and at the end of Dunmore lane we again had the return elevation of Tenement dwellings for the front of Norfolk st and this takes us to Norfolk st proper.

Buchan st, west side/east side.

We start on the west side of Buchan st and we have tenement dwellings numbering 34 to number 32 and next to that we have numbers 30/28/26 which was once a brass works but later became the store and garage of the education department. Then we came to number 22 and this was us at Oxford st.

Crossing over Oxford st we come to the Missionary dispensary building on the opposite corner of Buchan st /Oxford st, then tenement numbers14, 10 and 6 which then takes us to the John Knox Church at the corner of Buchan st /Carlton place and this now takes us to Carlton place proper,

That section of Carlton place was once known as Clyde terrace.

Going back to the start of Buchan st east side we had numbers 45 to 35 which were tenement dwellings, then we had the Victoria works warehouse which manufactured gas equipment.

Then next door we had the Jewish Synagogue at number 33 which was on the corner of Oxford st.

Crossing over Oxford st and continuing along Buchan st at number 42 we have the Janitors house for the Gorbals public school [Buchan st school] many of its early pupils were of Jewish descent. Then we have the playground and then the school itself which then takes us onto Carlton place.

Gorbals lane, west side/east side.

On the whole of the west side we have no numbers at all, we just had the return elevation of tenement dwellings at either end of the west side, although in the middle we had a Pend which gave access to the back of the Victoria works warehouse [which was in Buchan st].

On the east side we had the return elevations of tenement dwellings at the front and back of Gorbals lane. While in between we had tenement numbers 19 to 15 and next to that we had an engineering works at numbers 13 to 9, then 7, 5 and 3 were dwellings. That was us at Oxford st now. - - Gorbals lane ran from Norfolk st to Oxford st.

This is us now at the end of the "vertical streets".

Having finished all the streets [vertically] running from South to North, as in Eglinton toll to the River Clyde, we will now do all the streets [horizontaly] going from West to East as in Eglinton st to the Shawfield stadium direction.

Eglinton lane, south side/north side.

We start off with Eglinton lane just off the east side of Eglinton st and basically it was workshops that we had in this narrow passageway.

Catherine Clarke,
Down Eglinton Lane there was a bleach factory, a munitions Warehouse, that I remember being broken into and all the buttons from the uniforms and other stuff being scattered all over "The big back".

There was also stables there where Pat, the man who worked there toiled as a Cooper, he fascinated us kids who use to watch him create barrows! What a great life we had down that Big back!

Jean Wright ,
Our bedroom and kitchen window looked into Eglinton Lane and what we called "the Fishy Back " there was also some kind of factory that made clay pipes and figurines etc and we often found broken pieces lying around, which we used for chalk.

Peebles st, south side/north side.

Then next we had Peebles st [formerly Margaret st] we never had any shops here except the return of the car showroom from Eglinton st and along a wee bit up a close a man ran his taxi business from there.

This was on the south side of Peebles st. Many thanks to **Margaret Lyons** for this information.

Authors note,
I had the pleasure of meeting up with Margaret Lyons a few years ago when I was on my yearly trip back to Glasgow, we met up in Sharkey's bar on a Saturday night, quite a few people turned up that night including Carol Connolly her sister Sandra and their mother Alice, David Scott, Raymond Shannon, Molly Dooley, Maggie McKay, best pals Lorraine White and Barbara Carroll, Norah Greene and a few others and a great wee night indeed. It's always great to meet up with pals old and new on my returns back hame and look forward to it immensely. [the hangovers are worth it !!]

Kelty st, west side/ east side.

Next we come to Kelty st and I don't believe we had any shops here at all.

Neil Mathieson,
I was born and lived in Kelty St from 1948 till 1956 before moving to Castlemilk. I do not remember any shops on the street, only the Stags Head pub on the corner of Eglington and Kelty Streets.

Bedford st, south side.

Now we come to Bedford st which as **Jim McGukin** reminds me of the watering holes, The Mally arms, The Clock bar, The Double Eagle and The Tron. [Morven bar which stood on the corner of Bedford st/south Portland st].

Caroline Coyle Hastie.
The Tron pub, where I would have my tea break when I worked in the Mally.xxx

Bedford st had numbers 73 to 7 on the south side and numbers 104 to 2 on the north side.

The Bedford Picture hoose had the side of its building running along Bedford st from Eglinton st to Kilbarchan st.

[Then Bedford st crossed over Abbotsford place, Abbotsford lane, Nicholson st, Surrey lane and finally ending at Surrey st on the south side. While the north side was different as by this time Kilbarchan st had now become Coburg st, Abbotsford place had become South Portland st, Abbotsford lane had become Norfolk court. - Nicholson st stayed the same but Surrey st had became Portugal s.-]

We had tenement dwellings numbers 73 to 7 on Bedford st south side there was a Pawn shop here in Bedford st but I'm not sure if it was south side or north side,then we had the Clock bar at the junction of Abbotsford lane/Bedford st and there was a bakers shop just down from the Clock bar at number 40 I believe, then carrying on after the Clock bar we had number 29 and this was the junction with Nicholson st, crossing over Nicholson st we came to Surrey lane and the Bohreen bar and just 2 tenements, last one being number 7 and that was where Bedford st came to an end at the junction with Surrey st.

The Mally arms was at number 106 Bedford st, the Morven at 66, The Double Eagle at number 26, and the Clock bar at number 35 and the Tron bar at number 70. [there used to be the Beford bar an number 9 which was once called the Black Bull, Camerons at 79-81, Gallaghers at 35, Gardeners bar at 87, and Teachers at number 60] but with the passage of time some pubs close up and disappear while others change their names. So at least if we document them at lest people will know that once upon a time they did exist.

Bedford st, north side.

Nuala McFadden-Reid
Tells me that her close on the north side was one along from a private nursery which stood at 42 Bedford st and it catered for 3-4 year old weans.

Nuala lived at number 38 and remembers a lovely Indian man having a furniture shop at one side of her close-mouth.

There was Ellis's fruit shop at the corner of Bedford st/Nicholsoon st and **Bill Danks** had his motor garage here on Bedford st in between Nicholson st and Portugal st.

Bedford lane, south side/north side.

Next we come along to Bedford lane south side which had Lipton's Monumental sculptures yard here at the corner with Portugal st [The John Knox U.F.Church once stood here].

I remember standing here looking at all the monumental head stones when I was about 10 years old [in 1958] and thinking to myself what will I be like in the year 2000, I'll be 52 years old then !!!!

Well I'm now 72 but I clearly remember that day just like yesterday.

On the north side of Bedford lane you had the side elevation of Gorbals swimming baths.You had access to Bedford row from Bedford lane but it was more or less a short cut to Gorbals st [once Main st].

Herbertson st, south side/north side.

Herbertson st is the next of our [Horizontal streets] streets running west to east and here we had at one time a Hairdressers shop, a newsagents, a cobblers shop and a Chemist in it.

Dunmore st, south side.

Dunmore st was a fairly short street with the Princess bar on the south side with tenement dwellings going from 42 to 26 which took us to the junction with Bedford row.

In between these numbers we had 2 Pends, between 42 and 36 then between numbers 34 and 28. These Pends would allow access to any out-houses/workshops. Then crossing over Bedford row we had St Johns infants school and that was Bedford row and Portugal st.

Liz Donaldson, tells us that she lived above the Princess bar in Dunmore st.

Dunmore st, north side.

We had tenement dwelling numbers 1 to 39, number 1 was at the junction with Portugal st and number 39 was at the corner with Gorbals st. At numbers 5 and 7 we had Dunmore warehouse on the ground floor and numbers 11 and 13 were the

August Creameries and number 13 was right on the corner with Dunmore lane.

We now crossed over Dunmore lane and we had S, Stewart and sons at number 29 and tenement dwellings till we reached number 39 which was the end of Dumore st as it joined Gorbals st.

Norfolk st, south side.

On the south side of Norfolk st we had the British Linen bank [with Mr Devine the Dentists surgery above]

There were so many pubs along Norfolk st, so I will try my best to name them, the numbers on Norfolk st south side ran from 141 to 13 where we had Webster's pub at the corner with Coburg st, Thomas Pattersons pub at 119.

Then at number 99 we had South Portland st, crossing over we had the St Mungo Vinters [Gordon bar] at the corner.

We then crossed over Norfolk court with tenement dwelling numbers 83 to 71 and we crossed over Nicholson st [in between Nicholson st and Portugal st we had a Pend which took us into Portugal lane]

On the opposite corner heading towards Gorbals cross on the south side of Norfolk st we had Robin's bar at number 69, then numbers 65 to 47 and here at 47 we had McGovern's Central bar and crossing over Portugal st we had Ropers bar at the opposite corner at number 45.

Then moving along to number 29 we had Dunmore lane, and crossing over it we had numbers 23 to 13 Norfolk st. Then we had the Garry Owen public house at numbers 15-17. then after the Garry Owen we had numbers 11,9 ,7 and 5 which took us to Arthur Blacks gents outfitters shop.

Allison Carrol,
Arthur Black's Gents' Outfitters at corner of Norfolk Street, Munro the Butchers couple of steps further. Charlie the barbers where l was frequently sent for 'a half ounce of Condor Sliced' for Dad's pipe. No problem being served aged 7, all these shops were on the same side of the street where I lived, we lived at number 5 on the odd numbered side of the street.

Helen Carlin,
Favourite shops in Norfolk Street: Johnny Simpson's newsagent, Joe the Robber's, Joe O'Donnell's, Blackadder's ironmonger, the Co-op and Law's leather goods and toys. Mr. Devine the dentist at the corner with Eglinton Street.

Norfolk st, north side.

On the north side of Norfolk st, the numbers were 150 to 42 and we had a few more public houses which were Stevenson Taylors [The Glaswegian], on the corner at number 150, The Portland arms [Vogts/ McNees] at number 102 and the Norfolk arms at number 68-66.

We had Templetons, Norfolk Traders, a hairdressers, M Simmons &son, Rosses dairies ltd, Thos: Gall glazing and glass, a Cafe /Restaurant and Molle Anne gowns /dresses among other shops.

I couldn't name all the shops, this is the best that my research could come up with so please forgive me if there are any shops that I haven't mentioned and hope you forgive me.

Oxford st, south side.

Oxford st had 7 public houses going back to the early part of the 20th century but I believe the ones that were still standing in the 1950/60' were Mallarkey's on the south side at number 129, and the other 3 were on the north side which were the Club [Grahams bar] at 188, the Kings Arms at 130 and Quinns Tavern at number 106.We had numbers on the south side going from numbers 155 to 1, we had a multitude of shops, we had the large drapery warehouse then Pentinsky's knitwear shopt at 7-13.

Carol Connelly and her sister Sandra [above] lived at 9 Oxford st.

Starting at the corner of Oxford st/Bridge st we had the Commercial Bank of Scotland at number 155 and the Bank of Scotland on the corner of Oxford st/Gorbals st at number 1.

Oxford st, north side.

On the north side of Oxford st we had numbers running from 194 to 2, the Mission Dispensary at 50-46, a very large warehouse which was a shoe manufacturers at 36-26 among a few more shops and Harry Crown's woolen merchant shop right on the corner of Oxford st/Gorbals st.

Between numbers 43 to 65 Oxford st we had a three storey high factory which was built originally for a Mr James Wilson who was an iron tube manufacturer this changed hands many times over the years for other owners like, model makers/whisky merchants/bacon curers. Beside Quinn's tavern we had a shop owned by a H Brown then a toy shop /factory and an upholsterers.

I'm Helen Carlin.

I lived at 79 Oxford Street, opposite Quinn's Tavern, where our coalmans horse used to stop from force of habit, whether he was going in for a pint or not. Loved living there. Plenty of spare grounds, dykes and middens to play in and nipping into town over the suspension bridge with my Mum.

Now we come to the last street running from west to east in section 2 of my Gorbals street map.

Carlton court, south side/north side.

On the south side of Carlton court we had numbers going from west to east as number 2 to 22, number 6 was the Carlton bar public house with dwellings above it but overall Carlton court with numbers 2 to 22 south side and numbers 15 to 33 north side was a cluster of workshops and small factories, including the Carlton brass foundry, marine engineers academy, friendly bread association and small business's such as joiners, tinsmiths, and a hatters. There was access passageways either side of Carlton court to get to these small units but because it was narrow at some points some workshops would use sliding doors rather than traditional door opening methods. Altogether Carlton court was a site for small workshops and had its entrance from Bridge st right through to South Portland st.

This is the end of section 2 of my Gorbals street map.

Chapter 5

Gorbals People's Stories

Leonard Vine.

I was born in 1940 and as a kid I lived at 10 Abbotsford place, Gorbals, Glasgow where I stayed with my family till 1955 when I was 15, and we then moved to East Kilbride.

At Abbotsford place there was me and my mother, father and my sister Stella. We also had my two uncles staying with us, I went to Abbotsford school until I was 13, then onto Queens park senior secondary school.

I vividly remember walking to school daily along Abbotsford place past Cumberland street to Abbotsford school and for some reason, I don't know why, I always remember passing Geneen's restaurant and hotel. It stood out from the rest of the black tenement because it was painted white.

Many years later in Toronto, I would have a chance meeting with the granddaughter of the owner of Geneen's, but that's another story.

My life as a kid in the Gorbals was very typical. Some days for fun after the rain, we would race matchsticks along the flowing rain on the tram tracks at Abbotsford place. Yes, there used to be tram tracks there. I did some research and found that there was a short lived tram service on the street in 1925 that went all the way along South Portland street, but the rails never got tarred until sometime in the late 40's or early 50's.

I would have fun as a kid just by walking. I would often walk from Abbotsford place, cross over Bedford street and continue up South Portland street, then go across the suspension bridge and enjoy the view of the river Clyde.

I also remember that there was a great library at the corner of South Portland street and Norfolk street, which I often went into. Another time I would go along Bedford street to Eglinton street, and on the left was the Bedford picture house and on the right was the Coliseum. I thought I had died and went to Heaven. I loved going to the pictures. I remember my dad used to take me to the Bedford to see the double bill of the Jolson story and Jolson sings again.

One thing that was a constant source of disbelief whenever I would meet up with some ex-pat Glaswegian years later was the subject of indoor plumbing in the Gorbals, particularly the toilet facilities. They would talk with less than fond memories about the "stairheid lavvy" that was shared among 3 families and how you went to the public baths at Gorbals street once a week.

Of course, I could only relate to my own living conditions, and when I told them we had a full indoor bathroom at Abbotsford place they would say, "Naw, you're mistaken". they must have thought I was some kind of snob, but I was just telling the truth, as I saw it. Apparently at one time, so I have been told, Abbotsford place was quite a swanky place to live, long before the neglect set in.

One "celebrity" who lived on our street with his family was a band leader and musician Harry Margolis. He had a long career as a band leader in Glasgow, and was still playing at the Pivo - Pivo, on Waterloo street, well into his 90's.

I remember in 1953, seeing the Queen's Coronation on the telly. One of our neighbours was the first one in the street to get a TV, so naturally people would flock to her house to see this great event on her spanking new 13 inch Eckcovision floor console TV, with its highly polished wood cabinet.

Speaking of Royalty, another thing I remember around this time was when they changed the Royal cypher on pillar boxes to E11R, which incensed most Scots, because historically she is Queen Elizabeth 11 of England only. Needless to say, there were lots of vandalized pillar boxes.
But regardless, E11R remained on the pillar boxes, and the furore eventually died down.

My father worked as an engineer at Rolls Royce, East Kilbride, which facilitated us in getting a house there, as part of the tenement clearance programme, or whatever you wanted to call it.

So life began for us in East Kilbride in 1955, with a spanking new house at 21 Kirktonholme crescent, complete with modern fireplace in the living room, which we later replaced with a Cannon Gasmiser fire.

The other rooms had no heat, so during the cold weather, we had to get portable electric heaters in the bedrooms, aided by the good old hot water bottle in bed.

One of my uncles was interested in Photography, and that interest rubbed off onto me,which I still enjoy to this day, along with the latest video technology.

In 1956, I was employed at Rolls Royce as a trades apprentice for 5 years, working on components for jet engines. During this period at Rolls Royce, I was also put on what was called a day release programme, whereby I was sent to David Dale College in Bridgeton, one day a week, to learn various job skills. After my 5 year apprenticeship, I became a Jig and tool designer working in the Rolls Royce design office. At the newly built [in the 1950's]East Kilbride town centre, which was much smaller than it is today, we had a 5 pin bowling alley, a ballroom and a hotel, so our social life was pretty good, musically we listened and danced to the likes of Elvis and the Everly brothers.

In 1962 after 7 years, our family decided to leave East Kilbride and move back to Glasgow. We settled in the Victoria road, Queens park area.

In 1966 I made the monumental decision to emigrate to Canada, to pursue greener pastures. This decision puzzled my parents no end, who couldn't understand why I would leave my home and a good secure job behind, but, at age 26, I felt like a change.

In Toronto, I had no problem getting jobs, because of my engineering background. Over the years I worked at places like De Havilland aircraft, working on the Dash 8 commuter plane, and at Spar Aerospace, who built Canada arm for the N.A.S.A. space shuttle programme. I retired in 2001.
While keeping my passion for photography and video going on the side. I've been enjoying my spare time converting old super 8 movie films to D.V.D.

- - - -

My Name is Cathy Byrne

I was born in Lawmoor st but then we moved to Castlemilk although we weren't there long. We then moved to back to the Gorbals to Surrey st when I was about 4 but left when I was 7.

Then we moved to Priesthill and my oldest brother Eddie [born in 1955] still got the bus to the Gorbals as I still had to make my communion in St Francis and my brother was finishing his primary school.

I had another brother named Francis who was born in 1958 but sadly he died in that same year. In 1961 my younger sister Theresa was born.

In fact the years my brothers and sisters were born were =James [1951], Margaret [1952], Eddie [1955], Myself [1956], Francis[1958], Janice 1959] and Theresa 1961

I would love my wee granny to get a mention. She stayed in the Gorbals all her life. She died in 1969 and still had an outside toilet, she got moved to Yoker and lasted about 5 minutes lol and then back to the Gorbals, she passed away at 294 Florence st.

I would also like to give two of my cousins a wee mention, they are Rosemarie McDermid and Joan Coburn.

Authors note
Sadly, when typing this book-up my pal Cathy passed away, it was such a shock to her family and friends. R.I.P.Cathy. I can't believe I wont see you again, not on this earth anyway. xx

I always met up with Cathy and other friends when I pay my yearly return to Glasgow, we meet up in the Clutha public house in Stockwell st as it is in the Toon and easy to get to by bus from all areas. Its an open invitation to everyone.

Actually the Clutha vaults is ran by Gorbals man Alan Crossan and is a great pub for music, food and drink.

- - - -

Peter Mortimer

I was born in the Gorbals in 1956 and spent my young childhood growing up in the tenements, and playing in the streets. To my young eyes, it was obvious the Gorbals was in decline, but even so, I had a wonderful upbringing, and yes, like most it was tough, but I wouldn't trade my memories for a million pounds.

We lived in the traditional room and kitchen on Ballater street, with the toilet on the landing shared with two other families, and by 1964 the movement of families out of the district had begun, as Waddell court got populated and new high rise blocks rose from the ashes of the old streets.

My da saw what was happening and didn't want to live in a high rise or be sent to a scheme such as Castlemilk, so the active search had begun to find us a new house away from the Gorbals.

As my da was a bread delivery man, he favoured moving to the East End to be near his workplace, so two new developments were identified and and applied for with the Corporation. The first was at Greenfield, lying just north of Shettleston, and the other was Janefield street at Camlachie.

It was here that one of the strange quirks of fate happened that changed my life and that of my family. A postcard came in from the housing department telling us that we had been allocated a new house, and at the top right hand corner of the postcard, the letter "G" had been scored out and substituted with a letter "J ", meaning we had initially been allocated Greenfield, but for whatever reason, a clerk at the housing, had changed the letter and changed my life. I would never have met my wife had I went to Greenfield, had my two children, or been "Papa" to my three adorable grandchildren.

And so it was to be, Camlachie was to replace the Gorbals as my home district. I clearly remember getting off the bus at Gallowgate and walking round to Janefield street one afternoon, with my maw and da to ballot for their flat. I was struck by how smart the house looked, and intrigued by the football ground a few yards away.

After about half an hour we got the keys and went to view our new house, and wow, we were impressed. Living room, Kitchen, two bedrooms, bathroom and cupboards, and I distinctly remember the smell of fresh sawn timber and everything looking so good. We were three flights up, and lo and behold we had a veranda, and I excitedly went out to admire the view, which included half the park of Celtic park.

We left the Gorbals on 14 th of December 1964 and started our new life at Camlachie, and at the time, I don't remember missing the Gorbals, probably because I was so caught up enjoying our new surrounds.

Of course a new house also means having to make new friends, and the 15 closes of new houses at Janefield street were filled with people from elsewhere in Glasgow, but mainly Calton, Bridgeton and Parkhead, so more or less everybody was happy to strike up new relationships.

It didn't take long before I was enrolled in Camlachie primary school and was making friends around the district. Just before Christmas 1964, a few days after we left the Gorbals, I went back with my da to attend a Christmas party at St Mungo Halls, and this was the last time I saw my old friends, which looking back was such a sad thing, but I was too young to realise the significance.

Thinking back, the streets of the Gorbals were truly bustling, like all the shops on Cumberland street and Crown street, and I don't remember ever experiencing anything like that in the East End, somehow the Gallowgate didn't quite measure up to the "Sooside".

Growing up next to Celtic park was exciting, watching the crowds hustle into the park, then at the end of the game, watch the crowds leave from our veranda, and the movement of masses of people could make you feel a wee bit sea-sick, it was sometimes an awesome thing to see.

As I got a wee bit older we would go into the ground with twenty minutes to go when the gates got opened and watch the game. I enjoyed my formative years in Camlachie, but I always remember when asked by someone "Where do you come from" I would always answer "The Gorbals", something I do to this very day.

I didn't return to the Gorbals after we had left, I went on to get married and live in Cumbernauld, Falkirk and then back to the East end at Garrowhill where I now stay.

In the past few years I have however returned to the Gorbals on a very frequent basis, mainly to do with my passion for local history, and I now get such a buzz whenever I walk round the district.

I often think how my life would have played out had we stayed in the Gorbals, and I am still in contact with with my old neighbours from Ballater street, and they remained in the district,and weren't moved out to the schemes, but into a new house on Caledonia road flats.

I'm sure many of us have speculated how the Gorbals would look today, had the tenement refurbishments of the 1970's and 80's been started twenty years earlier, would we still be walking along Abbotsford place and Crown street, - - - we can only imagine.

- - - -

Helen Ann Congalton [Mortimer]

"Ma I canny get to sleep, it's too quiet".

It was August 1963 and I was 10 years of age and we had just moved from the Gorbals to Arden, but let's start at the beginning.

My name was Helen Ann Mortimer, my ma and da, Davie and Nellie and my sister Theresa all lived at 252 Florence street, Gorbals, Glasgow, right beside Dixon's Blazes and I loved the hustle and bustle and all the noise that went with it.

I attended St Francis primary school in Cumberland street and it was the best school ever. I remember my first day so clearly and how proud I felt. Sitting at my desk I couldn't wait to have access to all this schooling everyone kept talking about. I wasn't disappointed, the May procession after the first holy communion, will stay in my heart for ever.

My pastimes were playing skipping ropes, playing baws [against our room wall], kick the can and beds wae a peever in front of our close. Our kitchen window was in Kames street and was kept open until we came in. We would be out there all night playing except when "Champion the wonder horse" or "the Lone Ranger" was on the television. My ma would shout me and my sister and our pals in when these TV shows were showing, we lived low down [ground floor], very handy for drinks.

I would always be on the look-out for new baby's arriving with the "Green Lady" and when my ma said it was ok I would chap the ladies door and ask if I could take the wean out for a walk, then I would push the pram to Richmond park. This was a common practice amongst us girls.

Buildings had started to being demolished and these became another playground. We would play at houses in some of these buildings, my ma would have been horrified if she'd known. I can still remember the smell o stour as the buildings fell.

I had the pictures, the swimming baths and indeed the town all within walking distance. Cumberland street was where we went shopping and I loved the smells in the different shops. When the "shows" came to Glasgow green at the Fair we would walk there and back with my Da.

So in August 1963 I left the Gorbals for Arden. As it was the school holidays, I didn't have the chance to say cheerio to my pals, I was heartbroken. Our new house was at 1 Kilmartin place, one up to the right and it had two bedrooms, a living room, a kitchenette and a bathroom and a veranda. One of the bedrooms was mine and my sisters and it felt so strange falling asleep without the glow of the coal fire and no shutters on the windows to keep out the light [in days gone by these shutters would have kept out the glow from Dixon's Blazes].

It felt dreadful to think that I knew no-one and it was with apprehension I set out down the stairs and stared at that long path which would take me to unknown territory. Me and Theresa started walking down the path , only to be shouted back by the lady who lived in the close. "Have you been spitting in my close" she said. Horrified and crying I ran up to my ma and told her. She put her straight in no uncertain terms. My ma said we didn't do it in the Gorbals and certainly wouldn't there. Turned out it was the boy upstairs and we were given apologies all round.

There were lots of children playing and I bit the bullet and asked if I could join in and to my surprise they said yes. They were playing "tig" and instead of running in the streets we were in fields running through grass. Down the road we came to the "puggy" which ran from Arden to Thornliebank, we did lots of exploring ahead there.

The biggest change we noticed right away was that we needed buses to go everywhere like the pictures, the swimming and to visit my uncles, aunties and cousins[who had lived next door to us in the Gorbals] this of course meant more money, and as rents were a lot higher[I heard my ma saying that] it was money we didn't have.

After a short time my da took a job as a labourer in the Scottish special housing association yard in Arden.This was good both financially and meant we felt more a part of belonging.

By now I attended St Louise primary school, as I was 10 and in primary 7, having less than a year left in primary, my ma couldn't afford to buy a uniform so I stood out as the new girl. My first memory of this was being asked by someone in a very loud voice "Dae you come fae the slums ? " I answered with pride "No I come from the Gorbals". I have been asked that many times and I still give the same answer.

The teachers were lovely, I took part in all the activities and I soon made new friends, but still longed for my real pals. My playgrounds were now the fields and Rouken Glen park and of course the "puggy". when we walked along the "puggy" you came to the R.S.D. which was used during the war years.

We found gas masks and flat peevers. We took these home and were playing beds when someone said the peevers were actually in fact detonators left over from the war. The police were called and I can tell you my street cred went right up there and then. I was one of the crowd.

Maybe it was my young age, but I gradually felt at home, the main reason I think was after a short while I noticed faces I knew, there was Eileen who lived in the close facing me in Florence street, there was Betty from Oatlands and Helen from Kidston street. Oh my goodness some of my Gorbals was coming to me. In fact I passed my 11 plus [Quali] and could have gone to Holyrood but told mum and dad [I don't know what happened but ma and da became mum and dad !!!!] I wanted to join the friends that I had made and so went to St Robert Bellarmine. I am so glad that I did as I made friends, some of whom I still have and I met my husband there too.

I returned to the Gorbals for the firs time when I was 13 and I walked down my Florence street, and it was no longer mine. I couldn't bring myself to walk round to Kames street where our kitchen window would be, because my mum wouldn't be there. I felt like a stranger, the people I knew were gone and the ones left didn't know me.

Over the years, I have been back in the Gorbals quite often visiting my husbands family and saw it slowly vanishing. In my heart I don't think they had to rip us and all the buildings apart the way they did. I was last there a few months ago and passedced the library in Norfolk st and walked round the Citizens theatre. I kept walking and I was outside Florence street clinic but where was my Florence street, it had gone.

I still feel very emotional when I am there but my Gorbals of yesteryear will always be there in my fondest memories.

"Dae you come fae the slums?" - "No I come from the Gorbals."

- - - -

Allan Robertson

Around 1960 many households, including our own, were waiting and wondering what our fate would be when the powers that be finally decided where we would be shipped off to before our tenement in Lawmoor street, Gorbals was demolished.

There were new houses being built at the beginning of Pollokshaws rd which caught my mum's eye as she passed them every day on her way to do house-keeping in people's houses in the Pollokshields area of Glasgow.

"There's still a few left" was a fairly frequent comment from my mum as she hung up her coat after another days cleaning.
The day eventually arrived when a visit to the housing department was on the cards, so my mum and I headed out to take our place in the queue, full of anticipation and hopes.

The young lady who dealt with us must have thought a tornado had just passed as she offered the keys to one of my mother's much desired houses. In my eyes mind I see a doctor trying to reinstate the lady's arm in its socket after mum whisked the keys from her grasp. Perhaps the enthusiasm of the situation did overdo my imagination.

Roger Bannister would have been proud of the speed that we showed getting to our new abode, where we gazed in turn into each of the rooms in this mansion where we could now live. Not only were we to sleep in different rooms, but in addition to a kitchen with 11 cupboards and a double sink, there was also a living room and a Balcony. !!!

It is rather funny what sometimes crops up as your priorities, like sitting on the lavvy pan and of course just having to lie in the bath to see how it felt, an inside toilet let alone bathroom can be very enticing.

By the time my dad had finished work I had perused the instructions for our very own gas central heating, ready to show him it all worked, although I did have a numb bum after spending quite some time sitting in the lobby [sorry it was now called a hall] checking the valves and switches.

Wasn't modern technology great ??

I have lived in Perthshire since 1977 which is when we left our flat in Cumberland st. When we married in 71 we moved to Dalmuir, then Drumchapel followed by a return to the Gorbals in 1974.

- - - -

Ann Ward [nee Clark]

I was born and bred in hospital street, Gorbals, in 1959 and lived there until 1973.

My favourite pastime whilst waiting on my wee da finishing his pint in the Clelland bar, was skating up and doon outside the bar. It was a great street for skating on. My old skate would have been tied up with my ma's good American tan nylons. [tights].

After a while oot came my da and he would say "Take yer ma's wages up to her and tell her I'm having another pint, I wont be long !!". Off I went and to my delight my ma allowed me to go back oot on mah own with my skate !!.

Being the eldest of 8 this was a treat not having to look after others, so off I skated back doon to the Clelland with its big, wide smooth road, skating until my skate came apart in the middle !!.

I tried to put it back together tying my ma's nylons tighter n tighter but no, it just kept coming away. Heartbroken, I went into the bar to tell my da , who had moved to the lounge, watching the Go-Go dancers !!.

My da told me to go round the corner, opposite the wee swings and ask the man in the garage to put a "nut and bolt in". So off I went and asked the man for his help. "Nae bother hen, give me it here" and in no time my skate was sorted !!!. I was delighted and thanked the man.

Funny thing was I never ever got a "pair of skates", thought I was so lucky way the one !!. I played with it for hours and reluctantly let my wee sister Helen have a shot, but kept it secret fae my brothers Jim and John, in case they broke it. !!!

Telling this story to mah weans, they just can't believe how poor we were but happy just the same.

- - - -

Monty Borthwick

I remember the mail arriving one day. I think it was 1963 in Mathieson street, Gorbals where I lived in a single end with my parents.

My mum Jeanette Borthwick, opened the letter and shrieked with excitement. She picked me up and started swinging me around shouting "Oh my God, Oh my God,I can't believe it, I can't believe it".

Just for a moment I thought we had won the football pools, but it was better than that as my mum had just received notice that we we were moving to a luxury new 2 bedroom flat in Waddell court in the Gorbals not that very far away at all from where we lived in Mathieson street, in fact only a 5 minute walk.

In our single end we had shared an outside toilet with our neighbours, now we were going to have our very own flat with central heating, indoor toilet and bathroom. It's no wonder my mum was so excited.

I now live in Southsea, Portsmouth.

- - - -

Ann McLaughlin

My Granny lived at the corner of Cumberland street and Gorbals street facing the Granite City pub and it was a great house as it had windows in both streets, and we were always hinging oot the windae watching the world go by.

My Granny was always hinging oot the windae and could tell you who went in and out of the pub-time in and time out. You could see right down to Gorbals cross and along Cumberland street and then to Eglinton street. I think she had one of the best views in the Gorbals.

One time me and my pal Cath [R.I.P] who lived in Cally rd [Caledonia rd] decided to go to my aunty's house in Helensburgh as my uncle was the janitor for the Rhu yachting club.

So unbeknown to them we went out in a rowing boat and couldn't get back to shore. We just kept going around and around and had to take our knickers off to wave for help and had to get the rescue boat to tow us back in to shore. My aunt and uncle were not very happy and we never went back again.

Also when we were wee, we used to play Kiss, Kick or dare and I kicked the can and took my big toe nail off, and if we got kissed, there was one guy there who I will not name, that none of us would kiss and we pretended that we were sick or had to go home. Such a shame for that guy. !!!

Between Florence street and Crown street, the posh street in the back there was a big shiny tile thing that went the full length of 3/4 closes, and it was so slippery, we used to dare people to run across it, normally we used to shuffle along it on or on our bums, but there was still many a broken bone falling off of it.

I also remember the couch beds, you used to get that spring loaded and made it up into a couch. When I was a baby my Granny was watching me in Cumberland street and put me in the one in the big room, as we called it. My old Granda came in wae a wee drink in him and when my granny went to get me, she could not find me and asked auld Sammy"where's the babe"?. He said sure I don't know?. He had just shut up the bed/couch with me in it. Lol.

- - - -

Chapter 6

Section 3 of my Gorbals street map

The perimeter edge will be as below

Travelling down Cathcart rd and Gorbals st [Citizen theatre side] until we come to Adelphi st. Then going along Adelphi st until we come to Crown st, then travelling all the way up Crown st west side until we meet again with Cathcart rd where we started from. Then all the streets in between the perimiter edge.

Cathcart rd, east side.

We start at where St Ninian's Wynd Church used to stand at the junction of Cathcart rd and Crown st, we pass by this once magnificent Church and travel down Cathcart rd and next door at number 123 Cathcart rd stood the midwives hostel run by Glasgow corporation and next to that at 115 and 107 stood a large hall ran by the Church of Scotland which had a flat topped roof which was used as a "drying area" for clothes. It had iron railings in between the chimney stacks to save anyone from falling down to the ground or being blown over.

Then right next to the hall we had the Club bar at number 101, next to it stood a large shop frontage of a metal brokers, going down Cathcart rd we cross over Thistle st and come to the Govanhill bar at the corner of Cathcart rd/Thistle st, actually the 1877 built tenement that was above the Govanhill bar was built at an angle to accommodate the merging with Thistle st. This pub had a great reputation for good beer and when the tenements above were demolished the Govanhill bar stood alone at ground level as it was a going concern [as did a lot of public houses in the Gorbals].

We then had a run of tenement dwellings after the Govanhill bar with the old Cathcart bar standing just at the emerging of Hospital st junction with Cathcart rd.

Then travelling down Cathcart rd we come to the old public weighbridge that stood on a triangular island on its own.

I remember when I was an apprentice bricklayer that sometimes when I was being transferred from one site to another site that the lorry driver Joe Montague would weigh his lorry load on this weighbridge and both of us used to have to come out of his lorry cabin to get a "true reading" then when he got his ticket we headed off so I could be dropped off at whatever site I was required on. Its funny how some things like that always stick in your mind.

Just after and facing the public weighbridge stood the iconic U.F Church designed by Alexander "Greek" Thomson on Caledonia rd/Hospital st/Cathcart rd.

With its magnificent stone built tower it stands as a "beacon" in the skyline to that era of the old tenements that people of my generation grew up in. As I write it stands only as a shell of its former glory and hopefully in the future it will be used once again in some manner for the Gorbals people.

Next to the Church it had a Church hall abutted to it on Cathcart rd and then a run of tenements going down to the corner with Cumberland st and where once stood the Granite city inn public house [now the Brazen head pub]. Many a time years ago I drank in the Granite city with my work mate Jimmy Currie.

Now Cathcart rd has ended and its continuation becomes Gorbals st [formerly Main st].

Gorbals street, east side.

We had numbers 269 to 85 on Gorbals st east side. On the corner of Gorbals st/Cumberland st but going down Gorbals st east side we had a Chemist on the corner, a scrap merchants, a hairdressers, McLuskeys shop, [with a pawn shop above] then going by under the bridge we had a piece of "spare grun" use by Malcom + Allen to post adverts, Dr Connollys surgery, a shop for building trade workers, a sweet shop, the Glenbervie bar, [formerly Robbs bar], Johhny Hislops Pen[d] where he stored hand barrows and horses and carts, Johns second hand golf shop, a tailors shop, a wee greasy spoon cafe, Pacittis fish restaurant and lastly on the corner of Gorbals st /Cleland st stood the Falcon bar [but because a neon sign above the entrance said St John's bar, most people referred to it as St John's.

The Glenbervie.
Hughie Gallagher owned the Glenbervie, James McCreadie took it over when Hughie moved to the Tirconaill in Cumberland St, then moved to The Govanhill Bar.

I hope I have all the shops mentioned in the correct order but you have the general lay out and idea of the shops between Cumberland st and Cleland st on Gorbals st.

We cross over Cleland st and find the Kiosk cafe on the corner with Dr Anderson's and Dr McBeans surgery next to it, a few more shops then we come to the Palace Picture hoose.

Jeannette Cassie,
Tells me that later on when the Palace Picture hoose turned into a bingo hall, her mammy was the bingo caller.

Of course next to the Palace we had the Citizens theatre which had many famous actors/ actresses play in it over the years

The photo above shows the Princess cafe, with the Citizen theatre next to it and also the Palace Picture hoose further along, which later became a bingo hall. [the citizen theatre formerly name the Princess theatre].

We also had a dance hall at number 127 in between the Palace and Citizen's. Which I believe was on the 2nd floor.[?] Was this Joe Diamonds I believe it was.[?]

My name is **Dennis Smalley**, I still have an active Blues band in Glasgow called King Buddah.

In 1969 I won a talent contest at the Palace bingo and social club pictured here. The prize was £100 and the contest compere was Charlie Sim of the 1 o' clock gang fame.

I sang Ten Guitars and still will if forced by gunpoint.

James Brown,
Tells me that there used to be a passageway that ran underneath the Palace to the Citizens theatre, I wonder was it ever used by actors beating a hasty retreat after a bad performance !!!!

So in Gorbals st we had the Princess cafe where **Kathy Doogan** once worked, the Verretccia family owned it in the 1920's up to the early 50's. then it was taken over and owned by the Baggio family and their son Tony owned/ran it.

Immediately next to the Princess we had the Berta fish and chip restaurant, a few more shops including a Jewish Poultry shop, and then a newsagents, then we had John Verrico and co. ltd [tobacconists] then the Seaforth bar at the corner of [old] Rutherglen rd and crossing over we had the Citizen bar on the other corner of [old] Rutherglen rd and we are almost at Gorbals cross.

Just after the Citizen's bar we had a wholesalers shop, a hairdressers and at the "corner" with Ballater st we had Lena's fruit shop/florist at number 85 Gorbals st.

Crossing over Ballater st we continue going down Gorbals st and had a pawn shop at the "corner" of Gorbals st with Ballatter st and this was above McKellars public house [formerly the Athletic bar] which had a run of shops beside it heading north which included Maxwell's electricians shop, a Jewish deli's and the post office, a large billiards hall, a newsagents a few more shops then McLeans public house at number 9, then we come to the corner of Gorbals st and Adelphi st and we now go along Adelphi st.

Adelphi st.

We have numbers 1 to 242 [then Adelphi st turns into Waterside st, at the banks of the river Clyde, Waterside street before it came into existence was the continuation of Adelphi st and called Adelphi st].

So we start at number 1 Adelphi st where once stood the Horseshoe bar [Struans] right on the corner with dwellings above it, then the Adelphi filling station [petrol station] then crossing over Inverkip st [formerly Muirhead st] we had a run of tenement dwellings from number 18 to 28 which took us to St Ninian st with the railway line to and from St Enoch's railway station running parallel with St Ninian st with workshops in its railway arches all along St Ninian st.

We now come to Hospital st, crossing over it and continue along Adelphi st, on the west hand side of Hospital st, Adelphi st is just "spare grun" with a warehouse at number 43 Adelphi st.

This is us now at Thistle st and crossing over we have numbers 46 to 51 Adelphi st with the Old Burn foots vaults public house right at the corner with Crown st/Adelphi st.

John McLaughlin,
Tells me he lived at number 69 Adelphi st and spent his youth like most of Gorbals weans going to the Picture hooses and playing fitbaw in the streets, he tells me he played over in the Rosie graveyard opposite Twomax's. you can read more of John's story in chapter 11 of my book.

Crown street. - West side

We now travel up Crown st from Adelphi st and the Crown st that my generation remember was so full of shops, cafes, pubs etc. We had on the west side of Crown st, starting at number 2 to number 502.

At number 2 we had Jeans book shop, then a large area of "spare grun", next we had the Grapes bar at number 54, Jon's the Tailor, Wilson's butcher shop and Hooper's fireplace shop.

The photo above shows Stirling Hunter's shop in Crown st, where people could rent black and white TV sets on hire purchase back in the early 1950's.

James McCabe worked in Stirling Hunters as a TV mechanic and I will mention his story later in chapter 11. The Wheatsheaf Inn public house is just to the left hand side of Stirling Hunters shop.

Then we cross over Ballater st with Bata shoe shop on the corner of Crown st and along a wee bit was Jacksons bar and lounge, Carr's shoe shop,J.Daniels [Bookies?] **Stirling Hunter's** 2 shops and the Wheatsheaf bar right at the corner of [old]Rutherglen rd then on the opposite corner with [old] Rutherglen rd we had the Bank of Scotland, then Thomson's shop, R.S..McColls, Lombards chidrens wear shop, a Bakers and a newsagents among other shops till we came 164 Crown st where the Horseshoe bar stood at the junction of Cleland st. This pub was infamously connected to Gorbals gangster Jimmy Boyle.

Then we had numbers from 166 to 270 and in between we had wall to wall shops including the likes of Massey & sons ltd, City bakeries, McMasters the Chemist, the Post Office at number 194, a furniture shop, hairdressers, a dairy and other shops until we came to number 270 where stood Galls Drapers shop.

I meant to say at number 252 were the offices for the Jewish Echo newspaper as there was quite a large Jewish community in the Gorbals but later on they seemed to move out of the Gorbals area and mainly settled in the Giffnock/Newton Mearns area of south Glasgow.

We were definitely spoiled for choice of shops back in the days of the tenements and could take us ages to walk down the length of Crown st just looking in all those different shop windows.

Mind you many a man out with his wife would go into one of the many pubs to have a pint and a "hauf" and leave the shopping to her, eh !!!.

Crossing over Cumberland st and moving along Crown st we had Teaches pub on the corner at number 282 with again a multitude of shops including a Mrs Swains fruit shop. Newsagents, dairy, grocers etc.

Brenda Ferry,
Reminds me that Mamies cafe/ restaurant was next to my close at number 306 and lovely meals she certainly made as **Christina Milarvie Quarell** testifies to in saying she loved Mamies double pie with chips and stew gravy.

We now travel past all the shops and find ourselves at number 370 Crown st and here stood the Caley bar at the junction of Crown st/Caledonia rd.

Crossing over Caledonia rd we find ourselves on the opposite side of Caledonia rd and we have the Crown bar at the corner of Crown st/Caley rd.

Authors note

In the 1930's it was said that there were almost 140 public houses in the greater Gorbals area.

Shugi Coll, lived at number 394 Crown st and remembers lots of the shops that he used there including [up from the Crown bar heading towards Cathcart rd] we had Katie's cafe, then, a grocery shop, Doctors surgery, an off licence, the Hi-Hi bar, Deep sea chippy, Margaret's newsagents shop then further down towards the gushet with Cathcart rd we had a Charity shop, a petrol station with a car wash area.

Then this takes us back to where we started at St Ninians Wynd Church at the junction of Crown st /Cathcart rd. Which I believe was number 502 Crown st.

We now will go through the streets inside the perimeter edge of my map.

First of all we we start with the streets running south to north, ie, as in Eglinton toll headling towards the river Clyde.

Inverkip st, [formerly Muirhead st]

We have numbers 78 to 50 on the west side of Inverkip st, tenement dwelling from 78 to 62, number [78 was at the corner with Ballater st] then between 62 and 56, we had a Pend leading into a Bakery building in the back court area. We then had "spare grun" for a wee bit then we had the large Adelphi distillery which was number 50 and this backed onto the back of the Adelphi petrol filling station that had its frontage on Adelphi st.

Carol Campbell,
We lived at no 3 Inverkip street, Moved in 68. My memory is of a whiskey bond across the road. It had massive doors and a lot of stray cats used to get in from under the doors.

There was a saw Mill next to our close... Just a wee shop we used to get sawdust for the cat tray from there. Our living room was on the corner of the tenement and overlooked the Carrick on the Clyde. There was a garage around the corner facing the Clyde. Further down Inverkip St across the road was a bakery and some high backs. Memory sketchy as was only 8 when we left and was so long ago.

On the opposite side of Inverkip st we had Greens Picture hoose [Greens Picturedrome, to give it its posh name] this was situated right at the corner of Inverkip st and Ballater st. We had numbers from 19 to 1 on this side of the street.

Then next door to the picture hoose we had number 19 which was a large bonded warehouse [which was affiliated to the Adelphi distillery opposite in Inverkip st]. Then tenement dwellings from number 15 to number 1.
I remember as a wean of about 7 going to Greens Picture hoose but that was the only time I was ever in it and unfortunately can't remember the name of the film that my big sister took me to see that day.

Authors note,
Alan Pinkerton, was born in what was then called Muirhead st in 1819, he was a Cooper to trade and emigrated to America in 1843 starting up his Pinkerton's detective agency a year later. His agency's logo was "an eye" and was the first private agency formed in the States. Could be how we get the saying "private eye".

Cleland lane.

We had Cleland lane starting at number 82 [this was more or less in line with the back of the Glenbervie pub on Gorbals st] then "spare grun" until we came to number 70 which had an open passageway leading to a fair sized warehouse, then next door at 64 we had Hislops stables and a tenement dwelling right at the corner of Cleland lane and Cleland st.

Crossing over Cleland st we came to the side elevation of St Johns school with Cleland lane, [Ayrshire farmers had a place there] then skirted past the back of the Palace Picture hoose and then the back of the Citizens theatre [formerly Princess's theatre] and then next we had the children's playground right on the corner of Cleland lane and [old] Rutherglen rd. Here ended Cleland lane.

Crossing over [old] Rutherglen rd we had arches of the railway line leading to St Enoch's railway station, in between the arches we had a rag and bone man's in a Railway arch almost at Ballater st and after that we crossed Ballater st and here started St Ninians street.

St Ninians st, [later to be Mosque st]

On the west side of the street we had "spare grun" beside Greens Picture hoose and the first number was 48 which was the front entrance to that large bonded warehouse [which stretched between Inverkip and St Ninians streets]. Then next to that we had numbers 34 and 30 were the Cork works which was merged into the main structure of the bonded warehouse,[this Cork works was previously owned by Hodges tobacco merchants] then open space and then tenement dwellings at number 24 to 4 which took us onto Adelphi st.

On the opposite side of St Ninians st it was just the railway line above leading into St Enoch's railway station with loads of workshop spaces in all the arches underneath the railway line.

Hospital st, west side.

From the top end of Hospital st west side we had the Iconic Alexander "Greek"Thomson's Caledonian rd Free Church and what a masterpiece of architecture by Thomson indeed.

Next to that we had numbers 192 going all the way down Hospital st to number 18 which was the south side sawmills workshops.

From number 192 we had the usual run of Tenement dwellings with only a few shops at the intersection with Cumberland st at number 176. Crossing over Cumberland st we had Mr Christies shop at 170.

At number 110 we had Fords grocery/sweetie shop who had a broken down clock on the shelf, with a notice underneath it saying "no tick here" meaning no credit given, which was unusual because lots of shops in the Gorbals gave people "tick" until they got paid on Fridays.

Eileen Herald Boyle,
Says, In hospital st between Cumberland st and Clelland st was Charlie Duffy's grocery shop right next to Duffy's was Reid's dairy there was Leslie's further down past Cleland st on Hospital st, Leslie's shop was back up at the corner of Cumberland st and Hospital st. Christie's shop was opposite the Tirconal bar.

At number 96 Hospital st stood the Bluebird public house which was right on the corner with Cleland st.

Then crossing over Cleland st we had number 94 on the corner which was the Richmond park laundry service where people could get their laundry done for them [a kind of up market service laundry].

Leslie's dairy shop was next to number 94 at number 92, it was owned by Margaret & Maurice and their 3 weans worked there too, Angela, Bernadette & Joe and a lovely lady called Alice who was always on the ham machine (slicing), Hospital st weans used to get sent for "tic" but no fags on "tic"

Next to Leslie's shop was a "wee factory" where Mr Checkman made his tablet, macaroon bars, peanuts etc which he would sell from his wee shop under the bridge in Cleland st.

Then we had a run of tenement dwellings leading us down to Morton's sales-room shop, Pearl Bloch's bakery shop and right next to that we had the Turf bar at the corner of [old] Rutherglen rd.

Going over [old] Rutherglen rd we had a large shop front belonging to Fogell's wholesale grocers/Bakers and next to that we had the Clelland bar and music lounge.

Authors note,
The Clelland bar was a terrific place and I believe the first pub in the Gorbals to have live music bands. It was situated at the corner of Hospital st and Ballater st.

I used to go there with my girlfriend Rena Smith every Friday night to sit and listen to the Diplomats group who played there on Friday nights. The music lounge at the weekends was always packed to the rafters with punters having a relaxing drink while being entertained with the live music.

It was so busy that it was only table service from the barmaids who walked the floor taking your drinks order and bringing it to your table, When I used it there was a 10 pm closing time [back in the late 1960's] and unfortunately you would just be getting really in the mood when the last orders bell rang.

Lots of people would have got a "cairry oot" before the last orders bell and take their drink to their house or a neighbours house and continue drinking. I will always remember the Clelland with great affection.

I left Glasgow in September 1968 aged 20 to start my life of travelling. living/working in other countries and never saw the Clelland again.

I do remember after being away from the Gorbals/Oatlands area for 45 years that I decided on my next visit back to Glasgow I would go into the Clelland bar and have a pint and tell the barman how I used to drink in there 45 years previously, but when I got there the Clelland had been demolished as with all the tenements [well 95% of them.]

It was a sad day for me that day but I will always remember the magic of those weekend nights sitting in the music lounge with my girlfriend Rena drinking, clapping and cheering the music bands. I was 19 years of age with cash in my pockets and the world at my feet.

The Clelland bar and music lounge is pictured above.

Crossing over Ballater st and continuing down Hospital st we come to the south side sawmills factory at numbers 32 to 18 and then open space more or less till we come to Adelphi st.

Hospital st, east side

Going back up to the top of Hospital st we have numbers 245 at Cathcart rd end going down to number 25 which takes us to Adelphi st.

We had a short run of tenement dwellings form number 245 to 217 which took us to the junction with Caledonia rd and crossing over we had the Wallace bar at the corner of Hospital st at number 312.

From 312 to 153 we had a few shops and **Irene Catchpole** tells me I lived at number 157 Hospital st [above the bookies], there was Carroll's fruit shop on the corner, Mr Graddles butcher shop, Larry Bells fish shop, Weismans newsagents, and Walkers grocers.

And this took us to Cumberland st.

Going over Cumberland st right on the corner of Hospital st stood the Tirconnaill bar at 149 and we had a run of tenements down to number 101. Duffy's greengrocers was at number 115 Hospital st.

Brian Sweeney
Said I lived at number 149 Above the Tirconnaill bar.

We once again had a run of tenements with the usual shops until we came to **A. Tich** the Bookmakers that stood on the corner of Hospital st and Cleland st.

Authors note,
It was funny now when we think back but up to 1961 it was illegal for people to go into a bookmakers shop and place a bet and many a time the Polis would arrive in a " Paddy wagon" - "Black Mariah" and arrest all the people in the bookmakers, take them to Lawmoor st police station and they would be held in a cell.

On hearing people had been arrested in his shop the Bookmaker would go to Lawmoor st and bail them all out at usually anything from 10/- old money to a couple of pounds, that's why if you remember we had Bookies runners standing in close-mouths of the tenements taking peoples bets from them and he in turn placing the bets with the Bookie.

Of course if you won, you went back to the bookies runner and he would pay you out.

Changed days now indeed when you can go into a Bookies and sit having a "cuppa" tea/coffee and a snack while watching the racing or football on multiple TV screens, while reposing in an armchair.

Crossing over Cleland st and on the opposite corner we had L&J Allan Pawnbrokers at number 99 Hospital st, where Anne Ward tells me she sometimes was sent with the record player stuffed inside a pillowcase. She told me as if people didn't know what was inside the pillowcase but it had to be done back in those days to help our Ma's put a dinner on the table.

Between number 85 - 79 we had a Pend leading us into Number 81 dwelling and between 77-69 we had an open passageway gaining access to a Billiards hall.

At the corner of Hospital st and [old] Rutherglen rd we had the Sample boot&shoe company shop [later to become Concorde cash and carry].

If I remember correctly Hospital street had a lovely even surface and was great to use for your roller skates or maybe you made a boagie up and you went whizzing up and doon the street thinking you were Stirling Moss.

The photo above is of **Ann Ward** [nee Clark] born n bred in Hospital st , read her story in my Gorbals peoples story's in chapter 5.

Crossing over [old] Rutherglen rd and going down Hospital st we had the Central Synagogue for the Jewish community in the Gorbals [actually this building started off life as a relief Church in 1799 then later became the Hutcheson U.F Church before becoming the Central Synagogue] this building was at number 51 Hospital st, and then it was all open space and we then reach Ballater st.

Crossing over Ballater st we now come to numbers 49 - 25 Hospital st with a run of tenement dwellings, there was an open passageway between 27-25 which allowed access to the back of a Bakery. I'm afraid I don't have any names of shops for between numbers 49 to 25, only to say there was a vast open space "spare grun" from number 25 and that was us then at Adelphi st again.

Thistle st, west side.

We had numbers from 334 which was the Govanhill bar and ending with number 2 which was a warehouse at the corner with Adelphi st.

The Govanhill bar had a great reputation as a good pub serving good beer, we then had a run of tenement dwellings going to number 266 which was Mohammed Kushie general stores, his store was right at the corner of Thistle st/ Caledonia rd.

The singer **Alex Harvey** was born in Thistle st too.

Crossing over Caledonia rd we had number 246 Thistle st leading down to 210 Thistle st, we had the usual number of shops including a grocers a dairy, Mary Henry's shop [trade unknown] at 244.

At number 210 Thistle st we had Weisman's newsagents right on the corner and it was run for a while by **Margaret McGuigan Bonner**'s Da, as Mrs Weismans son was murdered and she gave up the shop. It must have been very hard for her to try and run the shop with her sons death on her mind.

Continuing down Thistle st we had numbers from 208 to 98. Number 98 was Kennedy's [Weirs] pub, which stood on the corner of Thistle st/Cleland st.

William McIntyre, says,
In this run of tenements between Cumberland st and Cleland st we had a few shops which included Isdales dairy, Hestons boot repairer at 100, Hugh McGinty's showroom at 114, James Lennon's second hand bookshop at 116 and then Fultons shop [trade unknown] at 146 Thistle street.

Margaret McConville,
I was born in Thistle street, there was a chip shop at the corner of Thistle St and Cleland street I used to hang about the corner with the cost boys and the owner Mrs Seickie who used to give us the crispies from the fryer on the cold nights for nothing I think she was Italian.

I never saw her for years as I got married and moved away until my Mum, sister Agnes and me went into a restaurant in Gorbals

St near the Palace Picture hoose and who do you think owned it Mrs Seickie and she remembered me which was amazing..

Once again we had the usual run of shops between 94 to 62 and number 62 was the Horn bar. [Nicholsons.]

Just before that at number 72 we had a large Billiards hall where many an unemployed man would go to while away the hours watching a game of Billiards being played.

The Horn bar was at the corner with Thistle st and [old] Rutherglen rd . The photo next/page will refresh your memory of where Thistle street met with [old] Rutherglen rd. Horn pub at corner. [PH]

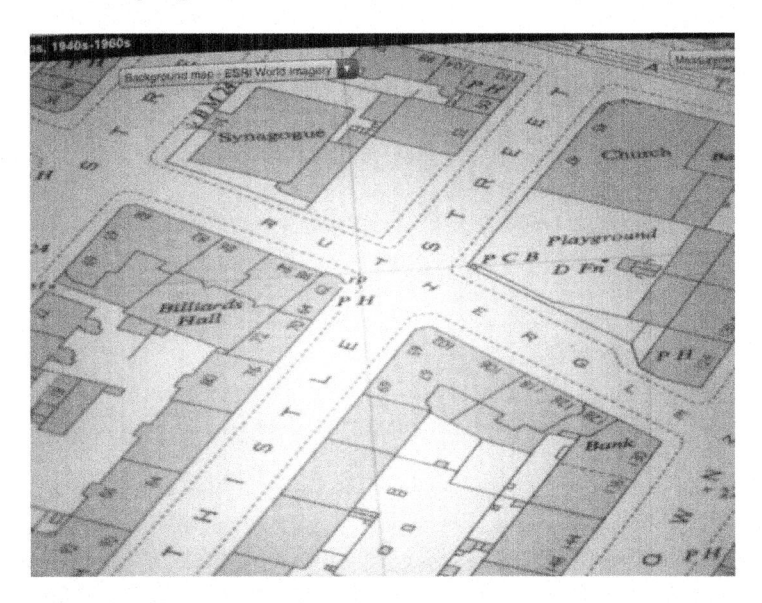

Now crossing over [old] Rutherglen rd we continue down Thistle st and find "spare grun" then we have number 52 and 50 dwellings with the Clady bar at number 46-48 and standing on the corner of Thistle st and Ballater st.

Crossing over Ballater st we had Taylor's pub on the opposite corner of Thistle st [of Stevenson Taylor fame, there were a few

Stevenson Taylor pubs dotted over the Glasgow area. Remember the one at the corner of Norfolk st and Bridge st]

Then next to that we had number 42+44 Thistle st and next was a warehouse at 34 and next to that was the large kippering works at 32-30, then an open passageway leading through to Hospital st.

Moving along we had dwellings at 28 to 20 and finally a large warehouse at numbers 8 and 2 and we reach Adelphi st and the river Clyde..

[Thistle street, east side.]

Starting at number 363 Thistle st we had the Club bar with a large shop front of a metal brokers, Boyd and Dunn bakers at 347, Anne Gordon's shop [trade unknown], Agnes Dundas [trade unknown] at 265, John Donnelly's showroom and next to that we had the Blarney Stone public house at number 259.

Frank McIlhone had a fruit shop near to the Caley rd end of Thistle st.

Frances Rogan, tells me that he later became a councillor with Glasgow city council.

The Blarney stone stood on the corner with Caledonia rd.

As we cross over Caledonia rd we have numbers from 251 to 209 which was Gallagher's pub [Havana bar /McCondachs/ Cosy bar.]. May's fruit shop was at 245, James Burt a dairyman at number 215.

Just remember that many pubs in the Gorbals area changed names over the years, [some more than once.]

At numbers 241- 247 we had open space which allowed access to any workshops in the back court and further along a wee bit we had number 219 which was called the "Local bar" [Star bar at one time]. Some people said I'll see you in my "local pub" and they meant it. Ha ha.

Alex Dundas, tells me that he lived right above this pub.

Then crossing over Cumberland st we had the Thistle bar at 207 and a run of tenement dwellings going down to number 111. We had a few shops including Daniel Schumachers a general dealer at 199, Mary and John McFarlane's dairy number [?], Mr Shaws at 197. Actually number 111 was Galloways Cooked Meat Factory and stood at the corner of Thistle st and Cleland st.

Steve Birrell, who founded the Old Gorbals picture facebook site was born at number 125 Thistle st.

The photo above shows my pal Barbara Carroll [right] with her sister Sandra to the extreme left and their pal Christina [McLaughlin] Gray in the middle standing in the back court of 222 Thistle street where Barbara was born and brought up.

I have met up with Barbara and her bestie pal Lorraine White on many occasions when I take my yearly trip back hame to Glasgow, we have met up in the Brazen head, Sharkeys and the Clutha bar at Stockwell st over the Toon.

After leaving the cooked meat factory we cross over Cleland st and we come to numbers 77 to 65 on Thistle st, again a run of tenement dwellings with Miss Duffy's shop [trade unknown] at number 77.

This now took us to the junction of Thistle st/Rutherglen rd. There once stood a large Playground area for children at this northern corner of Rutherglen rd and right next to that stood the Cunningham Memorial U.F Church and that took us to the corner of Thistle st /Ballater st.

Crossing over Ballater st we have on Thistle st numbers 41 to number 1 and we had Rachel Gilchrist's shop [trade unknown] at number 42.

Margaret Morrison,
Tells me that Gilbert's grocers shop at the corner of Thistle st/Ballater st had two great big Alsation dogs which frightened the life out of her every time she went into his shop.

Photo above shows the juncton of Ballater st- Thistle st

At numbers 33 to 27 we had a large engineering works [as shown in the photo above] then tenement dwellings with a pend at number 5 allowing access to the back courts for any workshops and arriving at number 1 and that was us back to Adelphi street again.

We now will go along the horizontal streets on my Gorbals st map

[Caledonia rd, between Cathcart rd and Crown st.]

South side + North side

Caledonia rd. South side

We had number 2 to number 22, Laing the newsagents was at number 4 then a very short run of Tenement buildings and number 22 was the corner of Thistle st/Caledonia rd.

Then crossing over Thistle st we had the Blarney stone pub right on the corner at number 30 Caledonia rd, again only a few tenement dwellings and then the Crown bar which stood at number 52 Caledonia rd/Crown st corner.

North side.

We Had Alexander "Greek" Thomson's Caledonian rd U.F.Church at number 1, then crossing over Hospital st we had the Wallace bar at number 5 with Mrs Kean's the newsagents beside it and a very short number of tenements which took us to the corner at number 23 and the junction with Thistle st.

Then crossing over Thistle st we had only a very few tenements from number 25 to number 47 Caledonia rd and number 47 was the Caley bar.

There were only a few shops on the above mentioned, with the usual newsagents and a dairy but I couldn't get the names of them, sorry.

Cumberland st south side, from Gorbals st to Crown st.

At the junction of Cathcart rd/Cumberland st we had the old Granite City Inn public house and I believe next to that was number 152 Cumberland st going onto number 166 at the junction with Hospital st.

Then crossing over Hospital st we had number 168 to number 190 which was where we came to the junction with Thistle st.

Then on the opposite corner of Cumberland st we had the Havana bar at number 194 and a very short run of tenements which ended at 282 which was Teachers pub at the corner of Cumberland st/Crown st. There were quite a few shops in that part of the south side of Cumberland st from the Granite City Inn pub right up to teachers pub at 282 and these included Carr's shoe shop, Tobias tobacconist's, Tommy Murry's newsagents, a wee Co-op shop, Davie Broons tobacconist/newsagents, McIndoe's dairy, Templetons, then a Launderette, a hairdressers and Carroll's bookmakers among others.

Cumberland st north side, from Gorbals st to Crown st.

A photo above of a very young Ann McLaughlin [who lived with her granny at 135 Cumberland st] at Saltcoats at the Glasgow fair fortnight holiday.

We had numbers from 135 Cumberland st to 163 which took us to Hospital st, then passing over Hospital st we came to number 173 which was the Tirconnaill bar, then just a couple of tenement numbers and we had the junction with Thistle st at number 185.

Crossing over Thistle st we had the Thistle bar on the corner at number 192 and only a few tenement dwellings which brought us once more to the corner with Crown st and Gall's the drapers shop at number 211.

Marion Maguire says,
This was Galls on the corner of Cumberland Street and Crown Street. In 1955 I was on the front Page of the Daily Record and the Express, as my mum was knocked down on the Zebra crossing by a motorcyclist who didn't stop.

She was pushing me in my big pram and pushed it away so hard it bounced on the pavement and either broke or cracked Galls window then bounced back towards the road, luckily a man caught it before it ran out in front of a bus. I was only one year old at the time and luckily my mum wasn't too badly hurt.

Once again there were quite a few shops from number 135 Cumberland st to 211 Cumberland st, again I'm not too sure of the exact position of the shops but I have tried my best to put them in order.

Starting at Number 135 we had McMasters the Chemist's, then a gift shop, the red star cafe at 155 [**Sandra Rmsay** lived above the red star cafe] Getlins shop, Woolfsons the drapers at the corner of Cumberland st/Hospital st at number 163, Crossing over Hospital st we had the Tirconnaill bar [Formerly the Empire bar] then Kelly's dairy, the Broadway Chippy and the Beehive drapers shop at 185 and the corner with Thistle st.

Leaving the Beehive and crossing over Thistle st we had the Thistle bar at the corner at number 192 Cumberland st, again only about a few tenement close-mouths and we then had Galls drapers shop at number 211 and the corner with Crown st.

Frances Rogan says,
Corner of Gorbals st / Cumberland st, Mcmasters the Chemist shop, Italy Ice cream shop I think it was called something "star", then a gift shop, then Woolfsons the drapers.

Corner Hospital st /Cumberland st pub then The Dairy, Dr's Surgery then the Beehive, travelling on we had the Thistle st egg store and Billy's newsagents then the Chippy then Galls, facing galls on other side was Templetons grocery, ladies fashion shop then the bakery then across Thistle st, Weismans newsagents, Victors fruit shop , McCready butchers, Larry's the fishmonger, then a radio shop that sold rechargeable Batteries and bike frames etc then the sweet shop and of course a pub at every corner, sorry I can't remember the names of all the shops.

We now come to Cleland st, south side – [formerly Greenside st].

At Cleland st **south side** we had St John's public house [whose proper name was the Falcon bar, but as it had a small illuminated St John's sign above the door entrance Gorbals people called it St John's]

St John's I believe was at number 79, and between numbers 75-67 we had Hislops stables, where he also kept fruit barra's then next we had a newsagents shop, then a few tenement dwellings which took us to number 67 and 63, with 63 which I believe was a rag and bone store at the intersection with Cleland lane and crossing over the lane we went under the railway bridge above which took us to McGowans confectioners and Cuthbertsons shop[?] then the Bluebird public house right at the corner of Cleland st and Hospital st..

Leaving the Bluebird pub and crossing over Hospital st we continue to the opposite corner of Cleland st/Hospital st and we had A.Tich the bookmakers shop.

Margaret Herd,
Says, my Da was Tich's best customers when he didn't have any premises, he just stood in a close with his 2 cronies then he got a place upstairs.

Then moving along Cleland st, after Tich's the bookies shop we had tenement dwellings from number 41 to number 27[?] with Crawford's fruit shop in between, then Weirs pub [Kennedy's] which stood right on the corner at Cleland st and Thistle st.

Then Crossing over Thistle st we had Galloway's bacon curers [meat factory] right on the corner with a big entrance/exit door next to it at number 17 which allowed access into Galloway's factory for lorry's/vans then only a few tenement dwellings which took us to Masseys grocers shop right at the corner of Cleland st /Crown st..

Actually, Galloways factory was originally built in 1911 as a grocery warehouse for Alexander Massey&son and it would have been only a short trip from Massey's corner shop to get their stock replenished from their factory just along the street.

Cleland st north side.

Going back to Gorbals st we turn into Cleland st and we had the Kiosk cafe on the corner, next to it was a sweetie shop, then William Andersons shop, next to that we had a shop front where you could pay for admission to the Palace Picture hoose stalls [and a passageway that took you into the Palace without having to go into the main entrance in Gorbals st]

Next was St Johns school which had a narrow passage way to its left hand side which led to the school playground at the back of the school, then on the other side of St Johns school we had Cleland lane.

Then after the school and just under the railway bridge you had the Ayrshire farmers right on the corner of Cleland lane / Cleland st and then we had and who will ever forget it !!

Yes Mr Checkmans hot peanut shop, selling all kinds of home made tablet, macaroon bars, toffee apples and the likes which were pure magic to us weans who visited there [including myself].

The "hoat peanut" man is such a great taking point for us who remember.

[Special thanks to **Gordon Smith**, and **Betty Gillan** brother and sister of the late Gorbals artist **Tam Smith** who gave me permission to show this image done by Tam. Gordon wrote a book called "Tam Smith, Art and soul of the Gorbals" and this is just one of the images inside Gordon's terrific book, available from Amazon].

After leaving the Gorbals swimming baths or the Palace Picture hoose us weans made a bee-line to Mr Checkmans [although as weans we never knew his name, we just called it the hoat peanut man or hoat peanut shop].

Next to Mr Checkmans we then had an open garage/repair place called Henry's motors, not sure if Henry was his first name or last name ? and of course next to that we had the Richmond park laundry. I can only think that people who had a fair bit of money would use this service as most women in my time as a wean went to the Steamie to do their weekly wash. Although there were a few Launderettes springing up from the 1950's onwards all over the soo-side.

So leaving the Richmond park laundry and crossing over Hospital st we had L&J Allan's pawnbrokers shop right on the corner and next to it was number 34 Cleland st and Jock Buchanan's newsagents shop and a few tenement dwellings which took us to the corner of Cleland st/ Thistle st at number 26, where I believe stood Mrs Seickie's chippy where you could sit down and eat or just get a fish supper or poke of chips to take away.

Crossing over Thistle st we had number 22 Cleland st right at the corner with Thistle st and a few tenement dwellings with Arthur Rose's drapers shop at number 16-17 [**Bridget McGee,** tells me she lived right above Arthur Rose's shop] and then a fruit shop at number 6 and finally we had the Horseshoe public house at the corner of Cleland st and Crown st. This pub was noted for being a hang-out for Gorbals gangster Jimmy Boyle in the 1960's.

There was an antique dealer named **Mr Altman** and I believe he had a shop in Cleland st , maybe near to Thistle st but I'm not sure [?].

Now we come to[old] Rutherglen rd, south side.

We had numbers 6 going onto number 130 which was the bank on the corner of Rutherglen rd/Crown st.

We start with the Seaforth bar at number 6 at the corner of Gorbals st/Rutherglen rd, there were a couple of shops here but the only two I could identify was a clothes shop that sold fair-isle jumpers and Harris's dairy then a Pend that led through to the back of the Citizens theatre then tenement dwellings and next was the weans swing park, which had a couple of sets of swings and a roundabout to keep the weans happy.

This playground was at the corner of [old] Rutherglen rd and Cleland lane. The railway line was right beside Cleland lane, so going under the railway bridge we had number 64 a tenement dwelling and right next to that we had the Turf bar at the corner of [old] Rutherglen rd/ Hospital st.

Continuing along [old] Rutherglen rd we had Samples boot & shoe company shop right on the corner [would become Concorde shop later] with a few shops next to it, then we had Thistle st and a few more shops.

Sarah McGrory says,
Hi Danny,
Rutherglen Rd facing the swings ... The bank on the corner at Crown st, Coyles fruit shop Tommy Murry's, McGowan's dairy, Maxies, an old Jewish man had a second hand shop, a hairdressers and the blinds making store = they had a van saying "a blind man drives this van". Which was a bit puzzling at first until you realized that it belonged to the blind making company shop.

As Sarah said we had those shops and the last one at the corner of [old] Rutherglen rd at the junction with Crown st was the bank.

We now go back to [old] Rutherglen rd, north side.

We had number 1 The Citizens bar going to number 109 which was the Wheatsheaf Inn pub at the corner of Crown st.

We had quite a few shops including among others Green brothers wholesale merchants, an engineers supply shop, A. Tich bookies, then a 2nd hand clothes shop [called Maggies ?]

Seems that over the years we had quite a few 2nd hand clothes shops in the Gorbals, not forgetting the rag and bone man coming round the streets and getting clothes off the weans in return for a balloon that usually never lasted the night or if it did, it was deflated in the morning but what a thrill getting the balloon and showing it to your wee pals.

Robert Brower says,
My dad was the manager of Tich's bookies in Old Rutherglen Road there was a second hand clothes shop next to it I think it was Maggies ? it was always busy.

The photo underneath is of [old] Rutherglen rd and the 2nd car after the Rover car on the right hand side is where A. Tich's bookies shop was, further down at the corner on the same side is the Citizen's bar on Gorbals st at number 1 [old] Rutherglen rd.

Passing by these shops we went under the railway bridge and came to just one tenement dwelling right at the corner of Hospital st.

Crossing over Hospital st we then came to the Jewish Central Synagogue, next to it an area of "spare grun" [which later became a post office] and then we had Thistle st. We had another weans playground here at the corner of Rutherglen rd and Thistle st and next to that was the Wheatsheaf Inn public house at the corner with Crown st. [this would later become Lennox's shop].

Ballater st, south side.

We had number 2 Ballater st [right at Gorbals cross] going all along to number 132 which took us to the corner with Crown st, starting at number 2 we had a newsagents shop, then Evans shop, a dairy, the Old Hampden bar public house, and a wholesalers shop among others which took us along to the old Cork works at number 42 and an open alleyway which had a rag store/ scrap metal in one of the ground floor railway arches of the railway line above.

Going under the railway bridge we then had the Clelland bar and music lounge at Hospital st/Ballater st and then crossing over Hospital st and we had "spare grun" on the corner of Ballater st/ Hospital st.

As we move along Ballater st we had numbers 96, 98,104 and at 110 we had the Clady bar.

Passing over Thistle st we then had the Cunningham Free Church and next to that was the Glasgow savings bank and the Bata shoe shop on the corner with Crown st.

Ballater st, North side.

We have numbers 1 going all along to number 145 which takes us to the junction with Crown st..

We start with number 1 which years ago was Arrols shop and I believe a Pawnbrokers above it, then at a later date we had a two or three shops there which were probably a newsagents and dairy and this took us to number 17 and the corner with Inverkip st.

Crossing over Inverkip st we had Greens Picterdrome Picture hoose at number 21 then,

Harry Jarvis says,
We lived at 24 Ballater st, had a Brothel upstairs and a couple of Nazis next door. There was a newsagent on the corner called Wullie Cousins, a fruit shop run by Teresa, a Printers owned by Evans, a butcher....I loved it even though we were dirt poor, We left when I was 9 in 1959 to go into the big time, upmarket flat in Govanhill that had two rooms, a kitchen and a bathroom with a real bath...

Then after where Harry Jarvis lived we moved onto St Ninians st and the railway line overhead that took the trains into St Enochs railway station. Moving along Ballater st we once again come to Hospital st which had the south - side saw mills on the corner and moving over we had number 91 on the corner of Ballater st/Hospital st to number 111 which was Taylor's pub right on the corner [of Stevenson Taylor fame].

Then leaving Taylor's pub we cross over Ballater st and we came to tenement dwellings numbering 119 to 145 and this took us to Crown st.[I'm sorry I have no information of shops between 119 - 145, as much as I searched in reference books or asked, no shops were made available to name, sorry.

This now brings us to the end of section 3 of my Gorbals street map.

Chapter 7

Topics

Co-op Divvy number.

How many of us can still remember our Ma's divvy number at the co-operative shop?. Well it was drilled into us all when we were weans and I still remember my Ma's – 57824. The last thing your Ma shouted to you as you were going down the tenement stair to the Co-op was "And don't forget mah number". Our Ma's got a dividend twice a year [or was it once ?] and she would get some money back as a rebate.

With this money she would buy some clothes and a few other things that were on her list and us weans always got a few penny's to buy sweeties didn't we ?.

I still remember the Co-op shop my Ma used it was on Rutherglen Rd/Snowdon street in the Hutchesontown area of the Gorbals. I stood there next to Ma as a 5 year old boy mesmerised as the cashier took Ma's money, placed it in a wee cup that was attached to an overhead wire and it zipped its way up to the main cashier sitting at her place high above us.

She took the money and put the change back into that wee cup and it zipped its way on the overhead wire back down to us.

To me through my weans eyes it was like something out of "Flash Gordon".

Oh and I just remembered there was always sawdust spread all over the floor, yes the Co-operative shops were very popular with Glaswegians with that dividend pay-out. How many of you reading this can remember your Ma or Granny's divvy number ??

- - - -

Hogmanay

Oh how I loved seeing in the new year years ago, I clearly remember my Ma would have the hoose in the old tenement cleaned spotless.

All of us weans were scrubbed clean and put to bed but at 11 am we were roused out of our beds to see in the new year alongside our parents and all the first footers who would come to visit us and wish everybody a happy new year.

My Ma and Da had a wee black and white TV set in the mid-1950's and we would sit there looking at Andy Stewart bringing in the Ne'erday, the countdown was on and it was 10, 9, 8 etc and then the bells chimed and the boats on the river Clyde would be blowing their horns [we lived beside the Clyde].

Our tenement house door was left ajar and soon we had our first footers coming in with a lump of coal for good luck and Ma and Da always had whisky, rum and beer on the kitchen table with enough Dundee cake and currant bun and mince pies to feed a battalion.

My sister and me would be sitting either under the kitchen table or hiding behind the sink windae curtain drinking cordial wine and shortbread while listening to everyone taking their turn to sing a song. Of course back in those days the TV ended by 11 pm usually but because it was the bells the TV finished at half an hour past midnight, just as Andy Stewart was getting into the swing of things lol.

I always remember saying to myself when I was about 8 or 9 years old, oh I wish I was grown up so I could drink whisky and sing a song, well my wish came true when I turned 18 and I never needed any persuasion to sing a song at the bells.

Those days in the auld tenements were the happiest days of my life, everyone knew each other, we all helped each and other whenever we could, our Ma's would never miss their turn of the stairs and you played with all your wee pals in the streets while under the watchful eyes of the neighbours who were doing their windae- hingin duty.

As I grew up into a young man I had a few Ne'erdays back in Glasgow but I left Glasgow when I was 20 years old and it just wasn't the same celebrating the bells in other countries.

I live here in south London in sheltered housing and no one celebrates the Ne'erday but I always sit watching the countdown to the bells on the TV, [opening my living room windae, to let the old year out and the new year in] and I raise my glass of whisky to the memory of my loved ones no longer with me and my toast is always a happy new year to all my own family and friends but at the same time my mind flits back to the old tenement days when we were all one.

- - - -

Old Phone boxes

Do you remember the old phone boxes in the streets with the A and B buttons, you put your 4 old penny's into the box then you dialed the number and if the person answered you pressed button A and you got connected and spoke to whoever you had called.

If you didn't get connected you pressed button B and your 4 penny's came down the wee chute back to you.

Of course some "bad boys" would shove bits of old newspaper up the B button chute to stop the 4 penny's from coming back to you.

The person who "lost" their 4 penny's would storm off in "the huff" while the "bad boys" would see all this happening from afar and come and pull away the bit of newspaper, get the 4 penny's and off to the nearest shop to buy sweeties or a couple of "single fags".

- - - -

Saltcoats by the sea

How many of us went away for the Glasgow fair fortnight or a week down to Saltcoats for your summer holidays, it was great, the pure excitement of packing all the suitcases and getting ready to go over to the Toon and St Enoch's railway station to catch the steam engine train to Saltcoats.

Then as the train pulled out of St Enoch's with the steam belching out of its funnel, you felt you were on top of the world. Your Da put all the suitcases on the overhead rack and you passed through the Gorbals with all its tenement buildings as you were on your way to the coast.

Then you arrived at Saltcoats railway station and immediately you could breathe in the sea-air, Oh what a feeling, then you walked to your wee place where you were going to stay for the next week or two.

As soon as you had unpacked you all went for a walk about the shops and took a wee walk along the shore, then us weans could play in the sand on the beach while your Da tried to set up the beach deck chairs for him and your Ma.

Lots of folks would paddle in the water while throwing some salt water from the sea onto their face to try and get a sun tan. Sometimes your wee Granny came with you too.

The joy of being bought a pokey-hat ice cream cone and playing in the sand was pure magic and they even had their own wee "Shows" down there.

Again us weans would be getting spoilt getting rides on the different things like the hobby horses and getting a stick of candy-floss and at night when you and the family went for a walk along the promenade you'd be looking at all the wee boats laying on their sides that the fishermen used and us weans playing on top of them.

It seemed every day the sun would shine [well maybe the odd wet day] and you made a bee-line to the beach after Ma had made the breakfast in the place you had rented.

It seems like half of Glasgow went to Saltcoats at the fair fortnight and my parents always bumped into someone they knew back in Glasgow. Then at night time on the way back to your wee place your Ma or Da would buy you a poke of chips with plenty of salt and vinegar and this was pure dead magic.

Then all of a sudden it was time to go back to Glasgow and you couldn't wait to tell your wee pals who unfortunately had no summer holiday about the great time you had.

Your Ma always made sure that you brought back a stick of rock for those wee pals [remember it had Saltcoats printed all the way through it].

Oh what a great place for your summer holiday although some other people preferred going to Dunoon or Helensburgh, it was great going away but great to go back to your tenement and play all your games.

- - - -

Midgie Rakin

Well how many of us done it ?, I was one of them and loved the thrill of trying to look for a find a "lux" or "luxy". Of course we would be on the look-out for Ginger bottles that people had thrown into the open middens because at that time [the 1950's for me] there was a penny or two deposit on them and if you found one, you couldn't run fast enough to the nearest shop to get the penny or two deposit money so you could buy some sweeties.

Although some shopkeepers said "that bottle never came from my shop", so you had to keep going to to find a shop that would accept them and give you your sweetie money.

Lots of times you didn't do "midgie rakin" in your own back court but went further afield to other tenements and this was all part of the adventure to us weans. You might come across a toy that was thrown out into the auld midden bin but to you it looked perfect.

Some days in the school summer holidays you spent the whole day midgie rakin going from one back court to another.

Then when you found a "luxy" you'd shout out Aw look what I've found and immediately the shout went up ["Hawfers" or "I'm baggin Hawfers"] from your pals, that was the unwritten law of the "Midgie rakers".

At the end of the day if you had found a toy that looked in good order you could actually sell it for a penny to some wean who liked the toy and more importantly who had a penny or two to spare.

Then when you eventually went hame for your tea and your Ma would be screaming at you "You been midgie rakin again hivin't ye" and you always answered "Naw no me Ma" then she said "well how come your covered fae heid tae toe in ashes". !!!!!

Of course that wouldn't happen today as "health and safety" would go bananas but it never did us weans any harm did it ? and nowadays how could you "midgie rake" a Wheelie bin anyway eh.

I look back now on those days and didn't we truly have a wonderful childhood growing up in the tenements, no computer games for us or videos, just playing our own games in the streets under the watchful eyes of our Granny's or Ma's or neighbours who were doing their windae hingin".

I honestly feel sorry for the weans of today who will never experience all the games and adventure that us weans of that era had.

- - - -

The Steamie

Nowadays most of us have washing machines in our kitchens or utility rooms but for our Ma's and Granny's years ago it was a different story for them.

They would have paid in advance for their weekly slot at the Steamie nearest to them, or to give it its official name "The Washouse". first of all all the clothing and bed-sheets etc was piled into a pram and then your Ma or Granny "bumped" the pram down the tenement stair and then pushed it along the street until they reached the Steamie.

Then they would sweat hard for a few hours doing their washing and then trying to get them dried before placing them back in their pram and pushing it all along the street until they came to their tenement close-mouth and proceeded to "bump" the pram back up the stair till they reached their door and put all the newly washed clothes into the drawers or cupboards/wardrobes. Or maybe aired them on the pulley overhead.

Then sat down to have a well earned cup of tea.

Of course while they were in the Steamie they got talking to the other women there and lots of news [or gossip] was exchanged and if anyone had been up to no good then their ears must have been burning as that person became "The talk of the Steamie".

There was another service that the Steamie offered and that was a hot bath and for threepence [or was it sixpence, I can't remember] you had the luxury of having a hot bath. In the tenements most of us never had inside bathrooms with a bath or even an inside toilet !!

You would climb up the stairs in the Steamie and sit on a bench waiting your call while the attendant filled your bath up with hot water using a "turn-key" from outside of your bath cubicle. When you lowered yourself into the bath [usually the water was red-hot] the attendant from outside your cubicle shouted more hot or cold water, you always shouted more cold but just as you were getting used to the heat of the water and using the carbolic soap given by the office down below where you also got your towel from, the attendant banged on your door "time up".

You then stood on a wooden duck board and dried yourself. Oh How you felt great and actually felt six-feet tall!!

Yes today we think nothing of waking up in the morning and having a hot shower or bath in out homes then chucking your clothes in the washing machine but oh how it was different for out Ma's, Granny's and Great Granny's back then.

- - - -

The Southern Necropolis

The Southern Necropolis is a cemetery in the Gorbals district of southern Glasgow. It was opened in the year 1840 to provide an affordable and respectable place of burial for the people of the Gorbals and the surrounding areas of the city of Glasgow.

Over 250.000 individuals have been buried within the many lairs.

The cemetery was established in response to the crowded state of the old Gorbals burial ground on [old] Rutherglen rd.

Proposals for a new cemetery were put forward in 1839 and the following year land was purchased from William Gilmour of Oatlands.

The first burial, that of a 16 month - old child took place on 21st of July 1840. There are three sections to the cemetery, central opened in 1840, eastern in 1846 and the larger western section opened in 1850.

Myself as a wean used to play in the Southern Necropolis with my pals and were always on the look out for "Vampires".

I only lived a 5 minute walk away in Fauldhouse st. It has been my pleasure to donate my royalty payments from my books over the years to help with the upkeep/promotion of the graveyard ran by my good pal Colin Mackie and his wife Elsie and all the other good folk who do such great work alongside them.

- - - -

Bridge street Railway Terminus

Lots of people today take for granted that the Central station has always been the "end of the line" for trains but they would be wrong because before the Central station was built all trains terminated at Bridge street terminus in the Gorbals [no not the subway station].

Bridge street main line station line terminal was built between 1839-41 and opened in 1841, then the railway line was extended over the river Clyde to become what we know today as Glasgow Central station. [formerly Gordon street station] The Central station opened in 1879, between 1901-1905 the Central station was refurbished and extended over Argyle street with 13 platforms being built.

- - - -

In the Summertime

Do you remember those hot summers we used to know when we were weans growing up. It used to get that hot it melted the tarmacadam on the pavements and we got that thirsty we used to beg oor Ma's to buy us a Jubbly or was it a Jubilee ? [triangular shaped frozen orange lolly] and how it froze your hands it was that cold.

Your Ma used to whitewash your sannies and leave them on the windae sill to dry in the hot sunshine, when they were dry you put them on to go down the stair to play with your wee pals in the street but your Ma's last words to you were don't you dare get any "taur" on them.

It was time to play a game of "rounders" with your pals [a game the USA copied off of us and called it baseball].

Then you would be playing all day in the sunshine and if you got hungry while playing you would always shout up to your Ma's windae "aw Ma gonny threw me doon a piece on jam", of course your Ma always obliged and when she threw it out the windae wrapped in bread paper it would land with a splat at your feet and you had it devoured in thirty seconds flat because you wanted to quickly get back to the game you were playing with your pals.

Here's a wee question for you all, with that many weans living in the tenements how come your Ma knew it was your voice when you shouted up for a piece, but she did didn't she. ?

- - - -

The Sub crawl

Being away from Glasgow for so many years I never realised there was such a thing as a "Sub Crawl ", I happened to be standing in the Laurieston bar in Bridge street in the Gorbals having a drink in the lounge bar with friends that I hadn't seen in many a year [but met up through face-book] any way it was a Saturday afternoon and there was my company about eight people sitting cosy enough round our table and only a handful of other customers.

All of a sudden the Lounge door opened and within five minutes the lounge was absolutely packed to the rafters, there had to be at least 50 to 60 people and they had one or two quick drinks but within 25 minutes they had all gone !!

I was dumbfounded !! until I was told that people join this "Sub Crawl" do it for a charity of their choice, they meet up and visit every pub nearest to every subway station.

They have one or two drinks in the pub, [alcoholic or not] then get back onto the subway train and get to the next pub and have another drink until they have completed the 15 pubs nearest to the 15 subway stations.

Then after they had all left all the barmen came out cleaned all the glasses from the tables. Made the pub clean again and within twenty minutes another 50 or 60 people had came into the Laurieston bar and the procedure happened all over again. I think that people who partake in the sub crawl say they will give a certain amount of money to charity if they complete all the pubs or just give a donation.

I think its a good cause as long as you can hold your drink but what a shock I got when this happened to me, of course all the pubs on the "Subway Crawl" do a roaring trade Eh.

- - - -

Chapter 8

Section 4 of my Gorbals street map

Going from the east side of Crown st north to and along Adelphi st, then along Lawmoor st, then along Kames st and back to Crown st.

Crown st [east side].

We start off at the top of Crown st, which was number 473 and going all the way down to number 1 which was Gerry Hurrell's pub [on the corner with Adelphi st].

So we had a glass doors/window shop at number 473 [which was the corner of Crown st/Kames st] then Joyce's fruit and veg shop and a few tenement dwellings till we came to number 437 and this was Kidston st.

Crossing over Kidston st we had the United free Church right on the corner of Crown st/Kidston st. The Oriental cafe was next door at number 425 and a few shops including McGuinnesses's bookies [which became a barbers, who gave a wean a penny dainty or lollipop for getting their hair cut withoot greetin !!!] Paccittis cafe then we had the Waverley pub on the corner with Crown st/Caledonia rd.

Moving along and over Caley rd we continue down Crown st at number 369 on the corner and at the other corner as we move along we find Souters pub on the corner at number 281 which was at the junction with Cumberland st. In between 369 and Souters pub we had a few shops including [L]omax toy shop, then Walls ice cream shop, Rheme's Haberdashery's, ladies clothes shop, the Commercial Bank, Bakers shop, and a shop for reconditioned hoovers.

Moving on down Crown st we leave Souters pub, cross over Cumberland st and st and we have the Cumberland bar on the corner at number 279 Crown st and a run of tenement dwellings way down to number 133 which was Simsons furniture shop right on the corner of Crown st /Rutherglen rd.

Of course in the numbers between 279 and 133 we had the usual number of shops, newsagents, dairy and not to forget that magnificent building which was Hutchesontown boys grammar school, there were two doctors surgery,one to the right hand side and one to the left hand side of the school as you looked at it face on but I'm not sure what the doctor[s] name was/were.
Then at the left hand side [heading to Rutherglen rd] you had 2 shops side by side "Andy's stores" was next to the surgery with a shop owned by a Mr Gray beside it.

Then you had Lesley's sweetie shop a wee bit further on and who can forget the George Picture hoose where we went as weans. I remember one Saturday going there with my big sister and some pals and my wee pinky got caught in the fold down seat and cut it with blood everywhere, my big sister who was in charge of me said don't tell Mammy [as my sister was supposed to be looking after me], so she gave me all her sweeties to keep me quiet and I never told my Ma.

Then after Lesley's sweetie shop we had a few tenement dwellings and ended up at Simsons furniture shop at the corner of Crown st/Rutherglen rd which was number 133 Crown st.

Crossing over Rutherglen rd we came to numbers 129 to number 18, I believe we had either a Cochranes or McVitties grocery shop on the corner at 129, number 18 was The Royal bank of Scotland building and in between these number we had a few shops including a butchers and a dairy and of course a run of tenement dwellings. After the bank we came to Ballater st.

Going over Ballater st we had numbers 79 to number 1 which was Gerry Hurrells public house. In between 79 and Hurrells pub we had a few shops and pubs including Sammerops wholesale shop, a radiators shop, John's dairy and Inglis drapery which had that overhead tube where the assistant placed money in it and it was sent overhead by wires to the assistant who usually sat high above at her/his till and the change was sent back the same way, an Army and Navy shop and a butchers, the other pubs were from Hurrells onwards, the Moulin Rouge, Alf Grants pub and Wards [Dykes] bar at number 17.

Adelphi st.

Turning into and along Adelphi st we had numbers from 60 to 69, this was just a short run of tenement dwellings and like most of Adelphi st we had so very few shops it was more or less commercial premises. Although we had Peter Balsistis chippy at number 62. Then number 69 was right on the corner with Florence st.

Crossing over Florence st we then had Adelphi st school at number 85, then a tenement at number 91 and right next to that was a large warehouse with a vast expanse of "spare grun" which then took us to Commercial rd.

Crossing over Commercial rd we had a public house on the opposite corner of Adelphi st/Commercial rd **[in my research of the 11 public houses that once stood on Adelphi st the only pub I can find at this junction is a pub owned by a Mr John Mitchell, its stated the address was 116, so this must be it ?]** then a tenement numbered 126 next to it then again a large space of "spare grun" and a tenement at number 134 and this was us now at Lawmoor st.

Lawmoor st [west side].

We start at number 8 right on the corner with Adelphi st and travel along one of the longest streets in the Gorbals 'till we reach number 470 which faced onto the perimeter/boundary wall of the Southern Necropolis graveyard.

Starting at number 8 where we had number 14 tenement abutting against it and then a a large piece of "spare grun" which showed the back of the Bee's Picture hoose, then we had tenement dwellings next at number 40 right down to number 76 which was Andrew McFarlanes public house which was on the corner of Ballater st. In between number 56 and 62 there was an open passageway to allow access into the back.

Crossing over Ballater st we then came to the Brechins bar on the opposite side of Lawmoor st/Ballater st which was number 88 and we then had a run of tenements from number 88 to 162 which took us to [old] Rutherglen rd. Between number 158 and 154 we had an open passageway to allow access into any workshops in the back courts. There weren't many shops here in this run of tenements just the odd one dotted here and there.

Going over [old] Rutherglen rd we had numbers 164, 170 and 172 tenements and Galbraiths shop stood there as did Campbell's newsagents and a wee dairy I believe, then after 172 was "spare grun" and this took us to Spring lane, crossing over Spring lane we had tenement number 184, 188, 190 and 192 then "spare grun" again and tenements numbering 204 to 246 and next to that we had Lawmoor police station.

Just before we reached the Police station we had Betty McLellands dance studio.

I always remember the air raid siren on top of the single storey flat roof of the police station, and it didn't half make a din when it was tested. This took us now to Cumberland st.

Not forgetting the guy who stood with a barra selling whelks on the corner of Lawmoor st /Cumberland st.

Going over Cumberland st we had number 274 on the corner of Lawmoor st/Cumberland st which was Georges fruit shop and this ran to number 364 at the corner with Caledonia rd. There was a bookies shop on the corner of Lawmoor st/Caledonia rd. **John Knotts** lived at number 311 Lawmoor st.

This photo is of my pal **Cathy Byrne [R.I.E.P.]** born in Lawmoor st read her story in Chapter 5.

Then as we move over Caledonia rd we had the Welcome Inn public house [formerly the Black Swan, or "mucky duck" as it was nicknamed]

Rena Devlin,
I lived at 378a Lawmoor st, my husband John Devlin worked in the Welcome Inn pub.

Moving along Lawmoor st the tenement numbers were 378 to 440, and at number 440 we had a pub on the corner of Kidston st and Lawmoor st, which was Jimmy Mahers pub.

Going over Kidston st we then had tenement numbers from 456 at the corner to 470 and this was the end of Lawmoor st west side, with the gable end of this last tenement facing Dixon's blazes iron works.

Kames st.

Then we had Kames st which only had 2 close-mouths in it, Kames street was sandwiched in between Florence st and Crown st and we had a Glaziers shop on the corner of Crown st/Kames st and this takes us back to Crown st itself where we started from.

This is us now at the end of the perimeter edge of section 4 of my Gorbals street map.

We will now travel down all the vertical streets [south to north] inside the perimeter edge of section 4 of my Gorbals street map.

Florence st, west side.

The photo above is of a young Helen Ann [Mortimer] Congalton, standing in Florence st, the street she was born in. The view is looking down towards the river Clyde. Read Helen's story in Chapter 5.

Florence st again was another one of the longest streets in the Gorbals with the lower end of it being once called Rose st. We start on the west side and start at number 352 which was on the corner with Kames st and we had four closes of tenement dwellings where we then had number 340 which was at the corner with Kidston st.

Crossing over Kidston st we then had number 336 going on to number 286 and the junction with Caledonia rd. At number 306 we had Hones provision shop, which was directly opposite the entrance to Camden st school [you would have thought that the main entrance would have been in Camden st ?]. There was also Arthur's dairy shop near to Caledonia rd.

Moving over Caley rd we had number 280 Florence st on the opposite corner and a run of tenements with a second hand bike shop in it.

Janice Docherty says,
Wee Lizzies dairy had a slot machine on the premises, my wee sister spent every penny she had in there. We had a dairy among other shops and then we came to number 204 Florence st and the junction with Cumberland st.

Crossing over Cumberland st we had the Moy bar right on the corner of Florence st/Cumberland st [once ran by Charlie Tully]. Immediately after the Moy bar we had number 196 Florence st running down to number 110 which was the junction with [old] Rutherglen rd.

Between numbers 178 and 174 Florence st we had a Pend giving access to any workshops/stores and between 174 and 164 we had the back entrance to Hutchesontown boys grammar school as we move down Florence st we had Knotts restaurant at number 120 and many a good meal was served there by Mr and Mrs Knotts who were from the Scottish Highlands I believe.

They used to have a giant sized dumpling in the front window.

Jane Carberry Marley,
Says I lived in close number 118 which was right beside Knott's restaurant.

I think there was a pawn shop next close [upstairs] after Knott's restaurant which would be the last close before [old] Rutherglen rd. at number 114, Then we had number 100 Florence st which brought us to [old] Rutherglen rd.

Marilyn Allan, says,
I stayed at 174 Florence Street and used to draw a chalk house with chalk table and chairs and sit in the middle of the street . Nae traffic!

Moving over [old] Rutherglen rd we had the Hutchesontown Parish Church then numbers 90 to 72 with a small electric sub station between number 76 and 72 and then right beside that we had The Tavern bar public house, which was right on the corner with Ballater st.

Margaret Fullerton,
"Hi, Danny,
My granny stayed at 51 Florence Street across from the Tavern pub owned by John Adams, we used to always shop at a bakers called Wullie Marks in Ballater Street, all our family loved the morning rolls, pies etc the cream cookies were to die for.

I remember my granny sending me down to the shop one Saturday morning at 6 am to ask Wullie if I could use the phone to find out if my mother had her baby yet I phoned the Ross hospital in Paisley and was told she had a lovely baby boy my brother is 49 years young what a lovely memory".

Now crossing over Ballater st we had the Ballater arms pub on the corner on Florence st/Ballater st at number 66 and an open passageway gaining access for shopkeepers or for the Florence st clinic whose main entrance was at number 26 then just after the clinic there was another open passageway which once again allowed access to the back of the clinic. Then we had number 6 and number 2 which was us at corner of Adelphi st. Remember that Sammy Wilson who was Benny Lynch's manager had his gym here in what was once named Rose st.

Here is a Gorbals street map of the aforementioned to refresh your memory.

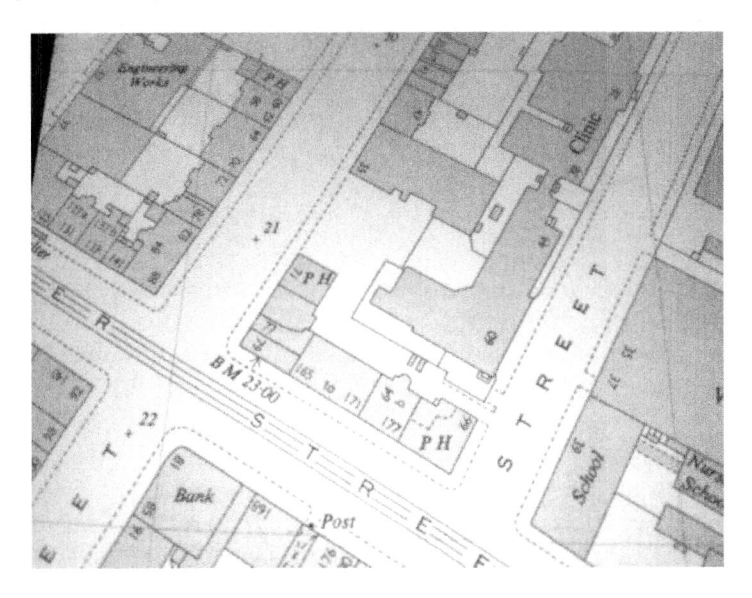

The "PH" on the corner is the Ballater Arms public house on the corner of Ballater st/Florence st, next to it is the "passageway" and the "L" shaped building is part of Florence st Clinic.

Florence st, east side.

We now travel back up to the top of Florence st and start with the odd numbers starting with number 353 and 347 which was us at Kidston st.
Then crossing over Kidston st we had Camden st infants school right on the corner of Florence st, a playground then next door was Camden st school for the older children. Then numbers 295 to 289 and right next to 289 we had Derry Treanors pub.

Over Caledonia rd we had a long run of tenement dwellings and from numbers 281 to 199, Anne Nash mentions a few shops below between these numbers.

My Name is **Anne Nash**
Hi Danny I lived in 253 Florence St, there was a dairy 2 sisters owned it also a wee sweetie shop and it was owned by a wee lady called Lizzie, and shoe shop think it was called Stead and Simpson this was from Florence street to Cumberland Street, there was also a fish Barrow at the corner of Florence street and Cumberland street, don't know if this will help you, also there was another shop called "We have it" but that was further down the street.

Again folks I have tried my best to get the shops in their proper order but its hard to get it spot on [as much as I might try] but I'm sure that those who remember these shops will forgive me if I have got them slightly out of order. [please.]

Pat Duffy says,
Shops on Florence st were = Duffy's dairy owned by Mary Duffy [was Byrne's dairy beforehand], fruiterer's owned by James Duffy, Elliot's dairy, Knotts restaurant, Ritz bar, We Have it shop, Moy bar. Pat says my Ma had the dairy and my Da had the fruit shop.

Now we leave number 199 Florence st and cross over Cumberland st.

Crossing over Cumberland st we had numbers from 149 to 71 next to 71 stood the Ritz bar. At number 111 we had Rose street Free Church large hall right opposite the back entrance of Hutchesontown boys grammar school. At number 81 to 71 there was a narrow open passageway to allow access into the back courts for any workshops/stores that were there. There were a few shops dotted only here and there in this long run of tenements which would have been the usual newsagents or grocers.

Crossing over [old] Rutherglen rd we continue down Florence st at the corner number which was 67, we had a couple of tenement dwellings 67 and 65 and then a wide Pend allowing access into side and back of the Colour dye works that stood at number 61.

Then we had St Gabriels school at number 57, then numbers 53 to 45 and this was us now at the corner with Ballater st where stood Bells motor car spares shop.

Then crossing over Ballater st we had Old Rose street school and next to that we had a really large warehouse with a passageway on its side flank for access and right next to that we had the playground for Adelphi st school and Adelphi st school itself which now took us to Adelphi st.

Finally how could we ever forget that Scotland's very first ever world champion boxer **Benny Lynch** was born at 17 Florence st although at the time of Benny's birth that part of Florence st was called Rose street.

Camden st, west side.

We start Camden st at the junction with Kidston st with Camden st school [infants] and the entrance for that was in Kidston st,and next door to that was the main school which had its entrance in Florence st. Then we had a few tenement dwellings numbering 176, 170 and 166.

This took us to Caledonia rd and crossing over we had the Camden [Vaults] bar at 158 Camden st and above this bar is where I believe Gorbals social worker **David O'Neil** lived.

Then we had numbers from 150 going down to 88 which was the corner at Cumberland st. The Cam Inn public house was at number 98. On the corner of Cumberland st /Camden st a guy stood selling fruit from a barra.

George White,
Was born and bred at number 100 Camden st

Margaret Muir
Was born and brought up at number 118 Camden st in 1956, so we are now at number 96 and we cross over Cumberland st. There was also a dairy almost at the corner with Camden st/Florence st.

We have numbers 84 at the corner of Camden st leading down to number 2 which was the Holly tree public house which stood at the junction with [old] Rutherglen rd.

This was a longish run of tenement dwellings but I don't believe there were many shops at all here, although between numbers 48 and 34 we had the back of Rose st Free church, as I say there were few shops here in Camden st, unlike Cumberland st or Crown st where we had wall to wall shops next to each other. So after reaching the end of Camden st with the Holly Tree pub we will go back to the top of Camden st and travel along the east side of it.

A wee story sent into me by **Chic Junior Beaton** about Camden st,

Hi Dan,
A wee pal of mines lived in Camden street way his wee brother he and his wee brother wiz bigger than their ma and da who where tiny wee people, his ma and da had a bit of a falling oot his ma belted him, he retaliated, his ma ran oot the hoose screaming blue murder, two polis men ran doon.

He's in the hoose she screamed eye half shut, the polis drew their batons ran in the single end came oot, nobody there madam.

He's in there awe right, the polis said there's only three weans in the hoose in the bed, she said but I've only got two weans, he wiz in the middle of the bed in the hole in the wall pulled army coats over him, thought he wiz the wee brother got the nick!!

Camden st, east side.

We start at number 211 which was the junction with Kidston st and we only have a short run of tenements ending at number 193 which was the corner with Hallside st. At number 211 we had Byrne's dairy shop and a wee shop beside it which I think was a newsagents.

Now crossing over Hallside st we have a short run of tenement dwellings, numbers 177 to 163 and this was us at Caledonia rd.

Crossing over Caledonia rd we have numbers 167 to 155, and 155 which was The Russell bar public house.

William Milligan, told me that his Da used to call the Russell bar the "Bible class" because on Sundays when the pubs never opened, his Da and a few mates were asked to come in and "do some cleaning" if you know what I mean.

In between numbers 177 and 163 we had an open passageway running through all the way from Camden st to Naburn st, there were a few out-houses in this passageway.

After leaving the Russell bar public house at 155 we had Hutcheson square with its swings, roundabout and a bandstand in the centre where the local Salvation Army band would play and oh yes and a few trees.

This gave the weans of the day a chance to "have a shot on the swings".

Then crossing over Hutcheson square we had the continuation of Camden st tenements, from number 103 to Eadies bar which was at number 69, there was an other open passageway in the middle of 103 and 69 which ran all the way through from Camden st to Naburn st.

Then after leaving Eadies bar we had Cumberland st. Sutherland's had a bakers shop in Camden st, I think it was on the corner of Hutcheson sq and 103 Camden st but I'm not totally sure. So going over Cumberland st we had numbers 85 to 65 and in this small run of tenement dwellings we had a small open passageway allowing access to out houses in the back court.

After leaving number 65 Camden st we had Errol st and Harry Broons pub right on the corner with Camden st and very near to there we had a Pend between 33 and 35 and beside this was a wee shop that sold tablet and sweets.

Then a few tenements down to number 3 which was the Oak Tree pub ? [but in my lifetime in the soo-side - this pub had been demolished and was just "spare grun"] in between Harry Broons pub and the Oak tree pub we once had a cooperage works between numbers 31 and 29 and next to that we had an Engineering works at numbers 17 to 13 which later became Buccleuch works of Parking-Cowan ltd which was a gas meter making manufactures.

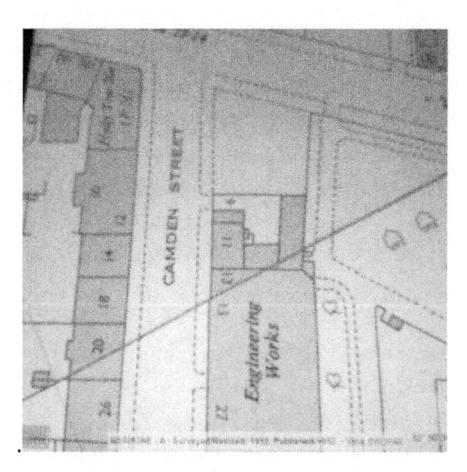

Photo above shows, the Engineering works and the Holly tree pub. The Engineering works backed onto the original Gorbals burial ground.

Naburn st, west side.

Starting at the top of Naburn st we had numbers 142b [There may have been a number before this but Naburn st on my digital street map is partly covered with the lay-out image of Dixon blazes grounds].

So we will start at number 142b and travel the short distance of tenement dwellings until number 130 which was the "Crookit Baw-Bee" public house which stood on the corner with Kidston st.

May Farries,
My mammy and her aunties and cousins were all brought up in Naburn st the closes on both sides of the street down at the end had relatives in each close. She was in number 128.

James McCabe,
Also lived at number 128 and Jim says I was born at 128 Naburn st and our windows faced Kidston st, the pub below our window was the "Crookit Bawbee".

[**I have story from James** which I will mention in chapter 11 in my book].

Crossing over Kidston st we had a piece of "spare grun" right on the corner [might have been caused by the German Luftwaffe aiming bombs at Dixon Blazes and fell short of their target during WW 2 ?].We then only have tenement numbers 120, 114 and 110,

Trisha Bolt was born n bred at 100 Naburn st in 1955.

Then we had number110 Naburn st and we arrive at Hallside st.

Going over Hallside st we had numbers 104 to 90 Naburn st and that was us at Caledonia rd.

We had Robert Todd's pawnbrokers on the corner of Hallside st and Naburn st which I believe was number 104.

Crossing over Caledonia rd we had tenement number 84 to 60 with a passageway in the middle leading through to Camden st and this took us to Hutcheson square with its bandstand in the middle and swings for the weans of the day and benches for all the Ma's to sit down on to keep an eye on their weans.

Susan O'Neill,
Tells me her Da , **Patrick Joseph O'Neill** was born n bred in number 60 Camden st and lived there till he was 16 when he moved with his family to Dougrie drive Castlemilk [in 1955].

After Hutcheson square we had tenement numbers 18, 14 and in the middle a passageway all the way through to Camden st and the Windsor bar stood at number 342 Naburn st right on the corner of Cumberland st.

Naburn st, east side.

We now start going along the east side of Naburn st and we start at number 147 to 127, which were a short run of tenement dwellings and 127 was right on the corner with Kidston st.

Crossing over Kidston st we started with number 123 Naburn st and going to number 83 which was at the corner with Caledonia rd. Mrs Scott had a shop in Naburn st, when that was pulled down she moved to Kidston st.

Robina Silvestro,
Lived at number 83 Naburn st, right across from us was Bob's book shop where you could exchange books and comics for a few penny's said Rena.

Leaving number 83 Naburn st on the corner and crossing over Caledonia rd we come to "**Barney Cousins**" pub **The Wee Hoose** and Barney says across from that was a newspaper shop. Continuing from The Wee Hoose pub we had a run of tenements going from number 65 to number 13, and St Bernard's Church hall was number 13 and next to it was St Bernard's Church itself right on the corner with Cumberland st.

Ann McAloon says,
Danny Gill well I'll look forward to reading your book my grandad and mum and all. Us kids we're born in the same house in 29 Naburn street my family were so proud to be a sou-sider, I left the Gorbals when I was 5 and went to Arden to live but still went up and down to my Granny's and Granda's house in Naburn street. We all stayed up the same close, lots of found memories of there I will surely enjoy reading your books I was born there in Halloween 1954, my mum was out for her Halloween when she had to cut it short to deliver me lol. My mother's maiden is Cameron and mines is Douglas.

Rita Horan Carrigan,
Stayed at number 21 Naburn st until 4 years old and then moved to Q.E.S.in 1964.

So as I said we came to St Bernards Church at the end of Naburn st and find ourselves at Cumberland st.

Commercial rd, west side.

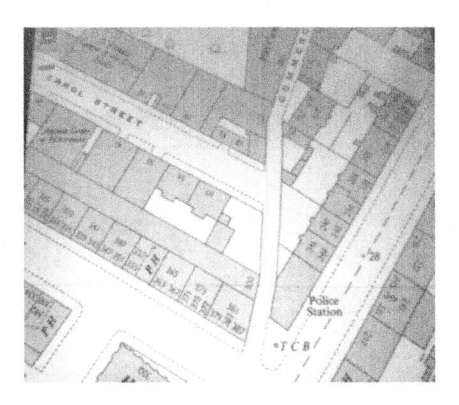

The photo above shows the start of Commercial rd, in between the 2 "PH"s either side of the street is Cumberland st, the police station is in Lawmoor st and over to the left is Errol st. Hope this refreshes your memory.

So we start our journey along Commercial rd starting at Cumberland st and ending at Adelphi st. We had a "rag store" as it was nicknamed and it stood at number 300 which can be seen on the map image above, it was directly behind Lawmoor st Police station, it sold old clothes from a few tables positioned out in Commercial rd either side.

Allison Carrroll,
The "Market" in Commercial rd was just behind Lawmoor st police station I remember it was quite small, probably two or three rows of stalls. My mother sewed wee boys short trousers, they had buttons for braces and button fly! Other people sold second-hand clothes from their stalls. I think maybe one woman sold jewellery.

We had just a few tenement dwellings either side down Commercial rd on the west side we had number 222 tenement and next to that we had the rather big fish curing works owned by John Kyle and at the end of his factory we had the Gorbals original burial ground and Rose[the Rosie] garden and this took us onto [old] Rutherglen rd.

Crossing over [old] Rutherglen rd we had a large Billiards hall at number 80 Commercial rd which I think was called the Globe, and next to that we had a passageway leading into the back and number 68, but what number 68 was I do not know.

William Wiseman's new Adelphi mill [cotton waste factory], was at number 58 and next to that was another passageway to a workshop of some kind in the back, then we had number 56 and then some "spare grun" and next was the large furniture works which stood on the corner of Ballater st.

Crossing over Ballater st we had numbers 38 to 20 which included a garage and another furniture works and then a vast area of "spare grun" where once stood Confectionery works and then we had arrived at Adelphi st.

Commercial rd, east side.

Now travelling back up to Cumberland st we will go along Commercial rd east side, we had the back of Lawmoor st Police station and the "rag store" tables outside, then moving along Commercial rd we had brick built boundary walls separating Commercial rd with the back courts of the tenement dwellings in Lawmoor st.

Along a wee bit further was John Mulvey's scrap metal store, this was covered with tin sheeting side and roof, there was a passageway leading into the back court beside this scrap merchants and next to it we had a few tenement dwellings numbered 231 to 191 and at this point we had the start of Spring lane.

We then had "spare grun" immediately after Spring lane and a couple of tenements numbered 87 and 91, number 91 was actually the Cecil public house, this now took us to [old] Rutherglen rd.

Crossing over Rutherglen rd we had tenement numbers from 81 to 49 with an open passageway between 61 and 59 to allow access to workshops in the back courts and also a Pend between 51 and 53 again to allow access as there was a dividing wall built in the back court so to keep private and no access from the open passageway at 61 and 59.

At number 49 stood the Commercial bar and this was us on Ballater st.
I couldn't get any info if there was any shops or not but I wouldn't think that there was [of course I could be wrong ?]

After leaving number 49 we crossed over Ballater st and came to tenement dwellings at number 41 all the way down to a public house at the corner with Adelphi st. We had a "Club" at number 25 which I believe was a fitness club/gym and along a wee bit at number 11a and 11b we had the Wellington Palace cinema but we called it the Bees Picture hoose .[I believe a film chain bought over the Wellington Palace cinema in Commercial rd, this syndicate was called "B B Pictures" or "B B Productions" and this is how in my view we called it the B's or Bees Picture hoose.].

I suppose it was a bit like the EE Picture hoose in Eglinton st where some people called it going to the E's.

Maria Cahill says,
My Gran cleaned the Bees Picture hoose in the mornings and evenings and also sold tickets and ice cream.

Authors note, she would be classed as a multi-tasker nowadays, then again all oor Ma's and Granny's were multi-taskers back in the day, eh.

There was a woman who lived low doon in Commercial rd and she sold tablet and toffee apples from her ground floor [low doon] window to us weans going to the Bee's Picture hoose.

After the Bee's Picture hoose we had a few tenements and ending with a public house on the corner with Adelphi st, there was at one time eleven public houses along Adelphi st and the nearest number that I can get to this pub was at number 116 Adelphi st and was owned by a Mr John Mitchell.

Just as a matter of fact at the bottom end of Commercial rd just up a few yards from Ballter st was a public toilet in the middle of Commercial rd. Years ago there were quite a few of these street toilets in the streets of the Gorbals.

This ends the "vertical streets" in section 4 of my Gorbals street map, we will now travel along the "horizontal streets" in section 4 of the map.

Kidston st, south side.

We start at the corner of Kidston st /Crown st, then we have numbers 2 to 38 which was a small run of tenements and as we reached number 38 that was us at Florence st. There was a Mr Paul's shop in Kidston street who used to make iron beds to fit into bed recesses.

Crossing over Florence st we had numbers 52 to 116 which was the "Crookit Bawbee" public house and this was right on the corner with Naburn st.

In between numbers 52 to 16 we had the Salvation Army hall which was between numbers 80 and 96.

Going over Naburn st we had just a couple of tenement dwellings numbered 130 to 146 and this was us at Lawmoor st.

A wumman at number 74 Kidston st keeps an eye on the weans playing in the street, the Gorbals dug is keeping an eye on the weans too.

Kidston st, north side.

We go back to Crown st and start with the United Free Church which is the start of Kidston st north side, then numbers 23 to 31.

Actually number 23 was a hall attached to the United Free Church then just a few tenements and we were at Florence st.

Crossing over Florence st we had a wee bit of "spare grun"then a part of Camden st school [infants I believe] and this was us at Camden st.

Hannah Gillon McCallum, said my hoose looked right into Camden st school. I loved that wee school.

Passing over Camden st we had numbers 95 Kidston st to 119 tenements and "spare grun" right at the corner with Naburn st.

Then we had Mrs Scott's wee shop in Kidston st, she used to sell tiny wee glasses of lemonade to the weans for a penny a shot.

Crossing over Naburn st we had numbers 137 to 155 and then we had a public house right on the corner which was Jimmy Mahers pub.

One side of the pub was in Kidston st and the other side in Lawmoor st and the Lawmoor st side looked into the Southern Necropolis graveyard, and how many of us played in the "gravie" over the years, eh. I know that I was one of them.

Hallside st, south side/north side.

Hallside st was only a wee street but nether the less whether a long street or short street it is an important part of our Gorbals street map and was home to good Gorbals people, **north side** we had numbers 41 to number 1 and **south side** we had numbers 42 to 2. There was also Robert Todd's pawn shop on the corner with Hallside st/Naburn st.

Ann Walker,
Stayed at number 34 then moved to number 13, I attended Camden st school 1958-63.

William Milligan says,
There was a wee sweetie shop on Hallside Street the shopkeeper used to give you a sweet for Farthings 2 years after they went out of circulation.

Caledonia rd, south side.

We now continue along Caledonia rd [we have done it in part up to now].

We start south side at the Waverly public house at number 54 [also called Dixons Blazes] which was right on the corner of Crown st/Caledonia rd and then we had a wee electric sub station at number 64 among the tenement dwellings then onto number 76 which took us to the corner with Florence st.

Crossing over Florence st we had number 84 on the corner of Caley rd which was Treanors pub [also known as "Tuckers", "Pullman bar","Ben Cleuch" and "McCutcheons bar"] we had a short run of tenement dwellings and number 108, which took us to the corner with Camden st.

In between Crown st and Camden st on this side of Caledonia rd we had quite a few shops including Mr Gilmours tobacconists, a fish shop, a licensed grocers, a fruit shop and Bobby the butchers shop.

After crossing over Camden st we had number 112 going to number 160 which was where we had the junction with Naburn st.

Jim McCarthy,
Says I stayed at number 118 Caley rd, Hunters bakery shop was directly opposite from my close.

Crossing over Naburn st we had number 162 to number 184, and 184 was the Welcome Inn public house [once called the Black Swan and nicknamed the"Mucky Duck"] and this was us at Lawmoor st.

Caledonia rd. north side.

Going back to Crown st we had tenement dwellings at number 51 to 73 and this had us at Florence st. Jimmy Munro had a newspaper shop between Crown st and Florence st and Wullie Whiskers grocers near to it, Lizzies dairy and old Hams shop.

Crossing over Florence st we had number 81 Caledonia rd to 103 on the corner which was the Camden vaults pub on the corner at Caledonia rd/Camden st. We had a cobblers shop and another shop before it.

In between these tenement numbers we had a Galbraith's, a sit in cafe where you could get hoat peas and vinegar, Phyliss's the hairdressers and the Havana chippy.

Nan Kurilla says,
Crawfords bakery (best pies), Alan's wet fishmongers Phyliss's ladies hairdresser, Mr. Gilmour's newsagent shop from "Crown st to Florence st". Then butcher shop next door Cochranes, Joe Gizzie tally shop in between Florence st. and Camden st..

All these shops were on Caledonia rd.

Crossing over Camden st we had number 105 Caledonia rd to number 157 Caledonia rd and this was us right at the corner with Naburn st.

Authors note.
I'm sorry I have done my best to get the shops in their proper order [and side of the street] please forgive me if I have made any mistakes.

Going over Naburn st we had the "Wee Hoose" public house right on the corner of Caledonia rd/Naburn st at 161 and then numbers to 181 and that was us at Lawmoor st.

Hutcheson square, south side/north side.

Actually this was a playground for weans with swings, a roundabout and seat benches for Ma's to have a rest and keep an eye on their weans.

Cumberland st, south side.

We now go back to Crown st again and start at number 281 which was Souters pub and number 228 beside it going to number 250 which was at Florence st.

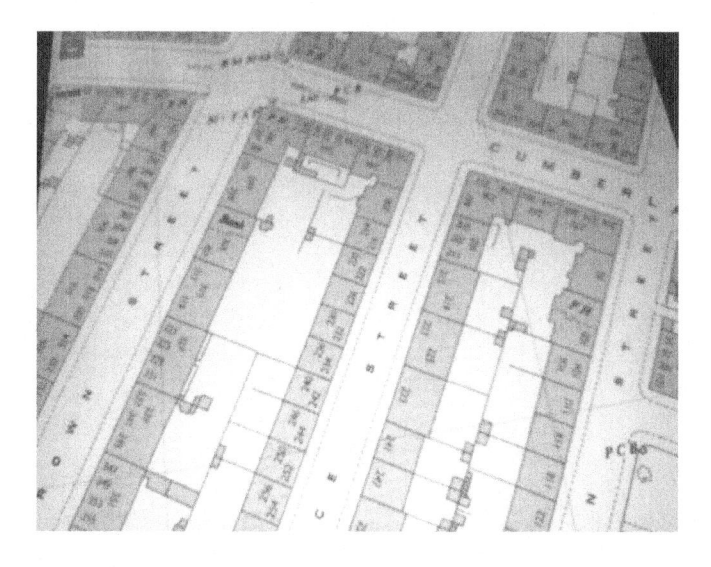

The photo above shows the junction of Crown st and Cumberland st, at the top of Crown/Cumberland st we can see the "PH" this was Souters public house and do you notice the public toilet in the street in the middle of Cumberland st ?. which says "Lav".

How many shops were there in Cumberland st, it seemed they went on forever, it was wall to wall shops next to each other, Galls, Galbraiths, Florists, Bakers, Coyles the fruiterers, newsagents and tobacconists galore. We had every shop imaginable in Cumberland st and there was no need to go over the Toon because we could get what we wanted right there. It was unbelievable the number of shops we had there and there was always a buzz about the place.

Margaret Donaghue says,
I remember a Wool shop, Simpson's dairy, Frank Stuarts-butchers. There was a fish and chip shop, a newsagents and an ice cream shop next to St Francis Chapel, Co-op and Guthries the butchers.

Crossing over Florence st we had numbers 252 to 276 which took us to Camden st.

Going over Camden st we had the Cumberland public house at the corner of Cumberland st/Camden st and was number 278 Cumberland st, then we had numbers to 342 Cumberland st which was the Windsor bar standing at the corner of Cumberland st/Naburn st.

Crossing over Naburn st we had St Bernards Church right on the corner at 350 Cumberland st and just a couple of tenement dwelling to 364[fruiters] Cumberland st which was us right at Lawmoor st.

Cumberland st, north side.

Once again we go back to Crown st and start with the Cumberland arms [Archibald's] at the corner of Cumberland st/Crown st and we have a few tenement dwellings till we get to the Moy bar [once owned by Charlie Tully] at number 249 Cumberland st and this is us at Florence st .

When you turned into Cumberland st from Crown st [same side as St Francis] you had a Holy shop that sold Rosary beads, Holy statues, prayer books etc, across the other side you had a shop that sold jars of sweeties, boxes of choc's and assorted sweets all on different shelves.

Authors note, I remember when I was about 8 years old my Ma used to send me to Quinn's the barbers to sit on a board resting over the armrests and get a bowl planked on my head and get my hair cropped. He was cheap so that's why my Ma sent me there, I'm sure his barbers shop was next to the Moy public house. [Quinns ?]

Crossing over Florence st we had number 253 to 273 of tenements which took us to Camden st,

Now going over Camden st we would reach number 275 Cumberland st going all the way along to number 387, which was where Commercial rd started.

There was a fishmongers and a Chemists right next to Commercial rd which were numbers 381 and 379[?].

At number 359 we had a public house owned by a Mr Andrew McLaren.

We never needed to go to Sauchiehall st or the Toon for our messages we had everything from Linen shops to barbers, bakeries to shoe shops, undertakers to hosiers, fishmongers to newsagents and everything else we might need. The Gorbals was actually a city within a city, we had at one time 10 Picture hooses, a swimming baths, 3 Steamies, great libraries and that's only to mention just a few. It was stated at the 1930s to 1940 we had almost 140 pubs and over a thousand shops, some going,eh.

This is us now at Lawmoor st west side.

Errol st, south side.

We start at number 2 which was at the corner with Camden st, and we had numbers going along to number 60 on the south side of Errol st, we had Frank Stuart's butchers next to the A.O.H. [Hibs hall] then a dairy, Cissies shop sold sweeties, biscuits, soda, tea, like most wee shops, she also sold Vantice raspberry flavoured syrup topped with a pint of soda, then a fish place was at the corner with Commercial rd.

Eddie Crawford says,
There was a shop in Errol st that we used to go into after playing for hours in the Rutherglen road Graveyard [then the Rosie] and she used to sell what was called a Vantice it was a Raspberry flavoured syrup topped up with a pint of soda I can still taste it now, the shop was across from the Legion hall but I can't remember the name of it maybe someone else remembers it.

Eddie Graham says,
My Auntie Katie & Uncle Jock MacDonald lived in Errol Street, when Jock died my Auntie Katie who was my daddy's sister came to live with us, Katie was blind but was a great singer two songs which I can clearly remember her singing were 'Oh Danny Boy' and I'll take you home again Kathleen which was her name.

Errol Street was waiting to be demolished, all that's left is memories of the streets of Gorbals Past. "Keep up the good work Danny, this book that you are working on will be a Belter".

Errol st, north side.

Going back to the other side of Errol st we had Harry Broon's pub on the corner with Camden st and numbers from 1 going to 81.

Maggie Boddy, lived at number 3 Errol st.

Noreen McCauley, lived at number 28 Errol st.

Cath Dorran lived at number 21 Errol st, the photo below shows Cath as a baby with her Ma to the right and her Auntie to the left outside of her room and kitchen window.

Next door to where Cath lived there was the St Francis League of the Cross halls.

My name is **Cath Dorran**,
As you'll remember, not many shops in Errol St. At the corner of Camden St, was Harry Broons pub, that was on the same side of the street as me. It was all houses on this side, the last close being mine no 21. Next to that was The League of the Cross hall. Early on there was a fish mongers, I remember the smell , it was like a factory of some sort. Maybe someone else will remember it better than me, next to that was St Francis halls, where the pipe band met to practice. At the bottom of the street was Commercial rd, there was a wee market, you walked through to take you to Cumberland St .

I was very young so hopefully my memories are accurate, on the other side was Frank Stuarts butchers, their vans were always in the street loading up orders for the shops. Then the Hibs hall, many' a night the music kept me awake . We Lived directly across the street from it, there was s dairy on that side too.

That side of the street the tenements got demolished very early 60 s. We were there till Feb 69, the Hibs hall and Frank Stuart's survived and stood derelict for as long as us.

Just a note the wall in our back courts was the same wall as the Rosie. We climbed over the palings to get into our very own garden. I hope this helps. X.- - - - [Cath now lives in N.S.W. Australia.]

Authors note,
Errol st was a mixture of works + tenements - William Henderson &sons fish curing works was near to the League of the Cross hall.

Spring lane, south side/North side.

Starting on the south side of Spring lane we had a small run of tenement dwellings starting with a tenement standing on its own at the corner with Commercial rd and then "spare grun" and then numbers 9 to 1, it was only a fairly short cut through from Lawmoor st to Commercial rd.

On the north side all we had was one building a large hall standing at on its own at number 6, which I believe was "The Band of Hope"or officially known as"The Carters Mission" - - "The Foundry boys" was like a Sunday school meeting at the hall on a Sunday. It was ran by Alex Robertson for many, many years. Thanks to **Irene Young+Jean Jack** for this info.

[old] Rutherglen rd, south side.

We start at the south side of Rutherglen rd and we had Simsons furniture shop right on the corner with Crown st, then a few shops including, a newsagents, D'Arcy's dairy and Lockies [hardware shop ?] then we came to Florence st.
Crossing over Florence st we had the Ritz bar at number 166 [old] Rutherglen rd a few of the usual shops and the Holly Tree public house right on the corner with Camden st.

Going over Camden st we had a large piece of "spare grun" and then the original Gorbals burial ground with the Rosie park next to it.

How many of us over the years had a walk through the graveyard or played there as weans in among the graveyard tombstones, although the Rosie was a better place to play for us weans.

Moving past the Rosie we then had Commercial rd with the Cecil bar right on the corner of Rutherglen rd/Commercial rd with tenements numbers 266 to 282 a very large piece of "spare grun" and tenement numbers 292 and 294 which meant we were now at Lawmoor st.

[old] Rutherglen rd, north side.

We now travel back to Crown st and the start of [old] Rutherglen rd north side at number 107, 111 and 115. I believe the shop on the corner at 107 was either McVitties or Cochranes grocers shop then Lombardi's cafe where you could sit in and have a wonderful Italian ice cream with plenty of sarsaparilla over it.

Next door to that was the hall belonging to the Hutchesontown Parish Church, then the Church itself at number 117 and what a fine building this Church was, as was all the Gorbals Church's, Chapel's Synagogues etc. This now brought us to Florence st. Passing over Florence st we had tenements, Church's, Mills starting at number 135 on the corner of Florence st and going all along till 215 which was Commercial rd.

We had a few shops between number 135 to 153, then a wide Pend which allowed access to "the Steamie" in the back court at number 155.

Next to this wide Pend we had the Hutchesontown Congregational Church at number 157 then "spare grun" and then we had St Margaret's and St Mungo's Episcopal Church at number 171.Then once again "spare grun" and next to that we had a passageway to the side of Twomax's woolen /knitwear factory at number 187/189 and next to that we had at number 203 the New Adelphi Mills [cotton waste] and lastly we had [the Globe ?] Billiards and Snooker hall right on the corner with Commercial rd which was at number 215. There were quite a few Billiards/Snooker halls dotted over the Gorbals area of that era.

The street image above shows number 135 [top left hand side] then the Congregational Church, then St Margarets+St Mungos, the electric- sub station at Twomax's woolen factory, the New Adelphi Mills and then the Billiards hall at number 215 which was us at Commercial rd.

Passing over Commercial rd we had tenements from 217 to 251 [pictured above but some of the tenements had been demolished in this photo] which had a few shops including a barbers shop [**Connie Friels,** granda had it] and Anderson's drapers shop among others.

You can just see the McEwans sign at the corner of the Kick - Off public house which stood on the corner of Rutherglen rd and Lawmoor st. The McEwan sign is about 12 feet up from the pavement, just above the guy on the pavement.
We have now reached Lawmoor st west side, so we will now go to Ballater st.

Obviously Rutherglen rd will be continued when we get to section 5 of my Gorbals street map, which will be the last section of my map.
Ballater st, south side.

We start with the Royal bank of Scotland at the junction with Crown st and next to it was number 168 to 186, in between we had a Plumbers shop, a Post office and a Pend beside the Post office allowing access to the back court for workshops or outhouses.

Then going past the Pend we had tenement numbers 176 to 180, there was Chic McNeil's bookies which was upstairs, also just after the Pend was Agnes's dairy shop then at number 186 we had the Tavern bar right at the junction with Florence st,

Crossing over Florence st we then had number 190 Ballater st on the corner with the east side of Florence st. Here at number 190 on the corner was Bell's motor repair shop with a Hairdressers shop next to it [Phyliss's shop ?].

Mrs Wilkes shop which was at number 202 Ballater st and sold, rolls, halfpenny ice-lollies, candy balls and groceries.

Then we had Wullie Marks bakers shop at number 210 and onto the other corner was number 270 which was the junction of Commercial rd. In between number 206 and 216 we had an open passage way, [lane].

John McInch Senior,
I went to St Luke's from 1951 and as far as I remember entrance to school and Church was Ballater St, there was a lane between Florence St. and the school.

This if I'm correct led to St. Luke's B.G. hall in the back.

Of course we had a few more shops then we had the entrance to St Luke's school from Ballater st and this led us to number 286 attached to St Luke's and another passageway which used to be the entrance to St Luke's R. C. Church, there was an electric sub station to the east side of this passageway and the flank end of a large furniture works factory ran down this passageway, this furniture factory works factory also stood on Ballater st at number 270 and went all the way along to the junction with Commercial rd..

Going over Commercial rd we arrived at the Commercial bar at number 320 Ballater st, then we had numbers from 320 to 358 tenement dwellings with a few shops in between, this now took us to Brechin's public house at number 358 and that was us at the junction with Lawmoor st, west side.

Ballater st, north side.

We now go back and start at the north side of Ballater st and start at the junction with Crown st at number 161 Ballater st, we had tenement numbers 161 to 181. At numbers 165 to 177 we had the Factors rent office, we then had number 177 and then the Ballater arms public house at number 185 which was the corner with Florence st.

Moving over Florence st we come to the old Rose street school which stood on the corner of Ballater st and Florence st [once called Rose st] then next to it was number 201 which was the schools playground and access to the nursery school.
We had a couple of Pends at 241 and 247 Ballater st, the first gained access to a warehouse and the next gained access to the very large Fur and Hair works factory which stood on Ballater st at numbers 249 and 251. [this Fur and Hair works factory was almost opposite St Luke's school] then we had numbers 277 which had a furniture works at the back of its frontage, then number 285, then this was us at Commercial rd.

Crossing over Commercial rd we had numbers 329 to 359, which had a few of the usual shops, between number 339 and 343 we had an open passageway giving access to any workshops/outhouses in the back and at number 359 we had Andrew McFarlane's public house [I cant find the name of it, in the Gorbals pub guide it says its the Clachan but the Clachan is actually on the opposite corner of Ballater st/Lawmoor st] This now has us at Lawmoor st.

This ends section 4 of my Gorbals street map.

Chapter 9

People's Snippets

Rose McDougall,
Danny, thought I would tell you this about the buses, my Mother in law had 13 children and she was taking them out where she stayed in Barrow field and finally got got a house to accommodate them all, anyhow taking them all out and got on a bus, they were aw fighting to get oan the bus and she was skelping them round the lugs.

The conductress said to her are they aw yours, or are you taking them for a picnic?, the reply from her was aye they're aw mine and I can assure you its nae bloody picnic. God it must have been hard for her to bring up aw them kids, but a great wee wumman she was. Hard times but great memories, hope it gave you a laugh. Xx.

- - - -

Michel Livingstone snr.
Hello Danny,
Maybe a wee story for your book, we lived in Lawmoor st top end at the graveyard and Dixons blazes. Now you'll remember how when we played football the jackets would go down in the streets as makeshift goals. Well not for us toffs top end of Lawmoor st, we would climb into the graveyard so we could play on the grass and to my eternal shame we used the gravestones as goal posts. May God have mercy on us.

- - - -

David Morland,.
Hi Danny Gill I shall try my best . . When my folks moved from Florence St to 327 Caledonia Road across from the Necropolis.

On the east corner of Moffat Street and Cally rd a sweety shop right on the corner was named Emmy Grahams Along the Cally rd front of the shop we had grills on the pavement where some coins had dropped down. It was quite common for urchins like myself to have long poles with soft sticky soap on one end. There was mere change there than at a funeral. Aye you could be rich for a short while Ha Ha .

Further along we had Oatlands Primary School and Pine Street? not sure at the end of the next row was a dairy my mother would visit for her jug of milk and fresh butter.

That dairy was known as Alex's Dairy heading towards St Bonaventure's Church and the Coronation bar .. Across from there we had the terrace hoose's . And at the end we had the Ritz picture hoose ... In this case the wee shop it may have been part of the Ritz. My dad would send me along their to get Orange lollys' hopefully I have helped ... Danny.

I have searched myself for quite some time for a picture of Oatlands School main entrance Caledonia Road .. Also Oregan Street (play street.] That's where a learned to heid a baw in the school shed Ha Ha.

I have a cousin in California Who I know has given info in the past Emily Eaglesham. OK Danny Gill the work you have being involved with is a fantastic record of our past and long may you add to all info. Thank you.

- - - -

Jim Grant says,
Above Galls at Crown st/Cumberland st was the communist party rooms in the 1950's. My family stayed there temporarily

and my brother Colin and I remember playing in the many rooms. Our parents weren't communists but they would have been grateful for the accommodation.

- - - -

Helen Jordan says,
The Tavern run by John Adams, corner of Ballater st and Florence st he ran it in the late 50's when it was demolished he moved on to the Railway tavern at Waddell court 90's.

I remember in the 60's our building went on fire 192 Ballater street and big John Adams let us all into the Tavern, he was a gent, I was a child then, but I always remember that.

- - - -

Ann Ward [nee Clark].
We lived at 82 Hospital st, and Mr Checkmans factory [The hoat peanut man] was next close to us, where he made all the tablet & macaroon& peanuts to sell in his shop under the railway bridge in Cleland st. Mr Turnbull used to run it for him !! Loved their penny bars of tablet in pink & lemon (coloured) and the candy apples yum yum, Lesley's shop was just after the wee factory xx And at end of oor street was the Turf bar.

- - - -

Tom Foley,
In Portugal Street, Jean's Store was the place for bread and rolls and so forth. Ellie Estro's shop was a little closer to St. John's church. The fruit shop was Finnegan's at one time and Peter's fish restaurant was next door. Lena's fruit and vegetable shop was on Norfolk Street facing Portugal St. Can you tell who "went for the messages"? .

- - - -

May Bishop Sweeney,
Danny my first job was in the coop offices in Coburg st there was a pawn shop but don't no the name of it x.

- - - -

Thomas Houston,
My uncle and gran lived in Waddell street, I remember a sweetie shop were you could get a penny drink of ginger and the penny tray.

- - - -

Frances Rogan,
Corner of Gorbals st / Cumberland st, - McMasters the Chemist, then next Italy Ice cream shop I think was something star, then gift shop, then Woolfsons the drapers.

Corner hospital st /Cumberland st pub, then The Dairy, Drs Surgery then the Beehive, across other side at this Thistle st Egg store and the Billy's newsagents then the Chippy then Galls, facing Galls on other side was Templetons grocery, ladies fashion shop then the bakery then across thistle st Wisemans newsagents, Victors fruit shop , McCready butchers, Larry's fishmonger, then radio shop that sold the rechargeable Batteries and bike frames etc then the sweet shop and of course a pub at every corner, sorry I can't remember the names of all the shops.

- - - -

Carol Campbell,
We lived at no 3 Inverkip street, Moved in 68. My memory is of a whiskey bond across the road. It had massive doors and a lot of stray cats used to get in from under the doors.

There was a saw Mill next to our close... Just a wee shop we used to get sawdust for the cat tray from there. Our living room was on the corner of the tenement and overlooked the Carrick on the Clyde.

There was a garage around the corner facing the Clyde. Further down Inverkip St across the road was a bakery and some high backs. Memory sketchy as was only, 8 when we left and was so long ago xx.

- - - -

Maureen McCarrol,
We lived in the close between the two Stirling Hunter shops at 110 Crown st my mum bought our first TV and record player, I even remember her first record, Frank Ifield.

- - - -

Edward Friel,
My dad played the piano at matinees in the paragon on Saturdays and my uncle Wullie Docherty was the wee man wae the torch happy memories.

- - - -

Jean Wright,
There were no shops in Eglinton Lane apart from Lord Nelson's side door..at the bottom of the lane "it was called the stables" was a man named Pat..he made the barrels for butter etc. heating the metal over a brazier fire ..he used to let us watch him, nice and warm in the winter, also give us a "hurl" on the cart to the bottom of the lane. While researching ancestry some years ago, came across a lady whose grandfather (I think), had been a farrier and shod the horses for the police force from memory I think she said the Royal Greys........There was also a type of factory/ tool shop owned by a Mr Robertson who was always happy for us to visit. One of his employees was an "old" man that we called "auld Wullie "...he always had a white stubble and threatened to give us "beardie"..all perfectly innocent. Mr Robertson always gave us a present at Christmas.

- - - -

Denis Doogan,
In Carlton place you had the T.U.C club there, the Stella Maris and Communist club, all worthy watering holes and deeply appreciated. The Communist party owned the whole building from the basement right up the stairs to the Star club bar and lounge as well as all the offices above. This was the Communist party's headquarters.

- - - -

I'm **Noreen Campbell**,
Born at 9 Cumberland St in 1964 remember going across the road to Bulloch's off-sales Corner of Eglington St and Cumberland St to buy sweet tobacco. Moved in 1971 to 160 Oxford St opposite Malarkey's pub and went to St John's primary school in Norfolk St. Also remember Quinn's and Herrity's pubs being on Oxford St and a pawn shop at the corner of Coburg St and Oxford St. Remember wee Flo the woman who worked in Bob's the newsagents in Norfolk St.

- - - -

I'm **Bobby Smith**,
I was born 1952 at 94 Nicholson St .... attended Gorbals primary school in Buchan St. I went to the Glasgow medical mission Sunday school in Oxford St. left the Gorbals when I was 11 to go to Househillwood but still went to Sunday school for years after I left.

- - - -

Peter Mortimer,
Hi Danny Number 2 Abbotsford Place was once used as a meeting place of the Royal Ancient Order of Buffaloes or Royal Antediluvian Order of Buffaloes, founded in 1822 and modeled on Freemasonry, although completely open. Name

believed to have been taken from the song 'We'll Chase the Buffaloes'. Known as 'The Buffs'.

- - - -

Myra Hall,
Hi Danny my father was a Buff and spent every available minute in there, he was a committee man and also did a bit of singing down there at their wee nights.

Every Christmas me and my brothers had to get dressed up and go to the Christmas Party which I never really enjoyed for some reason .. when My Da died the Buffs were good to my family they paid for everything and gave my Mother some money and my dad was buried in John Knox cemetery next to the Glasgow Cathedral overlooking the city...every time I come home I always look at John Knox' statue and think of ma Da up there courtesy of the Buffs in Abbotsford Place .

- - - -

Alan Quinn.
My father John Quinn and Mum Betty, Mum and Dad had the barbershop next door to the Moy bar (also known as Charlie Tully's) on Cumberland Street since the 40s until they demolished it in the 60s and my dad was offered a brand-new shop next to the flats.

It was obvious he would not be able to afford the rent so he got a wee caravan, me and him painted it red and white and he set up shop for many years. I helped him park it in different places on Cumberland Street till he retired.

To the kids who don't remember his name he was the barber with the big blue hand(birth mark) but he always had a balloon or a lollipop for all of them.

- - - -

My name is **Susan Rigmond**.
The grain store [Motherwells] at Gorbals st/Cumberland st used to charge batteries for old radios obviously when people only had gas light. The Connelly brothers were our doctors all the time we lived there and there was also a rag store under the bridge where we took our rags to get money for going to the pictures.

- - - -

Margaret Herd,
My brother and I attended Abbotsford School, I started in 1944 and my brother in 1945. We lived st 56 Cavendish Street with our parents and had moved there in 1940 from Snowdon Street.

- - - -

Rosetta Connolly,
I was Born 1959 in Sandyfaulds st then later moved to Waddell court.

- - - -

Mary Llyod,
My Da's name's **Alex Burton**, back in the 1950's my Da used to sell coal briquettes from a cart [no horse, just a cart he wheeled about]. Everyone could hear his voice as he shouted "Cahoal Brickettttts", one day he parked his cart in the pend after his shift to come up for his dinner and someone stole it !!!.

Whoever stole it used it to break into shops, the Polis came looking for him as everyone knew his cart but they knew it wasn't him that they were after.

My Da gave up selling briquettes to work in a pub and on my birth certificate it says he was a "spirit salesman".

Tracy Tomlison,
Tells me, my Granda Tim Byrne sold the newspapers in the Gorbals, he was well known by loads of people because of his snow-white hair. Also my Da George Byrne sold the newspapers at Eglinton toll right at the Star bar, his brother in law Allan Hogan used to help him until 1972 Although I'm sure my Da was still selling newspapers after that.

- - - -

Peter Mortimer,
The 'Venny' was an 'Adventure Playground' built on the ground at the starch works, half of which was destroyed in an industrial explosion in the 1940s.

- - - -

Danny Gallagher,
There Used to be a shop on Norfolk street at Nicholson street that was called "Joe the robber".

- - - -

David Morland,
Birch Street Home Bakery No 62 ? Opening Hr 9pm a line up from 8pm for hot crispy rolls many like myself weans oot shoppin for their mams and dads, Emy Graham Sweet Shop Moffat Street No 421 Entrance Cally Road corner, then Oatlands Infants and Nursery school on Oregan Street (North).
Rag Store Big Netty's on Moffat Street at No 409 ?, Cally Road Church west of corner Moffat Street, Bosworths Fruit Shop, Comics etc appx 2 closes from church. Then the Ritz Picture house small shop attached to the west corner before the terrace hooses it sold Ice-cream and Orangemaid lollies etc.

- - - -

John McCardle says,
Remember when you came through the pen on the right hand side Kelly's shop sold tobacco I went for 1/4 of thick black for someone. then there was a dairy down at the bottom of Moffat st right side sold milk & orange in milk bottles. [this was the Pend from Sandyfaulds st to Moffst st.]

- - - -

Linda Adams,
I lived at Gorbals cross, up the Dentist's close, I remember my older brother going to visit the Dentist and taking his three soldiers with him to be brave.

Also if my Da won on the grand national we would get a wee treat of Fry's chocolate the one with the different colours.

Then I worked in the Clelland bar in 1970, best place ever to work, great music bands and wonderful customers with a great sense of humour. Then off to Portland halls for a wee dance after work, best days ever.

My wee Granda and Granny had a fish barrow outside one of the pubs at Gorbals cross.

- - - -

Jeanie Kirby says ,
In Moffat st [between Caley rd and old Rutherglen rd] you had Susan and Molly's shop which had a big mangle in the shop, It was massive. They sold groceries and 'Penny drinks' of lemonade.

They were next one down from the Harmony Bar. There was a big woman who had a second hand clothes shop the other side of the close from Molly and Susan's shop. I used to run across the back court diagonally to fetch her tea and piece from her husband. They lived on Orchard street.

Cochrane's was next to the pend which lead through to Sandyfaulds street. A couple of closes down from there was a fruit and veg shop. No name... sorry.

- - - -

Pat Duffy,
Tells me, Joe Steel the Tailors shop Crown St was next to Hutchie Grammer, Cumberland St end

- - - -

Liz Donaldson,
I stayed up the high back in Dunmore Street above Derry Treanors pub.

Chapter 10

Section 5, last section of my Gorbals street map

We will travel the perimeter edge of section 5 of my map from the east side of Lawmoor st down to Adelphi st, then along Adelphi st till it meets up with Waterside st then onto [old] Rutherglen rd, then along Caledonia rd until we meet with Lawmoor st again.

Lawmoor st, east side.

Starting at the top end of Lawmoor st at the junction with Caledonia rd we had number 371 Lawmoor st leading down to number 275 which was the junction with Cumberland st, at the corner with Caledonia rd we had a large fronted "shop" but it was boarded up when I saw the photo of it [I think it used to be a Bookies ?] and next to that was a shop with "Self Service" in bold letters above its entrance. Which I believe would have been a grocers shop.

Then we had a few shops further along including Maggie McGlennins newsagents shop, Eddie McGee's grocers store, a Laundry and Bert's dairy among others. In Bert's dairy he sold macaroon bars, if it was pink in the middle you got a free one said **Sandra Gillon.** Also Flemings had a grocery shop on the east side at the corner of Lawmoor st and Cumberland st. There once was a furniture shop at the corner of Lawmoor st/Cumberland st

John Todd, Ann McFadden [Gallagher] and **John Knotts** all lived at number 311 Lawmoor st.

John Knotts, says I was born here in 1951 until 1963 when we moved to Provanmill. We stayed 3 up and our neighbours on our landing were **Nelly** and **Mick Quinn** and the **McCues**

Crossing over Cumberland st we had E. Smyths pub [formerly The Lantern] on the corner and next to that we had number 257 leading down to number 173 and then Teachers pub on the corner with [old] Rutherglen rd.

Along from Smyths pub we had a shop which I believe was named "Continental grocers" and going along the tenements we had a large open space [where once stood a tenement] this was between number 225 and 207, then moving along we had Mathieson lane between number 199 and 191. Actually Mathieson lane was shaped like the letter **T**, we had part of the lane running through from Lawmoor st to Mathieson st horizontally and the middle part of the **T** ran vertically from there right down to Cumberland st and crossed over Cumberland st and carried on for a fair bit before it ended.

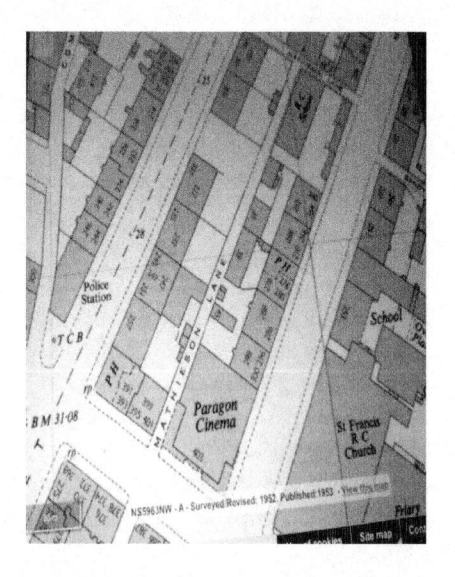

The map image above shows Mathieson lane from the Paragon Picture hoose going up to form a **T** as the top of the **T** heads to Lawmoor st to the left and right to Mathieson st.

190

Also on this section of Lawmoor st [east side] we had Mick the cobblers shop, Negrinis chippy and Shields sweetie shop, they were all in between [old] Rutherglen rd and Cumberland st on this side of Lawmoor st.

Now going back to Teachers pub at the corner of Lawmoor st and [old] Rutherglen rd, I have it on good authority from **Irene Tierney,** that this was definitely Teachers pub as she lived next close to it at number 173 Lawmoor st.

Authors note,
I had great trouble finding out the name of this pub as it is not mentioned in all the Gorbals pub guides, in 1900 we had 26 pubs and 3 off sales shops on Rutherglen rd and even the street number of this public house is not mentioned but yet it clearly shows on my digital street map that there was a pub here. I tried googling it too but to no avail.

So I asked People on the Gorbals face-book sites and Irene and a few others remembered it clearly so a big thanks for all your help. I can only remember so much myself I'm afraid, so a big thanks folks.

Passing Teachers pub and crossing over [old] Rutherglen rd we come to the Kick-Off pub on the corner here at Lawmoor st and past that on the east side were a few shops including Flood's sweetie shop, Isdales dairy and Holmes Butchers shop to but name a few.

The photo above is of a young **Allan Robertson** who lived in Lawmoor st, read Allan's story in chapter 5 of my book.

From the Kick Off pub we had tenement dwelling numbered 157 going along to number 89 and this then took us to Ballater st.

Crossing over Ballater st we had the Clachan bar on the corner of Lawmoor st/Ballater st and a run of tenement dwellings down to Adelphi st. Which were numbered 79 [beside the Clachan] to number 1 at the junction of Lawmoor st /Adelphi st.

We had a Pend in between numbers 37 and 31 allowing access to outbuildings in the back.

Adelphi st. [continued]

Starting at number 136 and going all the way along to number 242 [which was the end of Adelphi st as it then became Waterside st].

We had number 136 Adelphi st at the junction with Lawmoor st and it continued along the banks of the river Clyde. As I have previously stated there weren't all that many shops along Adelphi st, it was commercial premises with only a smattering of shops and from Lawmoor st onwards I can only make out one shop which belonged to a Margaret [Peggy] Galloway's confectioner shop [formerly a hardware shop].

So on Adelphi st from Lawmoor st to Mathieson st we had numbers 136 to 146 and between Mathieson st to Waddell st we had numbers 149 to 156. Being an only one sided street Adelphi st had even and odd numbers on it. The Strathclyde Distillery at [170 -72 ?] then a large gateway next to it gaining access to the Distillery followed by tenement number 176 / 180/ 183. This now took us to Moffat st.

Between Moffat st and McNeil st we had the U.C.B.S. building which stood for the United Co-operative Baking Society.[although in Gorbals colloquialism it stood for Uncle/Cousins/Brothers and Sisters].Which employed thousands of people over the years making bread, biscuits etc. What a magnificently built structure this was indeed. This large bakery took up all the width between Moffat st and McNeil st. Remembering that at the bottom of McNeil st we had the St Andrews Suspension bridge which took us over to Glasgow green.

Crossing over McNeil st we had a large annexe to the U.C.B.S and this took us on a curve of Adelphi st following the curvature of the river Clyde. Number 242 was an outhouse building adjoined to this annexe and next to it was a large Timber yard, after this yard we had Ballater st to the west hand side and Kings bridge to the east hand side, the bridge took us to the ash football playing pitches at Glasgow green and it was also a thorough-fare that took us from the Gorbals to the Bridgeton area of Glasgow's east end.

Continuing along the banks of the river Clyde we now find that Adelphi st has now became Waterside st [although in the early

1900's this section was still called Adelphi st till about the 1920's/30's and ended at the Old Ferry bar at the junction with Rutherglen rd. The Old Ferry bar being named after a ferry service that crossed the river Clyde many years ago near to where the pub stood.

So crossing over Ballater st at Kings bridge and moving along Waterside st we had that large bonded warehouse, that brick built structure that stood way up high in the Gorbals skyline. Next to that we had Turnlaw st which was part of the "new houses" built in between WW1 and WW 2, we had these "new houses" which were only 2 storeys high as opposed to the old tenements that were 3 storeys high.

Authors note,
These "new houses" were built on what used to be the sites of the Adelphi dye works [nearest to the bonded warehouse] and down a bit the Springfield print works once stood. After Turnlaw st we had Benthall st and then after Benthall st we once again had a curve in Waterside st which took us to the Old Ferry bar and Rutherglen rd, it was known as Rutherglen rd in my time in the soo-side, later becoming known as [old] Rutherglen rd.

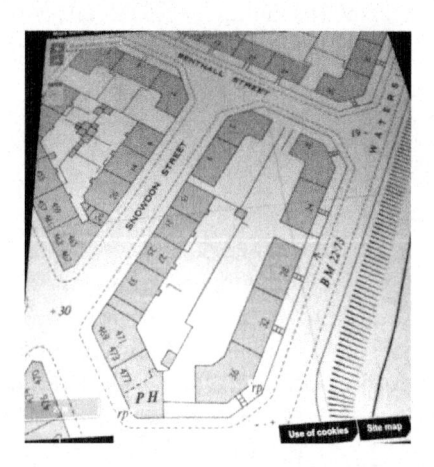

The street image above shows the Old Ferry bar as "PH", to its left hand side is Rutherglen rd and to the right Waterside st curves round to run parallel to the river Clyde. Also Benthall st can be seen at the top.

John O'Hara,
Who was in my primary class at St Bonaventures [Wee Bonnies] used to drink in the Old Ferry bar when Charlie Douglas owned it and Gordon and Landy [Orlando Antinon]were the barmen.

Rutherglen rd, south side.

From opposite the Old Ferry bar we cross over onto Rutherglen rd south side, we will move along the tenements eastwards to the direction of the Coronation bar. Here we had a newsagents shop that also sold American comics and books and along a wee bit we had a cafe [Derby ?] Then we had McLean's pub at the corner with Birch st/Rutherglen rd.

Crossing over Birch st we had a few shops including Whitelaw's licensed grocers, Donnellys dairy, a bookies shop then we had "Irish Paddy's" newsagents shop which was right beside the Coronation bar which was on Rutherglen rd.

Rutherglen rd, north side.

Going back to the end of Waterside st at the Old Ferry bar then we had [old] Rutherglen rd and wedged in between this part of [old] Rutherglen rd and the river Clyde we had a children's playground.

This playground was actually donated by William Dixon [of Dixon's blazes] and because of this the weans who used it called it "The Dixie" but when my pals and me used it back in the mid to late 50's, there was no swings there at all. It had a lovely even surface as all children's playgrounds have and my pals and me played football there until a big Polis man told us one day never to play in there again. [swings removed so no weans would play there]

It transpired that because of the proximity of the river Clyde [it was only a few feet away] a child who had been playing on the swings had ventured to the bank side of the river, fell in and drowned.

This was why there were no swings there any more and there was always a big chain and padlock on the entrance gate to it from Waterside st.

We now move onto [old] Rutherglen rd and travel up to the Coronation bar direction which was at the gushet of Rutherglen rd and Caledonia rd.

There were plenty of trees planted along [old] Rutherglen rd where this children's playground was and the playground ended at the public brick built toilets. This was used by not only members of the public but the 101 trolley bus drivers/conductors, the 101 trolley bus back then ran from Shawfield [later to Rutherglen] to Riddrie and back.

There were both men and women's toilets here.

Then almost opposite these toilets stood the Coronation bar at the gushet of Rutherglen rd and Caledonia rd. Which at one time had tenements above it when it was called Reids bar. Like many pubs the tenements above them were demolished but the pubs kept as they were making money !!

Caledonia rd, south side.

We had the Ritz Picture hoose right on the corner of Caledonia rd and Braehead st which I always classed as the Boundary where Oatlands finished and the Hutchesontown part of the Gorbals began.

The Ritz Picture hoose actually was built on the ground where once stood a Babtist Church.

The photo above is of the Ritz before its demolition in 1961. it was opened in 1921 for cine/variety, it started off life as the Hippodrome. Theatre and was equipped for "sound" films in 1929 and was such a success it was taken over by ABC in 1931.[Coronation bar to the right].

Then going along Caledonia rd we had a wee shop at the end of the Ritz which was used as Ed's cobblers shop but I believe was taken over at a later date and some electrical repairs were carried out in there. Plus as **Davie Morland** says he used to go in there to get ice-cream and Orange-maid ice lollies.

Authors note,
I remember going into Ed's wee shop back in the mid 50's and he was always working in his back shop so he had a wee bell at the top of his front door that rang when you opened it, to alert him someone was in the shop.

Next to Ed's shop we had a row of cottage type houses only one storey high, they were built for the railway workers and their families, the men worked at the railway gushet at Cathcart rd/Pollokshaws rd.

These cottage style houses had a nice wee garden in front of them with a picket type fence to separate them from the pavement, they did look nice.

These "cottage" houses then went along Caledonia rd and abutted against the Southern Necropolis graveyard side boundary wall, where many a wean played in between the tombstones [and I was just one of them !!].

Then the main Boundary wall of the Southern Necropolis went all the way along Caledonia rd and then returned back down Lawmoor street.

Caledonia rd, north side.

Starting with the Coronation bar at 447 Caledonia rd /570 Rutherglen rd [once called Reids bar with a water fountain outside it.] Donald MacLean was the last proprietor before it was demolished in the late 60's. he had a new pub built 500 yards away and he called it the Phoenix.

As we go past the Coronation bar we had St Bonaventures R.C Church at number 473 which was formerly the Buchanan Memorial free Church and then we came to Silverfir st where **Rose McDougall** lived and she says we had a rag and bone shop in Silverfir st and went in and came out "jumping with fleas", there was a wee dairy at the corner of Caledonia rd and Silverfir st called Alex's and he sold jugs of milk and fresh butter.

Crossing over Silverfir st we had numbers 391 Caledonia rd going all the way along to number 185 Caledonia rd which was us then at Lawmoor st.

So at Caledonia rd/Siverfir st we had numbers 391 which was Alex's dairy and then going to 361 Caledonia rd we came to Pine st.

Going over Pine st we then had Oatlands primary school and this school stood between all of Pine st and Gilmour st. Crossing over Gilmour st we had number 341 to 301 and 301 was Moffat st and here stood Emmy Graham's sweetie shop.

Also at number 327 stayed my school class mate **Robert Fairchild**, we played for St Bonaventures primary school football team, Robert at left back and myself at right back. I was always going along to Caley rd and up to Roberts door to see if he would come out to play fitbaw in Gilmour st which was just round the corner and had a lovely even tar Macadam road surface. Great for roller skating on too or "hurling" along on a home made Boagie-cart.

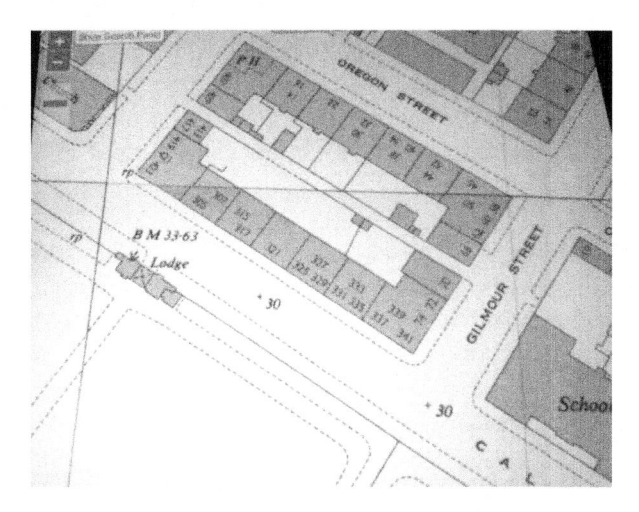

I'd also like to say that my pal Robert lived almost opposite the gatehouse [Lodge] of the Southern Necropolis graveyard which is shown in my digital street map image on the bottom of the last page.

I haven't met Robert since those days but he did send me lots of info for my book via his cousin **Davie Morland.**

Authors note,
Just as a matter of interest, in the image above in the previous page note the "open passageway" in that block of tenement flats that would allow access to any workshops/outbuildings.

It was surprising but there were lots of workshop units and outhouses in the back courts of the Gorbals which brought in more revenue for the greedy factors who only ever carried out only the very basic repairs on the tenements and workshop units.

Crossing over Moffat st at the other corner we had a United free Church with a hall attached to it, next we had tenement numbers 277 to 261 and at the corner with Sandyfaulds st was Moirs pub [Mac's bar] with **George Donnachie** living above it.

In between the United Free Church and Moirs pub we had Bosworths fruit shop and a newsagents which also sold weans comics, this was us now at Sandyfaulds st and crossing over Sandyfaulds st we had tenement numbers from 235 to 215 Caledonia rd.

Then at number 215 Caledonia rd we had the corner of Mathieson st and going past and over Mathieson st we had tenement numbers from 209 to 185 and this was us now at Lawmoor st.

This now ends the perimeter edge of Gorbals street/map section 5.

We will now go down all the "vertical streets" inside the perimeter edge of my street map, which all head south to north.

Mathieson lane, west/east side.

Mathieson lane was more or less a narrow lane wedged in between Lawmoor st and Mathieson st starting about 4 close mouths long up from Cumberland st.
It continued over Cumberland st and ended as a T shape with exits to the left hand side into Lawmoor st and to the right hand side it exited into Mathieson st. It did allow access to the back court workshops and the odd dwelling. You can see in the image below it only had a short length from

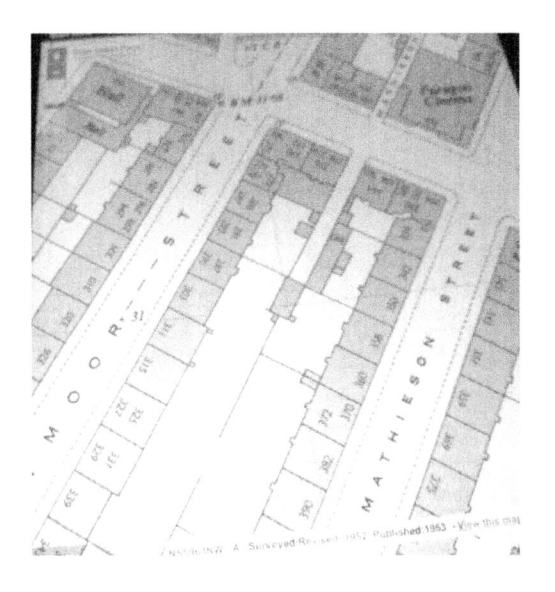

Cumberland st, just over the length of a few close-mouths before crossing over Cumberland st.

Mathieson st, west side.

Mathieson st was another fairly long street in the Gorbals going all the way from Caledonia rd to Adelphi st.

We start at number 426 Mathieson st at the junction with Caledonia rd and its tenement buildings went down to number 322 which was at the junction of Cumberland st.

Then crossing over Cumberland st we had the Paragon Picture hoose [which once was a Synagogue and a Church] and then numbers 300 to 216 on Mathieson st.

Along a bit from the Paragon was a public house which I believe was called the Bundoran bar ["Struans"?] and just after number 260 we had the entrance to St Francis's boys school which had on the top floor the older girls classrooms, then next to the boys school we had Mathieson lane which ran right through to Lawmoor st [Mathieson lane was actually "T" shaped as I mentioned before] then a few tenements numbered 226 and 216 and that was us at [old] Rutherglen rd.

At a **later date** boys would attend Hayfield st school instead of St Francis's. [It all depends on what decade you are talking about.]

Annie [Doherty]Ravizza says,
There was a dairy owned by Cissie McCafferty and her sister and they used to sell milk from a large urn [mid 1940's] the shop was about halfway between Cumberland st and Rutherglen rd on Mathieson st.

After that there was was a shop that hired out tables, benches and all catering goods like pots and cutlery for weddings and funerals. Next to that we had Livingstones [later changing its name to John Johnston's] this was actually 3 or 4 shops in the one including a pawn shop !!.

You could buy furniture and bed linen and some jewellery in the others, it was like an "Aladins cave" and it was always so exciting to walk into.

Brother and Sister Tommy and Betty Malarkey had an ice cream shop/cafe and used to wheel a wee trolley with sweeties etc to the schools gate at playtime.

Mary Mcnamara says Tommy and Betty do you remember would be all dressed up, he wore sports jackets and a bow tie, Betty wore smart day suits and always perfect make-up, thinking back now they were like a showbiz couple, I'm sure they were brother &sister. There was also a pawn shop not far from Tommy and Betty's shop/cafe. Molly Tiffaney had a fruit shop I believe among all the others mentioned.

Crossing over [old] Rutherglen rd we had numbers from 198 Mathieson st going down to number 118 which took us to the corner with Ballater st.

James O'Neill lived at 180 Mathieson st.

Con Butler says,
Doctors Freelander and Bateman had their surgery in between Rutherglen rd and Ballater st.

Going over Ballater st we had number 104 on the corner of Mathieson st and between 74 and 28 we had Mathieon st non-denominational primary school then tenement numbers from 24 to 2 and that was us at Adelphi st.

Trisha Bolt says,
Mathieson street public school. My big sister and brothers went there. My grandad lived in the street so did my mum.

Mathieson st, east side.

Going back up to Caledonia rd we will now go down the east side of Mathieson st starting with number 419 and going down to number 355 and then right next to that stood Ropers pub [once known as the White Horse by the locals]

At number 407 we had a Pen[d] allowing access to quite a few workshops/outhouses.

Authors note,
I never got much information on shops here on both side of Mathieson st I'm afraid, I tried my best but to no avail.

I did research and asked but couldn't find much shop info. But shop names or not I will still mention the close numbers as this will bring memories to the good Gorbals people who lived there.

Crossing past Ropers pub we go over Cumberland st and have St Francis's R. C. Church on the corner. with number 253 going to 217 and next to that stood a pub on the corner with [old] Rutherglen rd which was managed by Duncan Oliver in 1948, was this known as Oliver's bar ?

Again I looked up all the Gorbals pub guides but could not come up with a name for this pub other than being owned by Duncan Oliver at one time.

There was Campbells shop beside St Francis Church on Mathieson st.

Authors note.
Of all the magnificent places of worship we had in the era of the Gorbals tenements, to me St Francis has a special place in my heart as my Ma and Da were married in there in August 1940 and I was baptized there in 1948.

Now we have come to [old] Rutherglen rd and crossing over we had the Augustine Buchanan Church at the corner of Mathieson st and 283 [old] Rutherglen rd with its Church hall adjoined to it at number 189 and we travel down to number 121 and the corner with Ballater st.

Polycrisps shop/factory was situated here at the corner of Mathieson st/Ballater st but later moved to McNeil st. I believe it was only a small work shop with about a work-force of 6 people.

This was us now at Ballater st and as we go over we had the Ivy bar public house and numbers from 103 down to number 1 and this was the end of Mathieson st and we had arrived at Adelphi st.

Sandyfaulds st, west side.

We had tenement number starting at 176 at the corner with Caledonia rd and led down to number 86 Sandyfaulds st and the corner with Cumberland st. It was on this corner with Cumberland st that we had the surgery of Dr Emma Gibb + Dr Forbes with a Pharmacist beside it in Cumberland st [or the Pharmacist on the corner and Dr Emma Gibb + Dr Forbes beside it?].

We had only a couple of shops on the west side of Sandyfaulds st and Nesbitts dairy number 92 was next to the Pharmacist - or - Dr Emma Gibbs surgery. Michael Connolly also lived next door to Nesbitts dairy shop, I meant to say that Mr Nesbitt did a lot of baking in the back of his dairy shop, making the best fruit cakes ever.

A woman called **Bessie** had her shop about 5 closes up from Nesbitts.

Mary McLatchie was born at number 144 Sandyfaulds st.

Crossing over Cumberland st we had the Friary on the corner of Sandyfaulds st with a Pend down a wee bit on Sandyfaulds st to allow access into the back of it and also the girls school entrance could be reached from there.

Then we had tenements numbered 34 to 22 then we had Sandyfaulds lane which allowed access for the infants school and also to an electric sub-station.

Sandyfaulds lane went from Mathieson st through to Sandyfaulds st.

Wee **Mrs Murns** had a wee shop on this side of Sandyfaulds st, she was only about four and a half feet tall and had to stand on a wee box to serve you.

She sold penny drinks and a penny tray of sweeties for the school weans. She catered mainly for the infants school.

I believe there was a furniture shop on this side of Sandyfaulds st too.

Then after Sandyfaulds lane we then had numbers 18 to number 2 Sandyfaulds st which was a public house on the corner with Rutherglen rd and owned by Mr William Morrison. This was us now at the end of Sandyfaulds st west side.

Sandyfaulds st, east side.

Starting at Caledonia rd we had Mac's bar [Moirs bar] on the corner at number 261 Sandyfaulds st, then tenements running down to number 1 which was Neesons pub [Harvies pub].

Travelling back up to Mac's bar we had had tenement close numbers 171 and 163 then in between 163 and 159 we had a Pend which allowed access into lots of workshops/outhouse units, then down Sandyfaulds st [opposite Cumberland st] we had the Pend leading from Sandyfaulds st through to Moffat st which was actually called Sandyfaulds passage.

The street map image above shows Sandyfaulds passage.

In this passage we had Jackson's coal merchants horses and Hislop's[Hyslops?] barras kept horses and carts there too as did Barclay the coalman. The horses in the stable were looked after by Charlie who had a limp and also a wee bakers shop that sold hot crispy rolls . There was always a queue outside for their rolls after 11 pm at night time.

Then we had a run of tenement dwellings going along to number 1 Sandyfaulds st which was Harvies pub.

There were quite a few shops on this the east side of Sandyfaulds st including a wee dairy nearer to the Caledonia rd end, then the down a bit we had the Silver sea fish and chip shop and I think wee Jeanies shop then we had Sandyfaulds passage and after that we had Galbraiths, Boyds chemist, Lawlors newsagents, Orbs licensed grocers and a wet fish shop then that was us at [old] Rutherglen rd.

Mary McNamara lived at 105 Sandyfaulds st, **Peter Thomson** lived at number 49.

Waddell st, west side.

We had the post office at the corner of Waddell st/[old]Rutherglen rd then numbers 200 going down to number 110 and right beside that was the St Mungo vaults[St Mungo bar/Chathams] public house.

Next to the post office stood a Doctors surgery at number 198 and I believe Dr Cameron and Dr Freelander carried out their practice from there.

2 closes along we had two shops, one of which I believed was a newsagents and the other owned by Annie Bollen shopkeeper [circa 1948]. Then taken over by C.Young [circa 60's]

Grace Hynd,
Says Doctor Freedlander was definitely in a practice in Naburn Street however this may well be after Waddell Street as I remember my Mum saying how he went round personally asking people to join his practice when he went out on his own...

He was a wonderful doctor and even when we moved from Waddell Street to Castlemilk he would make house visits by bus!

He was our family's doctor until he retired. As well as having a surgery in Waddell Court he also had one in Shawlands Arcade at a later time.

Thomas Houston,
My uncle and gran lived in Waddell street I remember a sweetie shop were you could get a penny drink of ginger and the penny tray, oh the memories. !!

Michael Connolly says,
There was the chippie just up from Curries, we called the owner Bertie I can't remember the proper name. It was the same side as the Mungo bar and always had a queue outside it on a Friday night as Da's would go home with their pay-packets and Friday nights treat was a fish supper.

Oh and then there was a launderette where you took the washing in and he would wash it and you collected it. I think his name was John and I also think he was Polish, grey hair and thick rimmed glasses. That was just a couple of closes past Curries.

We travel down the west side of Waddell st and come to St Mungo's vaults [later called St Mungos bar/Chathams] and that is us now at Ballater st.

Crossing over Ballater st we had numbers 100 on the corner of Waddell st going down then to number 14 which was the corner with Adelphi st.

At number 26 we had a shop owned by R. McNeil. I don't know what he sold it just says shopkeeper on the post office directory.

Waddell st east side.

We start off at the corner of Waddell st/[old] Rutherglen rd and we have number 207 going along to 129 on this run of tenement dwellings.

Josephine Logan says,
I lived in Waddell street there were two fruit shops, a chip shop and Rose's shop where I bought my sweets from, a laundry where my mum worked but can't remember what the name of it was, the other fruit shop was at the bottom of the street. I lived at the Rutherglen road end and I think our close number was 107.

Con Butler,
Reminds me that there was a bakers shop here in Waddell st in between Rutherglen rd and Ballater st.

Marion Gillies Gibb asks **Rosetta Connolly,**
"Was there factories on the other side of Waddell street" ? Marion "aye the snowball factory and butchers I got sent over for ham ribs". [**Although** this wee mini industrial estate including a coffin makers, butchers, snowball factory etc actually came about in the late 60's early 70's after the demolition of some of the tenements in the clearance.]

We had D.Currie's newsagents at 131, Earlies greengrocers at number 159 and Rose Cowan's sweetie shop at at 189 among others.

We now find ourselves crossing over Ballater st and we have the Stag bar public house on the corner of Waddell st/[old] Rutherglen rd and immediately next to that we had tenement numbers 83 to 75 and next to number 75 we had a large gateway /passage leading into the Strathclyde distillery [can you remember the smell !!]. the Distillery took up numbers 71 to 47, then tenement numbers 37 and 31 then a Pend also allowing access to the distillery then after that a couple of tenement dwellings and then "spare grun" at the junction with Adelphi st.

Here ends Waddell st.

Moffat st, west side - Caledonia rd to [old] Rutherglen rd.]

At the top corner of Moffat st/Caledonia rd we had the U. F. Church [Shearers Memorial Church of Scotland] on the west side of Moffat st.

Then an "open space passageway allowing access into the back courts for workshops/outhouses, then number from 454 down to number 288 and then we had Dick Bartons pub right at the corner of Moffat st and [old] Rutherglen rd.

At number 409 we had big Netty's rag store. Netty's used to be owned by Louis Dublin rag + woolen merchant. **John McCardle** says I used to go in there and ask for badges.

At number 402 Moffat st we had a wee general store ran by **Michael** and **Elizabeth Kelly** who were the grandparents of **Brian O'Rourke,** their shop was one side of the Pend and Cochrane's greengrocers the other side of the Pend and along a bit, a couple of shops a dairy was one of them.

The photo above shows **Brian O'Rourke** on the back of "Pearl" the pony/horse in the back of the stable at Sandyfaulds passage [there was also a Joiners yard there and a coal merchant called Barclay, the horses/pony's could have belonged to either

Barclay or Jackson's for their coal carts] this photo was circa 1959/60.

Mary McNamara says,
I believe a Mr. Jackson owned the stables as most of the coal carts in there had his name in the back of them. A Mr. Dundas from Camden Street also kept his cart and horse in that stable, too.

Authors note,
When I was a wee boy walking through Sandyfaulds passage it was commonly known that Jackson's coal horses and carts were kept in the stables there.

Although I believe that at sometime Mr Checkman [the hoat peanut man] would keep horses in there too, he used to "rent" them out at Glasgow green and Queens park for weans to ride on them. Of Course Hislops [Hyslops] were involved with horses and cart hire too, could be different years that people owned them.

Not forgetting the other coalman Barclay who also delivered coal too in the Gorbals area.

Then between number 374 and 370 Moffat st we had Sandyfaulds passage with access through to Sandyfaulds st and between 370 to 334 we had tenement dwellings with another Pend between 334 - 326 which allowed access through to a large cooked meat factory.

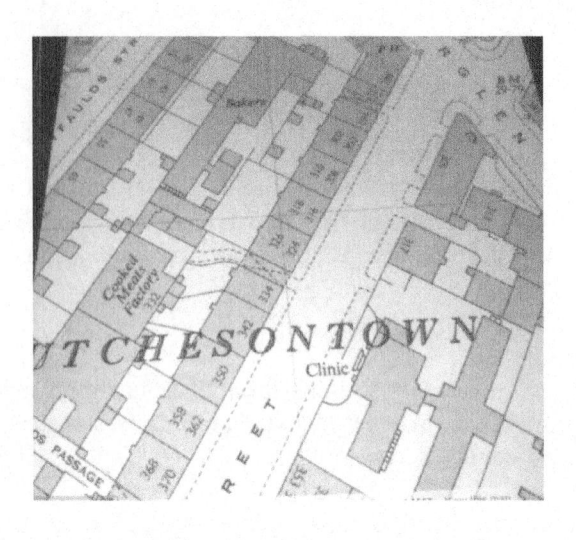

The map image above shows Sandyfaulds passage bottom left, then the Cooked meat factory and along a bit was the Bakery. The "PH" at the top is Dick Barton's public house.

Then from 326 onto 294 more tenements but another Pend after number 294 this time allowing access to a large Bakery, then numbers 292 and 288 and then next to that 2 shops one was a newsagents then next to that stood Dick Barton's public house at the junction with [old] Rutherglen rd.

Isn't it amazing the number of pubs that once stood in the Gorbals of old !! and just remember pubs never opened on a Sunday back then.[officially] We had to go to a Hotel for a Sunday drink.

Authors note,
I have done Moffat st west side and east side in this section but remember we have Moffat st crossing over and continuing as we go over [old] Rutherglen rd. I did it this way to make it easier for you. [and me!!]

Moffat st. East side [only to Rutherglen rd].

We start at the top of Caledonia rd again and we have numbers 423 going all the way down to number 305 which took us to [old] Rutherglen rd.

Actually from number 423 to 411 we had just a small number of tenements with Barnie's pub right at number 411 and that was also the corner with Oregon st. Also in between number 413 and 409 [in the middle] we had an open passageway running through all the way to the next street which was Gilmour st.

This open passageway granted access to a few outbuildings which stood there.

Now leaving Barnie's pub and crossing over Oregon st we had tenement numbers from 401 going to 369 and in between here we had **Martin Devine** who ran an illegal "bookies" from his "low doon" hoose and a fish and chip shop next close to him. Martin had look-outs positioned in case any Polis appeared.

Crossing over Orchard st we had the Harmony bar right on the corner of Mofft st/Orchard st and a tenement dwelling at number 357 and right next to that we had Moffat street "Clinic" it had high walls with barbed wire on top of it.

Mary McCnamara, says,
"I remember that "clinic", we used to call it the "scabby hoose" as there were always weans standing looking out the downstairs window. "We were all scared of it".

Leaving the "clinic" we had tenement number 317 beside it then an open passageway and number 305 which would become a taxi rank and butting onto this taxi rank was a garage but the garage was actually in [old] Rutherglen rd facing Greasy Peters fish and chip shop.

Moffat st west side, from [old] Rutherglen rd to Adelphi st.

Going along Moffat st we had Hayfield public school at the junction with [old] Rutherglen rd, at number 270, this school actually ran parallel along Rutherglen rd which I will mention when I get back to [old] Rutherglen rd when I do my "horizontal streets".

Next we have Hayfield school with its 2 large playground areas, [I always wondered why this school wasn't called Moffat st school ?]. I had a school class room pal from Wee Bonnies called Dennis Smith who lived on the other side of the school and past Hayfield street and some early evenings I would go down to his house and we would go into the school playground and play "fitbaw" with a tennis ball until the "Janny" shouted right that's it boys I'm locking the gate and we had to leave.

Next to Hayfield school we had the magnificent St Mungo halls which was built by the U.C.B.S Bakery building [which stood between Moffat st and McNeil st] for their workers to hold wedding celebrations etc. Of course as years went by St Mungo halls was open to the general public to hold wedding/ anniversary/funeral "do's". St Mungo halls ended at the junction of Moffat st/Ballater st.

Crossing over Ballater st we then had the Bonded Warehouse which was affiliated to the Strathclyde Distillery and almost abutted to it, we had numbers 34 then open space to allow access to the distillery and tenement numbers 12, 4 and 2 and that was us at Adelphi st.

Moffat st, east side from [old] Rutherglen rd to Adelphi st.

Starting on the east side we had the Rainbow cafe right on the corner which were ran by Italian people in my time and sold beautiful tasting ice-cream. Mushy peas and ice cream !!!

This was at number 297 and led down to number 161 which was the corner of Hayfield st and here stood wee Dougies shop.

Christina Quarrell Malarvie says,
There was a wee shop at end of Hayfield Street (Moffat st) Wee Dougie used to go over the Hayfield school with penny tray at the weans playtime.

Dougie was quite wee, the wife/woman was tall, and they would put their shutters up at night and Dougie would take a wee run at the door to kick it see if it was all secure.

This was circa 1964 me and my sister Jaqueline used to watch and get a wee laugh at his antics.

Just past the Rainbow cafe as I say we had a couple of tenements then at number 285-287 we had the aerated water works [Dunn&Moore ginger factory] and next door to that we had the large Confectionary Works for [W&J McLintock biscuit and jam makers] which had numbers from 281 to 265 with 2 gateways to allow access into the premises.

Then next to that we had tenement numbers 259 and 161 and wee Dougies sweetie shop of which I used a few times when going to visit/play fitbaw with my pal Dennis Smith. He had a machine on the wall and you put a penny in it and you had a wee handle at the side you clicked to "guide"a ball-bearing ball into a hole to win a bar of chocolate. I did win a few times !!

Then crossing over Hayfield st we had numbers 157/155 and 147, it was one up at number 147 Moffat st that my pal Dennis lived, then we had a an open space, then tenement numbers 135 to 121 and once again a large open space which had us at Ballater st.

Going over Ballater st we had the side flank of the U.C.B.S. Bakery building It occupied the block encompassing McNeil Street, Ballater Street, Adelphi Street and Moffat Street. It was built between 1896-1916. and employed thousands of Gorbals workers over the years. I always remember passing by it and there used to be loads of vans loading up bread etc to take to the Co-op shops all over Glasgow.

It really was such a magnificently built structure with such ornate brickwork/stonework. We now are at the end of Moffat st east side.

Gilmour st, west side.

Starting at the top of Gilmour st at Caledonia rd we had number 74 going to number 58 and in the middle of this small run of tenements we had an open passageway all the way through to Moffat st [to allow access to outbuildings]. at number 58 Gilmour st there was a newsagents right on the corner with Oregon st.

We then cross over Oregon st and have numbers 52 to 24 on Gilmour st.

Patricia [Hanlon] Shields says,
The shops that I can remember in Gilmour st are granny Brennan's that was at the end of Gilmour st that faced the swing park playground, the next shop was the dairy at the corner of Gilmour st and Orchard st.

The lady who owned the dairy was called Jenny I can't for the life of me remember her surname.

These two shops that Patricia mentions are in between numbers 52 to 24 and the dairy brought us to the corner with Orchard st.

Crossing over Orchard st we had numbers 16 to number 2 and number 2 was Sanny Broons public house and **Patricia Shields** tells me, "the pub on the corner of Gilmour st and Rutherglen road was called Sanny Broons all the men used to gather on that corner, that was a great Glasgow pastime for the men, they didn't have the money for the pub and the houses were so small so the men would stand at the corner as they called it and go home when the kids were in bed".

Gilmour st, east side.

We had Oatlands primary school which was a square surrounded by Caledonia rd/Gilmour st/Oatlands sq and Pine st. As shown in the image underneath.

Continuing along Gilmour east side we pass by Oatland school at Oatland sq and we had the children's playground where I used to have a go on the swings many moons ago. Passing by the children's swing park we had numbers 37 to number 1.

From number 37 to 19 we had tenement dwellings and just after number 19 we had an open passageway leading all the way through to Pine st.

After this open passageway we had number 15 and then "open grun" until we came to the corner of the tenements which stood at the corner of Gilmour st and [old] Rutherglen rd.

We now have reached the end of Gilmour st and are at Rutherglen rd.

McNeil st, west side.

We had numbers from 206 to 108 which took us to Hayfield st.

At the corner Of McNeil st/[old] Rutherglen rd we had Macs bar [known once as "the Challenge"] a couple of tenement dwellings then McNeil st library.

Authors note,
It was here at McNeil st library that I got my love for reading books from the age of 8/9 years old, I used to visit the children's library at the top of the stairs at the top of the building and looked forward to my weekly visits there with glee. I always remember the wee pouch just inside the front cover of the book where you placed you return date ticket.
After the library we had "Dunn + Moore Ginger factory" and next to that the biscuit/jam makers factory. The entrance to the "Ginger factory" was at number 140 and entrance to the Biscuit factory was next to number 132. I think the biscuit factory changed hands over the years. I think this is where Polycrisps relocated from its premises in Mathieson st. [?]

Then we had a couple of tenements at number 112 and 108, actually 108 was McPartlands dairy shop which also sold cigs, tea etc and gave "tic" until pay day. There were living quarters behind McPartlands shop, this was us now at Hayfield st. My Pal **Lynne Lees** lived here.

Going over Hayfield st we had the Pig and Whistle public house or as the locals called it "The Piggy". Later on at the time of the clearance the tenements above the "The Piggy" were demolished but "The Piggy" was left to stand on its own as it was a viable concern making money and is one of the very few Gorbals pubs left and still open for business to this day.

Danny Gill,
says I went in there myself to have a drink in "The Piggy" a few years back on one of my trips back hame on holiday and told the staff and punters that a "wandering son" had returned and was given a warm welcome by all. I loved all the old photos of the tenements that were on the pubs interior walls, they were just as I remembered it all those years ago.

After "The Piggy" we had tenement numbers 64 to 60 and a "bookies shop" then open space and numbers 44 to 28. Actually number 32 was a newsagents and right next to it at 30/28 was a transport cafe mainly frequented by lorry drivers [of whom many were drivers/workers from over the road at the U.C.B.S. Bakers]. The Transport cafe was right on the corner with Ballater st. Crossing over Ballater st we had as I said the U.C.B.S. Bakery building which ran all the way to Adelphi st and here we had the iconic St Andrews suspension bridge which took us over to Glasgow green.

McNeil st, east side.

We had tenement numbers 195 and 191 and this was the end of the old tenements, we had open space and then we had the "new hooses" which were built in between the two world war years as in 1918 to 1939. The "new hooses" continued past Benthall st and Turnlaw st until we arrived back at the old tenements again at number 55 McNeil st and led down to number 41 which was the junction with Ballater st.

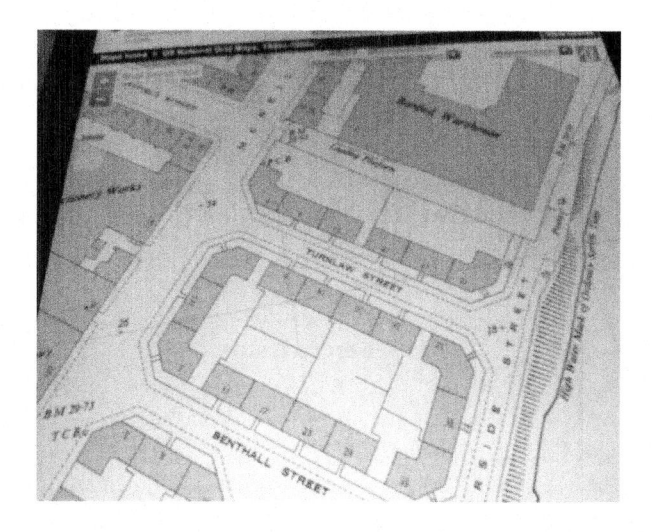

You can see in the street map image above the "new hooses" in between Benthalll st/Turnlaw st. Then after them were the old tenements leading to Ballater st.

Just as we passed by Turnlaw st we had an open space and an access passageway leading to a loading platform at the bonded Warehouse [shown on the map image].

Then we had tenement numbers from 55 to 41 and here almost at the corner of 41 we had a wee shop that sold woodbine cigarettes etc, this wee place was opened early in the mornings for people going to work say in the building trade or over at the U.C.B.S.

Going over Ballater st and continuing along McNeil st east side we had an annexe to the U.C.B.S. and this Bakery took up the whole of McNeil st east side from Ballater st to Adelphi st.. This was us now at the end of McNeil st as we had reached Adelphi st.

Pine st, west side.

Starting at Caledonia rd we had Pine st west side with Oatlands primary school which then took us to Oatlands square and the children's playground/swings and then crossing over Oatland sq we had tenement numbers 16 to number 12 and then an open passageway through to Gilmour st, this allowed access to an outhouse in the middle of the passageway. Next we had number 6 after the passageway and at number 2 was Alexander Hamiltons pub ["Hamiltons"] public house which was on the corner of [old] Rutherglen rd.

Pine st, east side.

Going back to Caledonia rd we now have Pine st east side and numbers 83 to 47, in between numbers 75 and 69 we had an open passageway leading into workshops/outhouses in the back court.. I believe there was a newsagents shop here but I'm not totally sure. Number 47 was at the corner of Pine st /Birch st.

Crossing over Birch st we had St Bernard's Church [which I believe was an annexe to St Bernard's Church which was at the junction of Naburn st/Cumberland st, it seems strange that two Churches having the same name only a fairly short distance from each other.]

Authors note,
I was passing by St Bernard's Church here in Birch st around 1955 when I was aged 7 and a woman and man came out of St Bernard's Church carrying a baby in their arms, the woman gave me a "Christening piece" and told me there was money inside it. Obviously their baby had just been Christened.

I looked and yes there was either a Florin [2/-] or a Half-Crown [2/-6d] in between two buttered digestive biscuits. I ran as fast as I could up to our tenement and showed it to my Ma and she told me the story/legend behind it. My Ma says it was mine and I could spend it, so I took all my wee pals to the sweetie shop and bought them all sweeties, I was very well liked that day!!.
After St Bernard's Church there was "spare grun" and then an electric sub station and a wee shop which I think was a newsagents then only a couple of tenements numbered 5 to 1 and that was us at [old] Rutherglen rd .

Snowdon st, west side.

Snowdon st started at the junction with [old] Rutherglen rd and we had numbers of the old tenements starting at number 26 [?] at the corner and going to number 8. On reaching number 8 that was us at the end of the old tenement buildings and we had open space and then number 2 which was one of the "new hooses" built in between the world war years and this took us to Benthall st.

I believe that on the corner of Snowdon st/Rutherglen rd we had a shop called " Wee Famies", it was a small shop that sold fruit & veg and some groceries. Of course you could say it was mainly a "gossip shop"as you could hardly get in the door for women "gabbing", the woman who ran the shop always made tea for them.

Snowdon st, east side.

At the junction with [old] Rutherglen rd we had on the east side the Co-op shop where I stood many a time with my Ma watching her getting her messages and the money placed into that small tube that whizzed over our head "zinging" up to the cashier sitting in her seat above.

At the corner of Snowdon st and numbers from 33 to 15 and then an open space as this was also the end of the old tenement buildings and number 9 and 3 were the numbers of the "new hooses".

At the open space we had access to the back where a bookies was situated. There were no more shops in Snowdon st. We now arrive at Benthall st.

Silverfir st, west side.

Starting at Silverfir st we had numbers from 40 to number 2, right at the corner there was Alex's wee dairy shop and along a bit was a rag and bone shop, then we came to number 2 and that was us at Birch st.

Silverfir st, east side.

Starting at the east side of Silverfir st we had St Bonaventures R.C Church and in my time Father Gilmartin was the Parish Priest [a right firebrand, if I saw him coming along the street then I would cross over to the other side]. we had numbers 33 to number 1 after St Bonaventures Church and that was us now at Birch st as we reached number 1.

So finishes all the "vertical streets" in section 5 of my Gorbals street map, we will now go along the horizontal streets.

Cumberland st, south side.[continued]

We had a Furniture shop right at the corner of Lawmoor st/Cumberland st, a dairy then Mathieson lane [only for a short distance] then Anderson's lady's fashion shop [which later became Galls] and a few other shops and we then had Mathieson st.

Crossing over Mathieson st we had Ropers public house and again a few more shops and finally a Pharmacists and a doctors surgery [for Dr Emma Gibb and Dr Freelander] then we had Sandyfaulds st and this was the end of Cumberland st.

Cumberland st, north side, [continued]

We had E. Smyth's pub on the corner with Lawmoor st [Lantern bar] and a few shops beside it including the Cumberland cafe and then Mathieson lane and then the Paragon Picture hoose [at different times a Synagogue, a Church and a bookies]. This was us now at Mathieson st and crossing over Mathieson st we had St Francis R.C. Church and the Friary beside it and this was us now at Sandyfaulds st.

Sandyfaulds lane, south side/ north side.

This was just a passageway to allow access to St Francis school infants and access to an electric sub station.

Mathieson lane, south side/north side.

Again this was a passageway through to Lawmoor st and Mathieson st with access to a few tenement dwellings on the north side numbers 2/4 and 8, as I have said before it was T shaped and the longest part of Mathieson lane ran parallel to Lawmoor st one side and Mathieson st the other side.[vertically].

[Old] Rutherglen rd, south side [continued].

We had Teachers pub on the corner of Lawmoor st and a few shops including Kings drapery shop next to Teachers then the Glen fish and chip shop [this chippy was owned by Andy Colalucca and it was his family that later owned "Marios" chippy in the Gorbals], The numbers after Teachers pub were 304 to 330 and 330 was on the corner of Mathieson st..

Crossing over Mathieson st we had a Public house managed by a Mr Duncan Oliver in 1948 [was this called Olivers bar?] and numbers 338 to 362 tenements and a few of the usual shops then a public house owned by a Mr William Morrison which stood right on the corner of [old] Rutherglen rd and Sandyfaulds st.

Authors note,
I am sorry I couldn't get more information on these two public houses, I tried all the Gorbals pub guides and asked around but all I could get was the owners names which would be circa 1940's.

Now continuing along [old] Rutherglen rd we pass over Sandyfaulds st and have another public house Harvies [once owned by a Mr Neeson] right on the east side corner of Sandyfauld st and [old] Rutherglen rd and numbers from 368 to 392, a few of shops including Hamilton's dairy and a newsagents and then we had Dick Bartons pub on the corner of Moffat st/[old] Rutherglen rd.

Crossing over Moffat st we had numbers on [old] Rutherglen rd from 402 to 438 and number 438 was Sanny Broons pub which was at the corner of Gilmour st.

Going back to number 402 this actually later became a taxi-rank and immediately beside it in Rutherglen rd was a garage [opposite Greasy Peters chippy] we had a few shops here including a Chemists called Todd's I believe, McCardles newsagents and a fruit shop. In between numbers 402 and 438 we had another pub called Eadies.

In between Sannie Broons pub and Eadies pub [the Oval] was a wee shop called May Dicks, May still dressed in the style of her youth she wore a long coat and a cloche hat,the shop was pitch black because it did not have electric light,she used to give tick and mark it up on the back of old cigarette cartons even as a child I would wonder if she got all the money back, the back room was stacked with old boxes and I don't think it was ever cleaned and yet she sold unwrapped bread, none of us died of food poisoning though did we says **Patrica Shields**.

Just before we got to Sanny Broons pub we had a Pend between numbers 436 and 432 which allowed access to the back court which had quite a few workshops out there. Sanny Broons pub was at Gilmour st.

Crossing over Gilmour st we had numbers 444 to 464 Rutherglen rd and just after 464 was another public house the proprietor being a Mr Alexander Hamilton and "Hamiltons" was what it was called by some. **Pat [nee Hanlon] Shields** tells me, another memorial shop was the cafe in Rutherglen rd between Gilmour st and Pine st it was owned by a couple called Wullie and Mary, in those non P C days they were fondly called "Wullie the Tally and Mary the Tally, my Da told us about the time when Wullie got interned during the war, when they came to get him he was pleading "me no Tallie me Glesga" all the neighbours were out shouting leave him a lane bloody shame. But of course poor Wullie had to go and Mary ran the shop herself for the duration of WW 2.

This was us at the end of Pine st and crossing over we had numbers 470 to 516 [old] Rutherglen rd and Mcleans pub stood just after number 516 but I actually discussed this section of [old] Rutherglen rd in my perimeter edge of section 5 of my Gorbals street map so I wont repeat my self again.

[Old] Rutherglen rd, north side. [continued from before].

We had numbers from 255 to 198 on this small section of tenement buildings,we had the Kick-off pub at the junction with Lawmoor st and next to that was the Clydesdale & North bank and a few shops beside it and this took us to the corner with Mathieson st.

Crossing over Mathieson st we had the Augustine Buchanan Church at number 283 [old] Rutherglen rd and tenements 287/289/291 and after 291 we had the Post office at the corner with Waddell st.

Going over Waddell st we had numbers 303 to 270 Rutherglen rd, we had tenement dwellings at 303 to 313 and then we had a quite long building which was the Hayfield public school, it was only one story high and was put aside for children to learn domestic skills, and had sewing machines for girls to practice making patterns which were drawn up on blackboards, these well lit large classrooms were also used for domestic subjects like needlework,cookery and laundry etc and for boys a woodwork class.

Authors note,
I fondly remember my big sister Jeanette attended an evening class here in the very late 1950's, I think the evening classes lasted for 2 hours and she told me about the boys woodwork class. I was always skilful with my hands so I went along and joined [I think we paid the teacher 3d for each time we attended the class].

I made a pipe-rack over the course of several weeks and when the classes were over at night time [always in the summer months] we went to "Greasy Peters" fish and chip shop nearby and bought either a penny worth or 3d worth of scrapings.

On the very last night of the summer classes I had my pipe rack in my hand and my big sister said [as we still had an hour to go] come into my class the teacher is going to teach us a French song. The song was "Frere Jacques" about a French monk/brother who overslept and forgot to ring the bells for the Matins [midnight or very early morning call to prayer.] Well when all us boys and girls left the school that night we were all singing "Frere Jacques" as we marched along to "Greasy Peters" and even eating our penny worth of scrapings we were still singing the song. "Us weans could sing in French" !!!!. What an iconic moment and it has stayed with me all these years. Coodny wait to run up the stair and say Aw Ma, guess whit " we kin sing in French" !!!

Anyway back to my Gorbals street map, this Hayfield public school was on the corner of Hayfield st and as we crossed over it we had The Rainbow cafe ran by Italian people and they sold lovely ice cream too and of course next to that we had "Greasy Peters" fish and chip shop. His real name was Peter Pagliari and he always wore a big hat as he worked behind the counter at the fish and chip frying trays.

We had numbers from 381 to 433 on this section of [old] Rutherglen rd.

Next shop to "Greasy Peters" was "Dirty Maggies" who sold second hand comics, it was always full of weans, she also sold firelighters and never had electricity in her shop, she always had candles lit. There were "millions" of old comics stacked everywhere and how her shop never caught fire was a mystery to me but thank God it didn't. Also I'm sure there must have been fleas in "Dirty Maggies" because every time you came out of there you would be scratching yourself. There were another few shops including a dairy and a Mr Staffa who fixed radios and recharged battery's [remember in the 1950's not many people had a TV set in their tenement hoose]. So we now come to 433 and the corner of McNeil st and here at the corner stood Mac's bar [or as it used to be called the Challenge"]

Crossing over McNeil st we had tenement numbers from 445 to 467 and that was us then at Snowdon st with "wee Famies" shop on the corner west side.

Crossing over Snowdon st we had the Co-operative shop on the corner where I stood many a time with my Ma watching her getting her messages and the money placed into that small tube that whizzed over our head up to the cashier sitting in her seat above. Also if I remember correctly there were three of the Co-op shops side by side, one being the drapers and one the bakers [?] and the other the shoe shop I do remember there was always saw-dust on the Co-ops floors. I also think there was a shop beside or part of the Co-ops shops that sold or gave away for free school uniforms for people who couldn't afford to buy them [I was told this by someone ?] then we had the Old Ferry bar which I had already discussed in my perimeter edge of my Gorbals st map.

Ballater st, south side. [continued].

We start at Lawmoor st and we had tenement dwellings numbers 366 to 388 on Ballater st. At number 388 was "Betty's shop" and I think she was a drapers shop but I could be wrong, but at least her shop was here on the corner of Ballater st/Mathieson st whatever she sold.

Isabel Knotts Kane,
Says we had Mary and Neil's shop which sold everything form cigs to bread and milk, fruit and veg.

My good pal Peter Mortimer below was born in Ballater st at number 437. Read Peter's story in Chapter 5 of my book.

After leaving number 388 Ballater st we had Mathieson st and on the east side corner we had Polycrisps which was a small wee shop/factory employing only about 6 people.

[Polycrisps would at a later date re-locate to McNeil st] then a few shops and the St Mungo vaults pub [St Mungo bar/Chathams] and this was us at Waddell st.

Crossing over Waddell st we had a few shops including a newsagents, the Shan shop [selling cheap price cake, bread, biscuits] Peters the butchers, Top Hat hairdressers and a dairy I believe, and where these shops ended we had St Mungo halls abutting to them which then took us to Moffat st.

Crossing over Moffat st we had "spare grun" then numbers 512 to 524, we had a few of the usual shops here with the Transport cafe right on the corner of McNeil st/Ballater st.

Brian Docherty says,
The transport cafe in my time was run by Davie McKell, we used to all meet there for football training over at Glasgow greens ash football pitches.

Crossing over McNeil st we had the return elevation of tenement dwellings then wide open space with that big brick built bonded warehouse set back in from Ballater st and then that was us at the corner of Ballater st and Waterside st.

Authors note,
Waterside st only became into existence with the building of the "new hooses" built in between the war years as before this it was still called Adelphi st and the "old Adelphi st" would run all the way along the river Clyde's banks until it came to the Old Ferry bar at the junction with what was then called Rutherglen rd and not [old] Rutherglen rd as it later became.

Ballater st, north side [continued].

We start at Lawmoor st and we have numbers 363 to 387, actually number 363 was the Clachan bar.

Margaret Cochrane,
Says we stayed at number 382, a butchers and a dairy either side of our close. As we reached number 387 that was us at Mathieson st.

Crossing over Mathieson st we once again had a pub on the corner which was the Ivy bar and we had numbers from 401 to 427 Ballater st which then had us at Waddell st.

Going over Waddell st we again had another pub on the corner which was the Stag pub at number 429 Ballater st with only one more tenement close next to it, then we had a large open space to allow access to the Strathclyde distillery and the Bonded Warehouse which abutted to it and that was us now at Moffat st..

Going over Moffat st we had the U.C.B.S. - Bakery which took up the length between Moffat st and McNeil st..

Crossing over McNeil st we had a few tenement dwellings from number 477 to 551 then an open access/passageway leading into the cooperage building which sat in a bit from Ballater st.

Then next door we had number 557 Ballater st which was once an old machine shop/factory but became the Empress Picture hoose sitting only 240 people but it only lasted a few years from 1911/12 to 1914 then closed later to become industrial units.

Remember in those days it was **"the silent movies"** as the **"talkies"** never came about to much later in the late 1920's. Then next door to the old Empress we had a small metal refinery at number 563 and next to that was number 565 which I believe was an office/dwelling for the large Timber yard beside it. This was us now at Adelphi st and Ballater st ended as we had the Kings-bridge spanning the river Clyde and taking us eastwards to the Bridgeton district of the east end of Glasgow.

Oregon st [formerely Lime st,] south side/north side.

In Oregon st formerly named Lime st we had Barnie's bar, a garage and a coal & briquette place also a newsagents and the entrance to the infants of Oatlands school.

On the south side we had Barnie's bar at the corner with Moffat st then numbers from 14 to 46 and at the corner of 46 we had the junction with Gilmour st.

On the north side we just had the return elevation of tenements at the Moffat st and Gilmour st sides and in between was Oatlands infants school.

Orchard st, south side/north side.

We had numbers 39 to 1 on the south side of Orchard st with a passageway school entrance for the infants of Oatlands school between numbers 39 and 37. My pal **Jean Friel** lived here at Orchard st.

Patricia Shields says,
I can remember the dairy at the corner of Gilmour st and Orchard st.

The lady who owned the dairy was called Jenny but I can't for the life of me remember her surname.

On the north side of Orchard st we had the Harmony bar at the junction with Moffat st and then numbers from 50 to number 2.

I believe there were two shops next to the Harmony bar but I can't get any info on them, I have a photo of them circa 1950's but it looks like they had been vacated for a good few years and their names unreadable, there was also a lock-up place next to these shops then no more shops until the end of Orchard st.

Hayfield st, south side/north side.

We had wee Dougies sweetie shop at the corner of Moffat st and Hayfield st south side which was number 2 then just a run of tenement dwellings until McPartlands wee corner shop at the junction with McNeil st.

On the opposite side we had numbers from 1 to 21 then the Pig and Whistle pub on the corner with McNeil st, no more shops here on Hayfield st north side.

Oatlands square, south side/north side.

On the south side of Oatlands sq all we had was class rooms/admin offices for Oatland school which faced onto Otlands swings playground, then at the other end of the swings/playground we had Oatland sq north side which had tenement dwellings number 1 to 21 and that was all.

Birch st, south side/north side. [formerly Elm st]

On the south side of Birch st we had numbers 43 at the junction with Pine st then numbers 31 to 27 and then an open passageway that gave access to work units/outhouses in the back court, the numbers 23 to 9 and there was a wee shop here on Birch st that sold penny Vanta drinks [tasted like sugarally watter] that was at the junction with Silverfir st then numbers 3 to 1 which brought us to [old] Rutherglen rd. [I think there was a wee bakers shop here ?]

On the north side of Birch st we had St Bernard's Church on the corner with Pine st which went along until we had an open passageway allowing access to the side of the Church building and also to some out-buildings.

Elizabeth Newall Paton says,
I was born in the Gorbals at number 6 Birch st, this was the only close in all of Birch st and it abutted onto McLeans public house then we had [old] Rutherglen rd.

Benthall street, south side/north side.

On the south side of Benthall st we had numbers 2 to 36 with a break in the middle for Snowdon st, also just before we got to number 36 we had an open space which allowed access to the back courts. as I say these "new hooses"were built in between the war years of 1918 to 1939, they were ground floor [low doon] and 1 up and 2 up, so only two storeys high as you can see in this photo here showing Snowdon st to the left and Benthall st heading along to McNeil st library which was in McNeil st.

Authors note,
Snowdon street holds family memories for me as my Ma, Da and big sister lived here right on the corner at number 2 until my Ma was expecting me and the family moved about a 5 minute walk away to Fauldhouse st.

Turnlaw st, south side/north side.

On the south side of Turnlaw st we had numbers from 2 to 32 with a couple of open passageways which I believe allowed access to the Mothers/Wives to get into the wash-line posts to hang up washing to dry. On the north side we had numbers 33 to 1 with an open passageway in the middle for access to the back court. There were no shops in any of the streets of the "new hooses".

So ends section 5 of my Gorbals st map and my Gorbals st map is now finished folks, I hope you have enjoyed the trip down memory lane.

Chapter 11

Gorbals People's Stories

Danny Gill

When my Ma was pregnant with me, she my Da and big sister left 2 Snowdon st and moved nearby to Fauldhouse st, so I spent my formative years up to the age of 13 living 2 up at 40 Fauldhouse st, where Big Bonnies [St Bonaventures junior school] and the Steamie stood.

At the bottom of my street you had Rutherglen rd and Hutchesontown bowling green, if you turned right it would take you a couple of minutes walk and you were at Richmond park which was "an oasis" to all us weans with its trees, swing park, rockery, "sonny pon" and the model yacht pond plus the white swans. Oh and a putting green in the summer months, pure magic for all.

Of course if you turned left at the bottom of my street in under two minutes you were at Braehead st which was the Boundary where Oatlands ended and the Hutchesontown part of Gorbals began. We had the Southern Necropolis graveyard or "the gravie" just on Caledonia rd and us weans were always playing in there. When I was about 8 years old I got my love for reading books at McNeil st library and can clearly remember climbing up the stairs to the children's dept on my weekly visits.

I was born in 1948 when all the auld tenements were still standing and I loved going for walks to Cumberland st with all its many shops, walking through the Pend [Sandyfaulds passage] from Moffat st to Cumberland st and the buzz of all the people doing their daily trips to get their messages and how

I loved the atmosphere. Of course we were spoiled for choice of all the Picture hooses in the greater Gorbals area and eagerly looked forward to Saturdays to hurry along so we could go and see the Lone Ranger or Flash Gordon in action.

I loved that feeling of "togetherness" that existed in the tenement buildings and we weans were loved unconditionally by our parents. Grandparents and neighbours. I also loved going to the Gorbals swimming baths and coming out of there with my wee pals and walking to Cleland st to the hoat peanut man or maybe to Greasy Peters fish and chip shop on Rutherglen rd for a penny worth of scrapings. All these memories have stayed with me all of my adult life, it was great being a wean back then, maybe not much money but happy every day.

Of course as I grew older I wanted to go and watch Celtic play at Parkhead but my Parents wouldn't allow it until I was eleven years old [started secondary school], same as some of my pals who wanted to go to watch Rangers play at Ibrox. So we had to settle for the second best and go and watch Clyde Fc play at Shawfield on Saturday afternoons. I was always playing with my pals Robert Fairfield in Caley rd and Dennis Smith in Moffat st and later James Gillfedder at Portugal st/Norfolk st and a few football street matches in Fauldhouse st too [and games of rounders, kick the can etc]. How I loved growing up in that era of the auld tenements, it was a part of me, it was part of my D.N.A.

Then disaster struck in December 1960, coming home from Holyrood school at 4.30 in the afternoon my street and back court was filled with policemen/ firemen, as when I was at school the back of our tenement had collapsed and the fire brigade were trying to shore up the back of our tenement with great big timbers. I'm afraid that was only a temporary measure and just before Hogmany we found ourselves living in the new housing scheme of South Nitshill. I never settled in South Nitshill and kept going back to the soo-side to visit all my pals.

Of course I met new pals and it was a novelty having an inside toilet and a bathroom with a bath, oh and a wee verandah too but it just wasn't the soo-side and even as I write my story today [aged 72] I still feel "cheated" on having to leave behind the tenements that were my home. As I say I kept going back to see my pals and to the Picture hooses in the Gorbals, plus when I started work as an apprentice bricklayer I was soon of drinking age and frequented a few of the Gorbals public houses. Of course the pub I loved the most was the Clelland in Hospital st and used to go there on Friday nights to the music lounge with my girlfriend Rena Smith.

Then on completion of my 5 year apprenticeship as a bricklayer I stayed in Glasgow for about 6 months and then I started my travels to other countries, with a good trade behind me I would always make good money be it in Sydney/Melbourne or Dublin 3 times etc. I always had the "travelling bug" in me. I left Glasgow in 1968 aged 20 and went to London for a few years with a short stay in Manchester and Birmingham although I must say I always liked London [and the pub life].

By this time I was "living in sin" with Maggie in London but left for the sunny shores of Australia then on returning went over to West Germany a few times [beer/schnapps and Frauleins.] I had a couple of stop overs in Holland and Belgium on my trips over to Germany to work and I must say overall I had a good time in Germany [it was just like the TV show Aufiedersehen Pet]. Then back to London and I worked most areas of London at my trade as a bricklayer and again made good money. Of course I married and had 3 daughters but my marriage sadly broke up but I never once stopped going to see my daughters on Friday nights and weekends and supported them morally and financially. My daughters and all my 7 grand-weans are all born in London and I see them at least once a month. [Nor forgetting all my trips to New-York-Philadelphia, France, Spain and Cyprus and the Canary islands. Wales, India and Isle of Man.]

Later in life when I was 50 I made my way over to Belfast to live and work and once again made great friends, then after a while went down to Dublin and counties Meath and Kildare to work and then after a few years went back to London to live and work again [still had itchy feet ha ha.] Back in London and after a few years found myself working down In Dorset/English coast for a builder in south London who was now living there and wanted work done, so Danny boy answered the call.

Now with all my travelling over the years I still went home to see Ma and Da and my big sister but sadly they are all gone now. I did go back to visit the greater Gorbals and Oatlands area for the first time about 8 years ago as I hadn't been there since I was 20. Oh what a shock I got, all the tenements that I had grown up in and loved had gone, it was like being on another planet !!. there was just a few of the auld buildings left and I felt like greetin.

I am now 72 years old now and after building bricks for over 46 years the wear and tear of it all has taken its toll on my body, I have to take daily heart med's, I have arthritis all over and I'm asthmatic among other things but I have had such a wonderful life here on earth and have so much to be thankful for. It gives me great pleasure to write my books about the tenements of the auld soo side and I'm proud to donate every penny from them to two great causes.

Yes the times may have changed but we have those great days to look back on when we were weans and as someone once said " you canny say you have lived unless you have stood in front of the auld tenement coal fire drying yourself after coming out the auld tin bath" eh.

I do travel back to Glasgow once a year on holiday and its great to meet up with pals old and new, I usually have a meet up in the Clutha bar and its an open invitation to all. Allan Crossan who runs the Clutha a is a Gorbals man too.

- - - -

John McLaughlin

I was brought up at close number 69 Adelphi street, like most young lads I played fitbaw in the streets, went to the Saturday Picture hoose matinee's at Greens playhouse, Palace etc, and sometimes played in the Rosie and old Gorbals burial ground opposite the Twomax building.

I attended St Lukes school on Ballater st and finally moved to Wee Bonnies and later Big Bonnies schools. I played for St Bonaventures footbal team alongside Billy Harvie and we won a few trophy's, when I attended Wee Bonnies school I was in the same class as Terry Dick [the son of Glasgow showman Glen Daly.] Terry was also in the same football team as me in Wee Bonnies.

Mr Smith was our school teacher at Wee Bonnies and he was also our football team coach, he was a nice man and always had a fag hanging from his lips.

I moved about a bit to Toonheid, Royston, Bridgeton and East Kilbride and became a self employed builder working as far away as Northampton in England for three years.

I remember all the shops and pubs in the Gorbals of my youth and my close number 69 was at the junction with Florence st/Adelphi st and Gerry Hurrells pub was along Adelphi st at the junction with Crown st, I also remember Wullie Marks the bakers and Granny Cossy's shop that sold toffee.

So many great times to look back on when I think back to those days of the old tenements and so many great pals.

- - - -

James McCabe

I was born at 128 Naburn st and our window faced Kidston st. The pub below our window was called the "The Crookit Bawbee" there were two closes by mine, numbers 134 and 142 Naburn st, then there was Dixon's blazes.

There were no other houses built and beyond Dixon's blazes was the area of Govanhill. We moved in 1966 to Aitkenhead rd from Naburn st and our old tenement was demolished, we were the last of two houses up 128 Naburn st, also the Salvation army building/hall was demolished in Kidston st, which was a land-mark.There were no inside toilets in Naburn st so we were delighted with the move to Govanhill where we had a bathroom.

At 16 years of age I was given an apprenticeship with "Stirling Hunter ltd" who were in Crown st, I served my apprenticeship there and became a fully qualified TV engineer, I was with the company for almost 20 years till "Visionhire" took over. Our workshop was moved from Crown st up to Pollokshaws rd in the early 70's.

I have to say that Mr Hunter was a thorough gentleman with good morals and always did his best to keep his staff and customers happy, he sold the company to "Visionhire" in 1969 and retired happily. He had only one daughter called Lesley along with his wife.

- - - -

Brian Morris

The leaving of Glasgow for a new life in Australia.

My parents migrated with their eldest five children to Australia in 1959, leaving Glasgow Scotland in July and arriving in Melbourne Australia on 18th August 1959 after a four week to five week voyage.

We sailed on the Peninsular & Orient ship SS Orion departing from Tilbury dock in England. After travelling by train from Glasgow and leaving the UK we sailed via the Suez Canal route eventually reaching Fremantle in WA, where we first touched Australian soil.

From Fremantle we sailed to Melbourne, disembarking at Station Pier (Port Melbourne). The original intention was to remain and settle in Melbourne, however we were placed on a train (the Overlander) and taken to Adelaide.

Upon arrival in Adelaide we were transported by bus to the migrant hostel at Smithfield, a hamlet type of location approx 30 kms north of Adelaide. In 1960 we moved into a new rental home on Knowles Rd, Elizabeth Vale, South Australia.

I completed my primary school and then Secondary High School education and in 1968 secured an apprenticeship as an electrician.

Married twice, producing 5 sons, rearing 4 step children and now having 16 grandchildren, life has been good and fulfilled, no doubt resulting from my parents and my early life in Gorbals/Oatlands which provided me with the ethics and values I have embraced all my life.

Brian Morris *1960, Smithfield Migrant Hostel, SA, 1960*

Authors note,
Brian's family like lots of others could see the start of the demolition of the old tenements and decided to take the "life changing decision" to emigrate to Australia [others would go to the U.S.A/Canada/ South Africa etc].

I have nothing but the greatest respect and admiration for any Father and Mother who take the monumental decision to move to another country and set up a new life and a new way of life in a country so far away.

I myself went to live in Australia for 2 years [1 year in Sydney and 1 year in Melbourne in the mid 70's] and worked at my trade as a bricklayer but to me it was a working holiday and I only had myself to look after and not a wife and family so I salute all the parents who emigrate with their children as it is a "daunting" task of "is it the right decision or not" ?

Brian and myself attended the same school St Bonaventures [Wee Bonnies] with only a few years age difference between us. When Brian left with his family in 1959, Braehead st was classed as Oatlands but everyone knew it was the boundary where Oatlands ended and the Gorbals area started and Braehead st is now officially part of the Gorbals now [as I always knew it was].

Fair play to you Brian for making a great life for yourself and family in Australia, I must say I really liked all the Aussies that I met when I lived in Oz, they're real down to earth people, just like Gorbals people.

- - - -

Margret Fullerton

This is a wee story for you about the pawn shop which our parents and grandparents used to all use [well a good many of us did years ago]

When my Dad john Kavanagh who lived in Florence st was much younger his mother Daisy Kavanagh told him to go across the road to the Tavern pub with my granadad's painters overalls as he had been to a funeral earlier on in the day and was wearing his suit, he then proceeded to change from his suit to his painters overalls [in the toilet] and then pretended he was going to work. This way then Daisy could take his suit to the pawn shop to help her get money to put food on the table and feed the family for the weekend.

Yes the Gorbals has changed over the years and a lot of people have moved away to all those new housing schemes after the tenements were demolished in the Gorbals clearance, but my own mother also called Margaret [nee Docherty] still stays in the Gorbals in Hallside place across from the police station in Cumberland st.

That's my wee story about the pawn shop and how it helped us out in our hours of need.

- - - -

John Hogan

I was born in Snowdon street, Gorbals, Glasgow and moved to live at 24 St Enoch's square when I was 5 years old. My dad got the job as a caretaker at the office block of the National Commercial bank. I attended Gorbals primary school at Buchan st until I was 11 years old in 1964, I used to cross over the suspension bridge every day and have many good memories of the Gorbals and my time at Buchan st school.

One story I would like to share with you is the time I and three pals skipped school [plunked it] at the afternoon break and went off on an adventure down by the river. Remember the wee ferries that criss-crossed the Clyde ?, well we had a great time going up and down the river from the Broomielaw to Govan and back again daring each other to walk round the little ledge that ran round the side of the ferry landing or seeing who would go the furthest down the steps at the ferry landing stage. If you recall the river was always being dredged in those days and the sludge kept in big wooden vats at the side of the river until they were taken away. It was a hot summers day and the sludge looked very solid when it dried out, we had a discussion about whether or not it was solid enough to stand on, only one way to find out eh, yes give it a go. My pal got in over the side and immediately sank up to his waist in sludge, it stank and he had to walk covered in the stuff.

He got absolutely battered when he got home. We all got taken in front of the headmistress the following day, I think her name was Mrs Smith or McKnight and received 5 of the belt each for skipping school, we also got it off our parents too. !!

I tell you what though it was worth it. We had a great day and solved the question of the solidity of dredged sludge. I have so many great memories of my childhood in the Gorbals and although I moved away in 1964 I will always consider myself as coming from the Gorbals and do so with pride.

- - - -

Everett Campbell Wylie

I was born in the Gorbals at 58 Eglinton st, there were 10 of us Wylies.

I remember having to go to the steamie after school to help my Ma with all the washing, a giant pram all full of it. She would send me and my sister upstairs to the hot baths.[as there were very few if any houses in the Gorbals that had a bath in the house, people were sent to the public baths where housed a swimming pool as well as bath tubs.] and we had to share the same bath and that was our weekly bath. !!

I used to love hanging oot the windae with my Ma chatting, we lived one up in our tenement and loved watching the day all the taxis took the weans to the sea-side. It was magical.

Ma's sisters would send us wee dresses from Kearney, New Jersey, U.S.A. so my sister and I would go to the subway and do a full circle, sitting quietly just so everyone could see our new dresses lol.[in Glasgow the subway/underground does one complete run around the city, therefore you can join at Bridge st station in the Gorbals and sit going "full circle" and get off at Bridge st again.

We sat there aw proud because we had new clothes on, oh how we appreciated the simple wee things, truly wonderful.

Chapter 12

Miscellaneous

Picture hooses

What other district in Glasgow can proudly say they had ten Picture hooses in their area eh. !!

[1] we had the New Bedford on Eglinton street.

[2] the Coliseum on Eglinton street.

[3] and the Eglinton Electreum also on Eglinton street.

[4] the Palace Picture hoose on Gorbals st/Main street.

[5] the George./Crown on Crown street.

[6] Greens playhouse on Ballater street.

[7] the Bees on Commercial road.

[8] the Empress also on Ballater street.

[9] the Paragon on Cumberland street.

[10] the Ritz on Caledonia road.

What a choice eh, as I have previously stated the Gorbals was actually a city within a city.

Of the above 10 Picture hooses I was in 8 of them at one time or another, the 2 that I wasn't in were the Eglinton Electreum and the Empress but the others I sat in either as a wean cheering on the goodies and booing the baddies or as a young man sitting in the winching seats at the back of the Picture hoose.

Of course as the Gorbals clearance was happening some of the Picture hooses turned into Bingo halls but like the tenements they were in turn sadly demolished but what memories people of my generation have of them still. I wonder if one day perhaps a new cinema complex will be built in the Gorbals of the future?

The Close Mouth

Weans greeting - Folks meeting

Toilets flushing - Lassies gushing

Men walking - Women talking

Sills sunning - Dogs running

Amaiddens clattering - Smells battering

Tenements throbbing - Stairheads sobbings

Couples winching - Doughballs mincing

EAST

WEST

NORTH

SOUTH

All life began at
The close mouth.

Christina Milarvie Quarrel c 1982.

Authors note,
Many thanks to Christina for allowing me to show one of her works here.

Tomboys don't wear white sannies.

As she opened her eyes, the first thing Ruby did was slide her hand down to the ball of her legs and after rubbing them she thought: "Good, that snowfire's worked just like mah Ma said it wid".

It cleared up the ring of scurvy that the wellies made around her legs. The good weather had arrived and she was dying to put on her new sannies and get out to play with her pals. After her wee sister had helped her fold the bed settee, she washed herself down at the sink before her Da got up. He was still sleeping in the bed recess with the curtain closed over, her Ma had just come back from the wee dairy across the road with rolls and two ounces of spam for breakfast and that was washed down with a cup of hot sweet tea.

One, two, three, four, five, six Ruby was counting with every beat she heard, she knew it was Mrs Henderson form the room and kitchen above who was in the back court the daylights out of her carpets that were hanging over the dyke. They were cleaned every second day, excepting Sundays.

"Hey", Ruby's Ma would say, ! they're only dirt collectors, widnae huv them furra fortune. Ruby knew her Da couldn't afford carpets: as he was on the buroo. Their floor was covered with waxcloth that was all brown patches from constant scrubbing but round the skirting board how brightly it had been when it was new.

They were listening to Housewives choice on the wireless when they heard a voice from the back shouting, "Any auld bits of bread, any draps a dry tea". Then they heard a tune bring blown out of a mouth organ. "Ruby, throw him a penny oot the windae, its the only thing that'll shift him. "Ah, God bliss ye hen, God bliss ye missus" he said then started all over again in the next back court.

Ruby sat outside her close mouth with her wee sister, Chrissie, waiting for her pals. She studdied her sannies as she knocked her feet together, they were just two days old, had just been whitened with pipe-clay and were brilliant in the sunshine now beating down on them.

Nell and Hennie were the first two to arrive, Aggie was next, she was eleven, the eldest and three years older than Ruby, Meg was last, Meg was always last. "Dae yeez want tae go midgie-rakin" ? said Hennie, "up the dibs". That was up in Govanhill where the toffs lived, they threw out toys that only needed washed and soap was cheap.

"Naw no the dibs" said Ruby,"Ah've goat Chrissie tae look after the day so ah canny go faur, whit aboot gaun tae the high backs?, ye get good lux up there". "Right lets go then gang" said Aggie "if anybody finds anythin, we sherr it right ?". Nobody answered her. They remembered the last time when Aggie found a a full book of scraps and she wouldn't share them because they were all sets. Then when a pack of dabbities were found, no one shared them either.

So off they went up Naburn street till they came to Cumberland street where each close had a flight of stairs that led to a door. Now some of these doors were locked and they had to try a few of them till they found one that was open.

"Here's wan" somebody shouted, the rest of them made a bee-line for the close and ran up the stairs two at a time. Hennie was in the back court first and was soon knee deep in ashes. She was stepping over the bins to get to the back of the bins first. They all knew that if there were anything worth finding it would be at the back.

Now they weren't all tomboys but Hennie was one, she could yodel better than Tarzan in the Pictures and she could whistle like a boy by just putting her first and third finger in her mouth and folding her tongue back and blowing. Now that was really good. !!

"Ah've fun a pen !" "Haufers", "ye canny sherr a pen ! anyway, there's nuthin else in here - oan tae the next midgie". the mad race began with Ruby dragging her wee sister at her back. Meg wasn't last this time, after getting to the fourth midden they were beginning to get fed up.

"Ah've fun a bag a jorries" shouted Nell, "Thurs hunners in it, thur must be nearly forty here .", "Haufers" cried Aggie, "don't be stupit, ye canny split a collection a marbles" Nell said. "How no? Ye said thur wiz aboot forty a thum, that's seven each at least".

"Well, if ah split thum thur widnae be a collection, wid thur?". Well were no sherrin anythin else we find, see" Hennie said. Ruby carried onto the next midden and as she was looking down at how dirty her white sannies were, she noticed at her foot a crumpled up ten bob note. She let out a shriek. !!. "Ah've fun ten shullins". Wee Chrissie started jumping all about, her shouting "ten shullin's! ten shullin's"."Oh that's great" Aggie said "that's wan and thruppence each", she was a quick counter but not as quick as Ruby. "Aye and ah don't think" said Ruby, "Me an wee Chrissie will get five bob each an youze lot cin sherr the pen and aw the marbles between yeez" and she walked away leaving them all gasping. !!. Ruby and Chrissie went skipping home and just noticed that the sun had melted the tar on the road and it was all over Ruby's new footwear.

Och well, she said "Tomboys don't werr white sannies!"

Rena [Ross] Silvestro.

Authors note,
Many thanks to Rena for allowing me to show her story here.

The winds of change.

In the mid 1930's there were discussions afoot about knocking down the tenements in the Gorbals area but with events happening in Europe around the rise of Adolf Hitler this demolition plan was put on hold as we were heading towards WW2.

After the end of the war and Britain suffering Austerity it took to the early to mid 1950's before the "clear the Gorbals" got back on track, in 1954 the new housing scheme of Castlemilk started getting built.
Of course Castlemilk would take a huge amount of Gorbals people when their tenements were demolished.

Yes the "winds of change" started blowing through the Gorbals in the the mid 50's when the tenements started to be demolished to make way for "new builds".

The first of these "new builds" were built at near to Commercial rd and Lawmoor st, in fact the first of these "new builds" were ready for habitation in circa 1958.

Everywhere you looked in the Gorbals there were clouds of stour/dust as the old tenements bit the dust, where generations of families had lived in a close knit community spirit and sadly this close knit community spirit would disappear and would not be "transferred" to the new housing schemes where thousands of Gorbals people moved to.

Ye it was nice to go to a housing scheme at first to have a bathroom and and an inside toilet too but that feeling of "togetherness" would not appear in these new housing schemes [although tenants associations tried their best to do this]. we still had to travel back to the Gorbals or Shawlands or whatever shopping centres were near your "new home" and we had to get buses to work, in fact maybe two buses. Whereas while living in the greater Gorbals lots of us could walk to work as the Toon was so close by.

In the Gorbals there were muti-story blocks of flats being built and maisonettes too, again these "new builds" had inside toilets and bathrooms and some form of central heating. It was good for Gorbals people who could stay in the soo-side but I have to say that when the tenements were demolished the "character and soul" left too. We used to get our messages on a daily basis and we had so many shops to shop from but with the disappearance of these shops, Pubs etc it just wasn't the same Gorbals anymore. I'm not saying that there isn't a Gorbals spirit anymore as Gorbals folks are very resilient and mainly happy go lucky folk but I have to say that the Gorbals of today is not what it was like when I was growing up surrounded by the old tenements.

But disaster once again struck as lots of the muti story's that were built to replace the old tenements actually were demolished themselves due to dampness and a multitude of other faults and in turn all the residents once again had to be rehoused elsewhere.

People born and brought up in say Q.E.Square, Waddell court, Caley rd flats etc are just as much Gorbals people as the folks born in the tenements but the era of the tenements is still held dear by people of my generation and the tenements with all their faults was our Hame.

Just think, if the orders from Glasgow city council etc could have been delayed by say 20 years or so we could have had so many of the tenements refurbished and still standing and all those fine Church's and other great structures could still be standing today.

Why is it that you can still go to other districts in Glasgow and their tenements are still standing [these structures have passed the test of time] whereas lots of the "new builds" only lasted 30 years or even less.

As I have previously stated the "greedy factors" were part of the problem as they would only carry out just the bare minimal repair work and let a lot of our tenements go to wreck and ruin. It really is sad that this happened as we lost our Gorbals tenements forever.Thankfully we still have our memories and photos to look back on.

Today we just have a few pockets of the old buildings still standing and I wonder when they in turn will be demolished, at least I am happy to say that I was brought up in the soo-side tenements and would not have exchanged it for all the tea in China.

Hi Danny,

My nana could remember some type of shops, but not always the name. Hopefully some of it is useful.

My nana's name is Margaret Donoghue, but her maiden name was Duncan and she was born in September 1925. She stayed at 100 Rutherglen Road which was her gran's house. She stayed there with her gran, her mum, dad and 3 sisters.

When she was 5 they got their own house at 129 Sandyfaulds street , she went to Oatlands Primary and then later to Adelphi. She left Adelphi and went to work in Twomax at the age of 14. At the age of 19 she got married to Patrick Donoghue and they lived with his parents at 67 Lawmoor Street. They had 3 children, but unfortunately her second child David was killed in a road accident. They moved to Castlemilk in 1960 and my mother - Margaret Telfer hated it, so much so that she moved back down to Oatlands (Logan street) when her and my dad Eddy Telfer got married. She couldn't wait to move back to the Gorbals. We moved to Queen Elizabeth Square in 1966/67.

My nana's first doctor was Doctor Gibb based in Sandyfaulds Street. Her next doctor was Gladstone Roberts who she said was the best doctor ever.

Shops - lawmoor Street

Wee Wullies - sweets and cigarettes
Holmes the Butchers (not sure of spelling)

Shops - Cumberland Street

Wool shop
Simpsons dairy
Frank Stuarts - butchers
There was a fish and chip shop, a newsagent and an ice cream shop next to the Chapel
Co-op
Guthries the butchers

Shops - Sandyfaulds Street

Furniture shop on Sandyfaulds street near Rutherglen road
Nisbetts Dairy
Mrs Ross's fruit shop
A dairy
A sweetie shop

Pawn shop on Mathieson Street

She remembers a guy who had a fruit barrow just off Camden Street and on a Saturday he would attract all the women shoppers with his patter. He also rented out the barrows to people who were flitting.

Her Dad used to work for the council and he drove a cart led by a Clydesdale horse called Sam. I think from what I can gather he picked up bigger stuff that people were getting rid of.

She tells us stories about her granny being a bookies runner around the back courts and how as a wee girl she had to run from the Police.

I think that's everything but if she remembers anymore then I will let you know.

Regards

Trisha

Authors note,
Thank you so much Trisha for giving me your Nana's story.

Chapter 13

Gorbals Bonus Story

Gorbals living in the 1930's and 1940's.

Preface.
My name is Alexander Neil, the purpose of this story is to give my stagnating brain something to do and attempt to show my grandchildren and great-grandchildren the huge difference between the living and social conditions of the 1930's and the present day. I don't profess to be a writer and I don't intend this to be a story about me. It's more of a snapshot of life as I experienced it in the 30's and 40's. I'll try not to make it too boring. It may only be of interest to my younger relatives and anyone who may be curious about living conditions in Gorbals in the title period.

The Gorbals.
I was born in the Gorbals district of Glasgow in 1933 and I think I had better start by giving people a brief glimpse of the Gorbals, there are plenty of old photographs, books, and articles about that and they are readily available on the internet. I have tried a few non fiction books about the Gorbals but all they seemed to do was focus on was violence and drunks. Everything seemed concentrated on negative aspects with very little positive views, in these books and in my opinion some negative things exaggerated.

When Gorbals is mentioned, people who never lived there have a look of disdain on their face because of things that they have heard or read about the Gorbals. I've no doubt there must have been abject poverty in some places [not just the Gorbals] but I never saw it or perhaps never recognised it. I want to show that things weren't all like that and that the Gorbals had a majority of decent hard working, neighbourly and friendly people.

That is why so many people today have happy memories of family life in the Gorbals and I am one of them. You can see more fights and drunks now on a Saturday night or morning when the night clubs come out [albeit it in the Toon where the clubs are and not in the Gorbals] because people can afford to get drunk more often now. There were and still are people who would spend too much money in a pub or the bookies to the detriment of their families. It angered me if I saw a man leaving a pub and I knew some of his family had holes in their shoes !!. Some men would "bleat" "I've worked hard all week and deserve a drink at the weekend". Fortunately my father wasn't one of them and fortunately he was a non-drinker and never kept alcohol in the house. If whisky was required for medicinal purposes [eg making a toddy for someone] you could take an empty bottle down to a pub and the barman would put a Gill of whisky in the bottle and charge you accordingly. No need to buy a full size bottle.

Conditions then and now.
Thinking back to those days I also wonder about the fact the first thing a family had to do at that time was pay the rent, if you didn't or couldn't pay your rent then after the usual obligatory warnings you were evicted, so paying the rent was the priority, food being a close second. There was no "housing benefit or council tax benefit" in those days and I wonder if there weren't any any of these benefits nowadays how many more of today's homes would look like slums?. Sadly there are plenty of houses today all over Britain that look like slums, at least on the inside.

Air Polution.
Glasgow, like lots of other big cities in Britain, was an industrial city and consequently lots of smoke was generated by factory chimneys and home fires that were fueled by coal. This deposited a fine coat of dirt and soot on all of the buildings in the city. This slowly built up over the years and stonework on

buildings became very black or dark looking. This gave the tenement buildings a rather sombre appearance. The clean air act 1956 was an act of Parliament of the United Kingdom. It was in effect until 1964. It introduced "smoke control areas" in some towns and cities in which only smokeless fuels could be burned. By shifting homes sources of heat towards cleaner coals, electricity and gas, it reduced the amount of smoke pollution and sulphur dioxide from household fires.

Smog.
Smog is a type of air pollutant, the word "smog" was made in the early 20th century as a portmanteau of the words "smog and fog" to refer to smoky fog through which you could hardly see. It was also dangerous to your health and caused a number of deaths to vulnerable people. In the late 1970's and 80's [I'm not sure of the date] sandblasting of prominent buildings in the city area was undertaken to remove years of soot and dirt. Some tenements not scheduled for demolition were also sandblasted.

The Gangs.
I won't dwell on the Gorbals gangs other than to say, "Yes. They were there" and bad things happened to some people over the years but fortunately not to anyone that I knew. I didn't have any serious trouble with them when I was young. I managed to avoid serious conflict with them by using a combination of common sense, cowardice, adrenalin rush and a pair of legs that could move like pistons when I felt threatened [that's where the adrenalin came in].

A big difference from then and now is that where I stayed, no gang member would harm or rob an old person. In fact they would "pay a visit" to anyone who had. Elderly people could go to the shops without the fear of being robbed or harmed. I had to run a few times to get out of trouble though. Regarding the Gorbals razor, Lord Carmont, a city judge in the 1950's, came on the scene and handed down some stiff sentences and is credited for curbing some of the gangs actions at the time. I believe that more young people who were not in gangs are carrying knifes nowadays.

I know a lot of old people say "this and that didn't happen in my day" well they are right it didn't happen.The big problem now is the widespread use of illegal habit - forming drugs. Drug taking and and the amount of cash needed to feed the habit is responsible for serious criminality of all kinds and affects people of all ages and classes. This wasn't known when I was young with the exception of smoking. I never heard of or knew anyone who took drugs when I was young.I should also add that there wasn't the same problems with lots of young people "binge" drinking and the various cost of dealing with that. There wasn't a problem with wide spread obesity either because children played outside most of the time and people did mainly manual work and walked a lot of the time, including daily walking up and down the stairs in the tenements. Plus we had food rationing, I'm not speaking of specific cases, I'm talking about situations "in general". I'm not trying to say that things were better then but life was simpler and and less complicated. Quality of life is obviously much, much better now and young children of today are much taller, healthier and very knowledgeable for their age.

On with the story,
It may be of some interest to know that the Gorbals has medieval origins and was at one time Glasgow's leper colony. Hospital street is formed on the site of St Ninian's leper hospital founded by lady Lochow in 1350. The Gorbals district is situated on the south bank of the river Clyde which is Glasgow's principal river which flows through the city. Our home was in Hospital street which ran roughly north to south, the north end of the street terminating at Adelphi street, which ran alongside the river and at the south terminating at near to the junction of Hospital st/Cathcart rd where Alexander "Greek" Thomsons Church still stands. [or just a short distance past there]. I also have to say that Hospital st had a wonderful smooth surface and it was great for roller skating on, go-carts[boagies] and cycling. After the Gorbals clearance/regeneration only a small part of Hospital st remains.

The remaining section is the north end of the street near the river Clyde, of course that was the last time I looked [it my have changed now ?]

The tenement buildings in the Gorbals were built mainly as four, three storey high blocks forming a rectangle, the space in the centre of the rectangle being the back courts where the rubbish bins were kept in three sided enclosures [which we called middens]. In some cases there was also a "wash-house" in the back court. There were also posts for attaching ropes to, to hang washing on to dry. These could also be used for "beating" carpets on. The courts were separated by walls that we called "Dykes" and us weans climbed them repeatedly. If there was any telephone poles next to the wall you could climb to the top of the wall and slide down the pole. Great fun but you had to beware of the jagged slivers of wood. We also jumped from wall to wall or wall to the roof of the middens etc. In addition air-raid shelters were built in some back-courts during WW 2. If there was a set of railings with spiked tops beneath you as you jumped it was called "a death jump", if a wall was too high to jump from, then you had to "dreep it". Dreeping involved hanging from the wall by your fingertips and then letting go. !!

We had "back-court singers" in these days, these were persons [usually men] who were down on their luck and would appear in the back-courts and sing simple songs for a few coppers or a sandwich [piece]. the sandwich was wrapped up in paper and thrown from the window down to the singer. If they were lucky they would be told to come up the stairs and get a sandwich and a cup of tea. They would sit on the stairs to consume their food, they didn't get allowed in the house.

There were also "rag-men" who came round the streets with hand carts or horse drawn carts calling "crockery for rags" or "balloons for rags". Many a still usable piece of clothing would disappear from a house and a child[wean] would suddenly, as if by magic acquire a balloon.

Going back to the rubbish bins, the bins were very large and the contents [mostly ashes from the tenement coal fires] were shoveled into large baskets and the baskets were carried on the backs of the "bin-men" out to the street and emptied into a horse drawn cart during the night. I think the workmen had a "carbide" lamp [which had a burning flame] on the front of their hats. Hard work, but that's how things were in those days. Think of the coal delivery men repeatedly carrying all those bags of coal on their backs up the tenement stairs. Some coal supply companies gave their customers a fairly coloured card which the customer displayed in their tenement window if they wanted a delivery. Each different coal company had a different coloured card which was about the size of a sash window pane. The stairs to the house were accessed via a ground level entrance which we called a "close" and each close had a number. This number, plus your street name of course being your address. Entering your close and proceeding upstairs brought you to the first landing, upstairs again to the second landing and finally up to the third landing [tap flair]. Each landing usually had three houses on it, meaning there were nine families living up each close and sometimes another two families at ground level [low doon].

In most cases you could also enter the close and walk straight through to the back-court. If I remember rightly, in some tenement blocks when you reached a landing on the stairs there was only one door, when you opened the door there was a hall or lobby as we called it, giving access to the other residential doors. The lobby [being warm] was a favourite with "down and outs" who had no place to sleep. They made themselves as comfortable as can be and slept on the bare floor all night, we called them "lobby dossers". If you were going out for an early start in the morning, opening the door and seeing a body lying on the doormat could more than startle you. It was not unusual in those days for families to have eight or more children and obviously there were lots of people living in a small area and the population of Glasgow in 1939 was over one million, its just over 600.000 [as I write].

Info from internet,
In 1930's and 40's Britain's children were born into a dangerous world, every year thousands died of infectious diseases like pneumonia, meningitis, tuberculosis, diphtheria and polio. Skin problems like scabies and impetigo were common. Infant mortality - deaths of children before their first birthday was around one in twenty. From 1945 more vaccines were developed to control childhood diseases. After the war the health of children was better generally than at any other time in history. Vaccines against polio, measles and rubella were developed in the 1950's and 60's.

There were many nationalities in the Gorbals including lots of Irish and a strong Jewish community. I read an article that said between 6000 and 9000 Jews stayed in the Gorbals at one time. I've heard the Gorbals cross area was nicknamed "Little Jerusalem" many local shops and businesses had Jewish owners. As they prospered they moved out to Pollokshields to live but still had businesses in the Gorbals. There was a large Synagogue, called the Great Synagogue in south Portland street near the Gorbals library. My Mothers sister "Jean Bain" and her family lived in the building opposite. There was a newspaper called The "Jewish Echo" available then. The "Sample shoe shop" at the corner of Hospital st and Rutherglen rd was owned by a Jewish man called Mr Barnett originally from Russia, I believe. Mr Jackman [or Checkman] had a small and rather famous shop under the railway bridge which crossed over Cleland st, it was between Hospital st and Gorbals st. He roasted and sold peanuts and toffee apples, tablet, etc and kept the stock round the corner in a disused shop in Hospital st. He also took a folding table to to fairgrounds to sell his produce, I went to assist him once to a fair somewhere in Springburn, on the left hand of the main road. I can't remember if I got paid with cash or some of his produce and didn't care !! as I'd been to the Fair and when you passed by his wee shop in the railway arch in Cleland st it was hard to resist that delicious aroma.

In our close we had Irish Catholics, Jews, Protestants and we all lived in harmony. When we were young we went to our Church or Sunday school and there was never any mention of divisions of religion in our home. I remember as a young boy about 11 being asked one time by two older boys was I a "Billy or a Dan or and old tin can" and I had no idea what these persons were talking about !!, someone had to explain to me that I was being asked was I a Protestant, a Catholic or Jew. I have never been interested in what anyone's religion was. If they were decent persons that was all I cared about.

Cafe's and fish and chip shops were mainly owned by Italians or persons of Italian descent, when Italy entered the war as allies of Germany on the 10th June 1940, a large number of these establishments had windows smashed by locals in towns and cities all over Britain, Glasgow I believe being particularly bad.

I've seen many photographs and films depicting the slums of Glasgow, showing dirty houses and permanently dirty children, but the houses of my friends and family were clean [as were the children]. All three flights of stairs, landings and windows in our close for example were washed twice a week by neighbours on a rota basis. You don't see many people doing that nowadays !!. Neighbours also cleaned them for any elderly, ill or infirm persons who lived beside us and who were unable to do so themselves. Being a close knit community there were always plenty of people willing to help neighbours when required. There was plenty of overcrowding though with large families in small houses.

The largest number of family members to stay in our home at any one time was eight, there being my Mum and Dad, myself and five other surviving siblings but I know of some houses where there was twelve persons. At that time we didn't consider our houses to be "slums" but they were miles behind today's standards. Some houses in Abbotsford place for example were grand affairs when first built in the mid 1880's having seven or eight rooms I believe. Sadly they became run-down too. People were poor so thick vegetable soup was a staple family food [as were "Stovies" which was a sort of hot-pot]. Some women would be worried because they were having another child and wondered how they would cope with an even larger family and invariably someone would say "just put more water in the soup". Poor people cared for each other and made the best of what they had without being depressed every day. Times were tough but I don't remember any "food banks" then.

Lots of people in the UK are still living in very poor conditions today which I think is a scandalous situation in this so called "modern age". At time of writing a lot of people are going to "food banks" to get free food from charities to sustain them [over 900,000 people in 2013/14 in the UK].

The following food-bank info from 2014 Trussel trust report - - Latest food-bank figure top 900,000. Life has got worse not better for the poorest in 2013/14 and this is just the tip of the iceberg.

Food banks have appeared all over Europe in the last few years. In 2012 a British politician stated that people were only going to the food banks because they were there !! I wonder what its like to live in a politicians world where you see only what you want to see!. They don't have a clue to whats going on outside of their own enviroment, I think a lot of them have what I call "Ostrich syndrome" !!. Of course there are some people using food banks who don't really need them, but as far as I know you have to be officially referred to them. There will always be people from all classes who will try to get something for nothing. Politicians would never do that of course just as rich people and global companies would never set up tax avoidance schemes would they ??

The Lamplighters,
The landings in the close were lit by gas lights and were lit every night by the lamplighters who would light and alternatively extinguish them in the morning. They carried a pole which had a small flame burning on the end. These poles also had a bracket fitted which was used to turn on the gas tap after which they lit the gas mantle with the flame. I think some

street lamps were gas at that time and were also basically lit by the same method. I believe after the street gas lamps got turned off in the morning, the lamplighter [on request] knocked on doors or windows with the pole to awaken people. The lamplighters were called "leeries" in some places. The chemical carried in the lamplighters pole to fuel the the flame was "calcium carbide" I believe. When they emptied the carbide usually near a drain, we kids used to put a little water on it and watch it fizz up. I've heard that putting a drop in a classmates inkwell was great fun of course I would never do that !!.

Home,
We lived in a palatial 2 storey town house in Hospital st, the house having a front porch held up by two fluted pillars and our entrance hallway had a Victorian tiled floor. A curved carpeted staircase led to the upper floors and we had a cook, a servant, a servant girl and a nanny to assist in our every day life. Our parents held many social events attended by many ladies and gentlemen in evening attire.

No, none of the above paragraph is true, I made it up, my Pinnochio nose is getting longer. Lol.

Home environment,
We actually lived 2 floors up at 103 Hospital st which was one of the 3 storey tenement buildings mentioned earlier. These tenements were built mid 1880's to house local factory worker and cotton mill workers, although I mostly remember the shipbuilders, dockers engineering and factory workers. The nearest cotton mills at that time that I know of were in Paisley although the Twomax factory on Rutherglen rd was a cottton mill at one time.

Our close in Hospital st was at the junction with Cleland st, our house had two rooms plus a kitchen and a large box-type room behind the kitchen, big enough for a double "built in bed" [recess]. We also had two double beds in the smaller bedroom, one of which was a recessed bed and one bed in the large room. Our two bedroom windows overlooked Cleland st and our kitchen window overlooked the back court, which was small as we were on the corner. We also had an indoor toilet and the toilet being inside the home was believe it or not a bit of luxury as most of my friends had toilets on the stair landing. These toilets were usually on a turn in the stair between two floors meaning you had to walk downstairs to use the toilet. Newspaper was used as toilet paper [no toilet rolls]. Newspaper cut to size, a hole in the corner of the sheets, string through the hole and hung on a nail. These outside toilets were shared by all tenants who lived on each floor which was commonly three families each landing. There was no wash hand basin in either the inside or outside of the toilets. Washing facilities in these homes were the black cast iron kitchen sink [cold water only] and a tin galvanized bath normally kept under the bed and brought out on bath night for the kids. Despite the absence of a bath in the house we were all taught and knew how to keep ourselves clean. "Soap and water's cheap" was a common expression or criticism if people were judged to be dirty. Carbolic soap was the common soap used and is a mild disinfectant soap that contains carbolic acid a compound that is extracted from coal tar, this soap was once the disinfectant of choice in operating rooms and private homes and it still can be found in some regions of the world. There were facilities for getting a hot bath in the Gorbals swimming baths, going "to the baths" enabled you to get a shower and a swim. There was also a section upstairs where there were actual hot baths you could get the use of these at a cost, towel and soap extra. Large deep baths with lashings of hot water, Great!! [always busy on a Friday and Saturday].

There was also local public wash-houses [commonly known as Steamies] where house wives could go with clothing or bedding in need of washing. A stall containing a sink could be hired and plenty of hot water and drying facilities were available. No launderettes then, an old pram was commonly used to transport the washing, washing board and soap to and from the steamie. There was an extra demand for the steamies at Christmas and New year time and consequently they were very busy. I remember in my early teens queuing all night at the steamie in

Rutherglen rd to get a "booking" for my Mother for the New year. My Father brought a flask of tea in the night and came and took over in the morning. It was fun listening to the banter and occasional arguments between the women in the queue.

1885 - April 17th Gorbals baths and wash house, 144 Main st - opened

1897 - October 18th Hutchesontown baths, 151 Rutherglen rd - opened.

Christmas and New year,
As you would expect Christmas presents were pretty modest in those days. On Christmas eve we hung a sock up on the mantelpiece above the kitchen fire and on Christmas morning we would get a few things in the sock. This usually included a tangerine or other fruit [which was scarce in wartime]. There would be a few larger toys which were often handmade. My Father used to make doll's houses with miniature furniture for the girls and wooden forts for the boys. I never found out where he kept them secretly hidden away until Christmas. There would also be a few dolls, cars and books etc.

At Christmas we looked forward to a large homemade "clootie" [cloth] dumpling. The cake mixture was wrapped in a cloth [sometimes a pillowcase] which was dipped in boiling water then sprinkled inside with flour. The dough was then inserted and leaving room for the mixture to expand, the cloth was tightly tied to keep it in shape, boiled for about 3 and half hours then the dumpling removed and dried in front of the fire. A few sixpence and three-penny pieces were wrapped in grease-proof paper and placed in the mixture before cooking. I can always see in my minds eye, a big round dumpling sitting on a rack in front of the fire, slight traces of steam rising from it, accompanied by a wonderful aroma. Delicious and I still love dumpling.

Homemade ginger wine was the drink for Christmas and New Year too. At midnight on Hogmany [New years eve] we could faintly hear the steam ships on the Clyde sounding their foghorns to signal the New Year coming in. At this point my Dad would line us up and shake our hand, wishing us a "Happy New Year". He usually had a coin in his hand which was transferred to each of us when he shook our hand.

Continuing with the houses,
There was one smaller block of houses on the opposite [west] side of Hospital st and slightly north from us abutting Cleland st which had bathrooms in the houses. It was a two story building which I was told belonged to "the railway" Which railway company I don't know, I knew a family called Moore who lived in that building. The railway lines ran behind the houses on that side [west side] of Hospital st at a height of three storeys. At home we only had gas lighting [no electricity] and cooking was done on the kitchen range which consisted of a coal fire which also heated the adjacent oven. [later we acquired a small two ring gas cooker on a metal stand - no oven]. As children we loved to toast bread by holding it with a special extendable long handled "toasting fork" close to the fire, delicious !!. the black part of the kitchen range had to be "black - leaded" every so often and the polished parts cleaned with an emery cloth. [Black - lead was a graphite composite I believe and emery cloth is a type of coated abrasive that has emery glued to a cloth backing, like sandpaper but finer]

I am indebted to my friend Danny Gill for his memories as a young boy as to how the the fire in the kitchen fire was lit. "I remember it well Alex, there was an art to lighting the old tenement coal fire. Getting old newspaper all crunched up and building the wood sticks like a Red Indian teepee but with spaces in between so that when you lit the newspaper inside you could blow air from your cheeks to help kindle the fire. Throwing a handful of sugar would act as an accelerant [although sugar was rationed in WW2] then placing a newspaper in front of the fire opening and you would hear "Whoosh" as the air drew the fire and the newspaper caught fire and disappeared up the Lum [chimney]. When the fire caught light it lit the previously placed wee lumps of coal that had also been placed next to the sticks. Then as the fire really caught alight you would add extra lumps of coal [bigger] and soon your coal fire was blazing. Worst thing about the coal fire was having to dump last nights ashes in the back court midden which was my job as I went to school in the morning. !!

Small bundles of firewood could be purchased in various shops, these being tied in wee bundles with string but lots of people just gathered their own sticks. Quite a few enterprising weans chopped up old wood tied them in wee bundles and went round chapping on people doors to see if people wanted to buy them. Zip brand firelighters became available in 1936, they were made from saw-dust, soaked in paraffin and bound into a block using paraffin wax. This made fire lighting much easier but of course at a cost. Handy if you were in a hurry to get the fire lit on a freezing morning.

We had a coal bunker in our lobby [hall]. It was a deep cupboard with a shelf near to the top and a board, maybe just over a foot high on the outer edge of the bottom. The coal was emptied in there by the coal man when he mad his delivery. Delivering coal to the tenements was hard work. There was no central heating, just coal fires. In later years we acquired a couple of "Paraffin heaters" also. As their name implies they were operated by burning paraffin which we had to purchase from an ironmongers shop, carrying the paraffin home in one gallon containers.. the only draw back with paraffin heaters is that every gallon of fuel that you use puts a gallon of moisture into the room. [same with bottled gas]. The amount of didn't affect the old tenements but it affects modern homes !

Chimney sweeps,
As the house fores were burning coal, sooner or later a chimney sweep was required. A chimney sweep is a worker who clears ash and soot from chimneys.. Chimneys may be straight or contain many changes of direction. Over a period of time a layer of creosote can build up on the inside of the chimney which can catch fire and could potentially set the building alight. The chimney must be swept to remove the soot, this was

done buy using a chimney sweep. In the tenements you could have a chimney stack with numerous chimney pots on it and the chimney sweep had to make sure he swept the correct one. He did this by climbing onto the roof and shouting down the chimney, when the tenant heard him and answered, he knew he had the correct chimney and could then drop his weighted circular brush down. Some chimney sweeps worked from inside the house. They covered the fireplace and hearth area with cloth sheets and through a joint in the cloth inserted his circular brush attached to a long pole and pushed this up the chimney [lum] to dislodge any soot, adding extra poles as required. No matter how careful they were soot invariably escaped into the room. No fitted carpets back in those days so not too much damage, just a mess to clean.

Continuing with the conditions,
There were no "spring interior" mattresses on the beds; mattresses were filled with clean "flock" [I believe it was called rag - flock by the manufacturers.] It was common practice to regularly empty the flock out of the mattress into the previously mentioned empty galvanized bath and sprinkle it with "flea powder" before refilling the newly laundered mattress cover. There may have been spring interior mattresses available but we didn't have them in our house. My Mother stayed at home to take care of the house and the children, which was the norm in those days. The women in those days didn't have the household aids that are available today. Washing clothes and bedding was all done by hand, as was mopping and sweeping floors. There were no disposable nappies, soiled nappies had to be cleaned, washed, dried and re-used !!. The floors were not carpeted, only linoleum [and rugs, if you were lucky] and any rugs were taken down to the back court, hung on a clothes rope and beaten with a carpet beater to remove any grit and dirt. [carpet beaters were typically made from rattan, cane or wicker, usually interwoven into decorative pattern but practical shapes]

Add dressing the kids taking them to school and the clinics when young, making the meals, washing dishes, washing stairs, cleaning windows, ironing, sweeping and washing floors, cleaning brasses, removing the ashes from the fire and of course shopping. You can see that a housewives day was very busy and tiring. We did not have a "throw away" society in those days. Torn clothes were repaired, socks with holes were darned and often boots and shoes were re soled or re heeled or had studs hammered onto them. Most houses had a mushroomed shaped piece of wood used when darning socks. No electric fires in those days, a "flat iron" was heated on the fire or gas ring and this process had to be repeated during ironing as the iron quickly cooled down. [best to use two irons]. Gas irons were introduced later, these had a flexible gas supply tube fitted to them and the gas actually burned inside the iron thus heating it. [there weren't many gas safety regulations in those days as stringent as they are nowadays]. No ironing boards, the kitchen table with a folded blanket or similar on top was used. We did not have televisions, washing machines, tumble dryers, refrigerators, freezers, vacuum cleaners, electric kettles or any of the common electrical household appliances used nowadays. We did not have any electricity installed in our home until after the death of my Father in 1950.

We didn't have many material possessions in those days and apart from a few minor squabbles among siblings, life was ok. We only had a radio in the house and a "wind-up" gramophone [record player]. You had to turn a handle on the side of the gramophone to tighten the spring which turned the turntable. Board games, cards, darts, table tennis, drawing, reading and hangman were popular forms of recreation when inclement weather kept us indoors. The radio was powered by an acid type of battery and when the power ran down, we had to take the battery to a shop [a cycle shop in Cumberland st in our case called Kitsons]. and they took the battery to recharge and gave you a fully charged replacement one. There was of course a charge for this service for the replacement. The battery's were called "accumulators". my parents seemed to have enough money to get by on but this changed in layer years when my Fathers health deteriorated and they had financial problems until his demise. No "social services" giving you assistance in those days like there is today but there was some assistance in clothing children from poor homes from the local "Parish". I don't know how it worked but I was the recipient of this assistance at one time. I believe my Mother was given a voucher which she took to a warehouse of some sort and I received a new suit and a pair of boots. I may have got some other clothing apart from the suit etc but I don't really remember. When you went to school you could identify everyone who had been given those suits and boots!!. The suits were herringbone material and all the same colour and the boots were what we called "Tackety boots". As I said this assistance was from the local Parish and people knew you were on "The Parish". [Parish suits and tackety boots was a common expression.]

Outdoors in the streets we played football [watch out for the Polis, I was caught twice] rounders, kick the can which was a form of hide and seek ledgy - ball/dodgy - ball, roller skating and we made go carts out of old prams and orange boxes. Girls played with skipping ropes, wall balls, hop-scotch [beds] and younger kids played with "whip and peeries" etc a peerie is a small wooden spinning top that you whip to keep it spinning. If we were feeling brave and mischievous we played K.D.R.F [kick door run fast]. We were never bored when outside. Glasgow green park with "Peoples palace" and winter museum and the winter gardens [hoat hoose] were within easy walking distance and we always enjoyed going over there. There was also a number of swing parks in the Gorbals, I heard that archaeologists were recently searching for old air raid shelters in Glasgow green. I remember as a small boy seeing mounds of earth on top of these shelters. It appeared as if the roofs were curved or it may just have been the mounds of earth on top. There was a number of short square brick "chimneys or vents" protruding above the mounds in various places. A boy at school told me had climbed down a ladder which was fixed inside the vent and saw long wooden seats alongside the walls inside. He must have had a torch with him !!]. Apparently no records had been kept of their whereabouts but if I remember correctly, they were near to the Winter gardens [hoat hoose].

We didn't have much money but generally we were happy with our lot for the simple reason that we didn't know anything else. In those days any adult could chastise a child for misbehaving. If you mentioned to your parents that someone had chastised you, parents would invariably say, "you must have been doing something to deserve it". Nowadays angry parents come to your door if you chastise their children, and if you don't chastise them and they injure themselves, you'll be told you should have stopped them from doing whatever it was that they were doing. !! Can't win. !

We got great enjoyment going to the cinema when we could afford it. [especially the Saturday matinee when we were young] there was no shortage of cinemas in those days ad we had about seven nearby in the Gorbals [The Eglinton Electreum [the EE'S], the Coliseum, the Bedford, the Palace [next to the Princess theatre and Diamonds Dancing Academy], the Crown cineam [the "Crownie" later becoming the George] Greens Picturedrome and the Wellington Palace [Bee's] which may have been in Hutchesontown adjoining the Gorbals. There was also the Ritz in Oatlands at the end of Caledonia rd. The Princess theatre later became the Citizen's theatre in 1945. In the Eglinton Electreum near Bridge st underground [subway station] the cinema was down in the basement and at times you could hear the rumble of the underground trains as they passed through the tunnels. There was also a Billiards/Snooker hall in old Rutherglen rd just around the corner from Hospital st called the Globe; but this was strictly off limits to any of us, this ruling by our parents. Snooker halls have a much better image now than then. In those days if you could play snooker, people said that was a evidence of a "miss-spent youth". I remember a fairly large group of men gambling in Hospital st. They were playing "pitch and toss" I'm sure that is what it was called. Betting on heads or tails landing or a combination of both as two coins were tossed in the air. A large number of people could gather at theses gambling sessions. The organisers had "cop watchers" placed nearby at the street corners to warn them if any sign of the police about as it was obviously illegal [as were the back court bookmakers at the time.] Bookmakers shops or the "Bookies" was legalised in 1961.

Tramcars,
When we weren't walking we travelled by tramcar or the underground [called the subway in Glasgow.] The old tramcars had a broad coloured painted band between the lower and upper decks. They had different coloured bands for different routes. By looking at the colour you knew the tramcars general route. They also had a destination board of course. If someone asked you which tram had to take to somewhere you could tell them to go across the road to the tram stop and take the "Yellow tram" for example. I think the yellow tram was the number 7 [the number also identified the route]. the tramcars had a flight of stairs to the upper deck on both front and rear platforms. As the driver stood on the front platform, the opening to which was facing the centre of the road, you could only board or get off at the rear platform which of course faced the pavement. Trams were powered by electricity and ran on rails, The electricity was supplied by overhead wires and an apparatus called a "Pantograph" and was attached to the roof and this conducted the current from the single wire to the tram. The return current was earthed through the trams steel wheels and rail tracks. Then new trams were eventually introduced [Coronation type I think they were called.] on which the driver sat in isolation in a little cabin, one at each end of the tram. Trams did not turn around to make the return journey, the driver simply carried the required hand controls from one cabin to the other to make the return journey. In other words what was the back became the front. All the double seats faced towards in the direction of travel and so for the return journey the conductor had to walk along between the seats pulling the backs of the seats [which were hinged] forward so that the new passengers were facing the direction of travel again. He also had to adjust the position of the Pantograph making it slope to the rear of the tram and he did this by pulling on a rope which was attached to it. Simple systems but effective!!. With the exception of emergencies all repairs to the tram tracks and surrounding cobblestones [which were the norm] were carried out during the night. The

workmen, tools and materials were transported to the area by a tramcar which was made for this purpose. If I remember correctly it was about half the height of normal tramcars which were double decked. In April 1949 Glasgow corporation transport started to replace the trams with "Trolleybuses" which also used overhead wires [two wires] to power them but did not require rails. They were much quieter than tramcars and you had to ensure that none was in the vicinity before crossing the road. The trolleybuses had two spring loaded poles to transfer power from two overhead wires to the bus. One positive and one negative to complete the circuit. The last Glasgow tram ran on on September 1962, the last trolleybus ran in May 1967 and were replaced by Leyland "Atlantean" diesel buses. At one time when I was about twelve, I decided I would try to "dodge the fare" on a tramcar. I was upstairs and when the conductor came upstairs to collect the fares, I stared out of the window and pretended not to hear him. The conductor tapped me on the shoulder and despite my protestations of innocence["I was deep in thought"] gave me a telling off in front of the rest of the passengers and collected the fare. I suppose he had plenty of previous experiences with fare-dodgers. Of course at the time I didn't realise that if a ticket inspector came on, the conductor could be in trouble. I bet my face was red !!

This also reminded me of the time that one of my neighbours from the 1st floor of our close and myself decided to "bunk off" school. We made our way to the fruit market which was near the city centre at that time and was a place of real hustle and bustle, with horses and carts, busy porters and dealers calling out prices. We had only been there about half an hour when I heard a well known voice from above my head ask " what are you doing here?", it was my Father at the top of a ladder and he was doing a bit of sign writing or painting on the front of the building. I never tried to dodge paying my fare or bunk off school again. !

I don't remember a great deal of my young childhood but I remember I had my tonsils removed at the Victoria infirmary. I remember walking along a corridor holding a nurses hand and she was telling me we were going to the theatre "to see Mickey Mouse" she said. I remember waking up lying on a large waterproof cover on the floor. There were other children beside me, some of whom were being sick and that's all I remember about it and because our throats were rather raw after the operation we were given ice-cream.

I also remember an unpleasant and very painful incident at home involving myself and a clothes wringer. My Mother had fitted the wringer to the kitchen table and was putting wet washing through the wringer to remove as much water as possible from the clothes. The bottom roller on the wringer was operated by turning a handle fitted to the end of the roller and this roller, by means of cog wheels, turned the upper roller in the opposite direction. I'm guessing I was about three or four years old and was watching my Mother working at the table. I was at the side of the wringer watching the cogs meshing together and whether by accident or deliberate action on my part, my second finger on my right hand got caught in the meshing cogs and they took the top off my finger. The wringer won that round [later models of wringers would have a guard over the cogs]

In view of the last three paragraphs, does anyone know where I can get some Lucky Heather from ??

I don't know where my Father was at this point but I remember him taking me by tramcar to the Glasgow Royal infirmary where my finger got the treatment required. I also remember that on the tram that some sympathetic adults gave me small amounts of money. From then my life was as any normal child in those days, playing various games with friends on the streets and back courts, going to primary school etc, etc.

School,
I went to primary school about 1938, the school being Camden st school with at least one "claim to fame", an MP had been educated there, his name was George Buchanan, he was MP for the Gorbals from 1922 -1948. In 1945 he was made "Under -

secretary of state for Scotland" and was made "Minister for pensions for Scotland" in 1947. He was sworn to be "Privy Council" in 1948, not bad for a Gorbals boy !! [the Privy Council is a formal body of advisers to the Sovereign in the UK.]

Strangely enough I don't remember much details of my education in Camden st school other than it was OK. I remember a newsagents shop in Caledonia rd, just round the corner from Camden st school that had an arcade machine on the wall into which put a penny to operate it. You then grasped two brass handles like door knobs [one of which turned] and an electric current passed through your body !. the more you turned the handle the greater the surge of electricity. Two or three persons could hold hands and the current passed all of those people. I believe these were battery operated, which is just as well!!. After Camden st school I went to Adelphi terrace school until I was 15. we walked to and from school in those days as they were in the locality.

Shopping,
In the 1930's and 1940's there were no supermarkets, there was no sliced bread and was not wrapped as it is now. There was no pre-packed food as we see nowadays. Cheese for example was displayed in the shop as a large portion and you indicated to the shop assistant the size of portion that you required. The assistant then cut the required portion, weighed it and charged you accordingly. Butter could also be purchased in the same manner. When rationing was introduced during WW2 the portion sizes were limited by weight of course. Children had their own ration books which were more generous than those of the adults. Pre-school children had allowances of cod liver oil and orange juice. The concentrated orange juice was okay [I personally liked it] but the cod liver oil was horrible and many children wouldn't take it, so it became available as "cod-liver oil and malt". this was a thick brown substance with the consistency I would say of honey and tasted fine. We did our shopping in local shops. Butchers, Bakers, Dairies, Fruit shops, Greengrocers, Fishmongers, Shoe shops, Clothes shops, Shoe

repairers, Cycle shops. Haberdasheries, Newsagents and Kosher Butchers for the Jewish community etc, were all in our neighbourhood or adjoining districts.

If I remember correctly, Cumberland st was one of the best streets for shopping, it was a long street and it had a great variety of shops and was always very busy. When there was a heavy fall of snow, shopkeepers cleared the snow from the pavements along the whole front of their shops using shovels, or if icy then sprinkle salt. This meant that in busy streets with lots of shops long lengths of pavement were cleared for pedestrians. There were no plastic bags back then. Your items were put into a paper bag where applicable. Other items were placed directly into your shopping bag or basket, there was no self service and there were no calculators. You asked the shop assistant for an item and the assistant wrote down the price of each item as they were given to you and then totalled the prices up and and charged you accordingly. With the exception of tinned foods there was no pre-packed food or "ready meals" only the ingredients to enable you to prepare and cook your own meals. Tea was made in a teapot using loose tea leafs, there was no tea-bags then. I also remember bottles of "Camp coffee" [coffee and chicory, which I think is still available]. There were no fast food outlets except "fish and chip" shops and some cafes who provided a snack. I remember my Father and Mother making jam and marmalade in a large copper jelly pan at home.

Wrapping,
Goods were wrapped in brown paper which was the common wrapping medium at the time. When purchasing clothes for example, the clothes were loosely folded [so not to crush them] and wrapped on brown paper and tied with string. Most homes had brown paper and string in a drawer somewhere. Brown paper was used to cover school books. I remember my Father wrapping parcels in brown paper, tying them with string and and then applying sealing wax to the knots to secure the parcel. Wax was sometimes used to secure the flap on an envelope if it contained something of importance. There was also a type of

waterproof brown paper available if my memory serves me right. It was brown on one side and black, like thin tar on the other side. This was useful for lining interwoven wicker hampers for example, which were commonly used in those days.

Carts,
I remember a person coming round our local streets with a small hand cart selling milk, buttermilk and also cream I think. You took a large jug down to the cart and the jug was filled with one of the above. I can't remember the cost but I remember taking a jug down to get buttermilk for my Father. It wasn't a flat handcart, it had a box type curved roof structure which contained urns and some measuring cups hanging from hooks. There were no ice-cream vans, flat handcarts were common then and could be hired locally usually from Mr Hyslop whose premises were in a lane just off of Cleland st, the lane may have been the back entrance. When people moved houses in those days they usually only moved a few streets away and hired these carts to carry their few belongings, making the number of trips required.

Currency,
Our currency was different then, we used Pounds , shillings and pence. 12 pence in a shilling and 20 shillings in a pound making 240 pence in a pound. We had farthing coins - one quarter the value of one penny and half-penny coins too. We also had threepence and sixpence coins, a one shilling piece, a two shilling coin and a half crown piece. We had £5 notes, £1notes, and ten shilling notes. Currency calculations were therefore a bit more difficult then. The decimal currency we use today was introduced on February 1971.

Note,
Old penny coins are still used to adjust the weights that control the time on the Great clock, in the Elizabeth tower in London commonly known as "Big Ben". big Ben is actually the clock bell [the tower was renamed the Elizabeth tower in 2012 in honour of Queen Elizabeth 11's diamond Jubilee.]

Linear measure,
The linear measure used then was yards, feet and inches not metres and centimetres. The UK joined the EEC in 1973 and were obliged under the treaty to adopt metrification within 5 years. You can see the old standard measures in stone on the front south corner of the Glasgow city chambers in George square. [the corner facing the square, I remember seeing it when I was young].

Recycling,
There was no recycling as we recognise it now but empty milk bottles were returned to the dairy or milkman for re-use. Beer bottles and soft drink bottles like lemonade for example were also returned to shops as you got a small amount of cash back on each bottle. These were the children's favourites and some weans worked hard to collect empty bottles. I've heard at one time this refund system was also used for glass jam jars.

The NHS,
There was no National health service. The NHS didn't come into being until 5th July 1948. If you required any medical help, treatment or prescriptions you had to pay for it. When you went to the Chemist you had to pay for it there and then. If you needed to visit a doctor or have him come to your home you also had to pay for it. You didn't make an appointment with the doctor, you had to go to the surgery and wait your turn. Our family doctor was Dr Percival Baird and his surgery was in Crown st which was near to our home. He was a brilliant man who had an amazing memory for the names and addresses of his patients and their previous ailments [and he didn't charge too much.]

Due to the overcrowding as I mentioned before, infectious illness and diseases spread quickly. Most children were born at home those days and all the experienced female neighbours helped with the birth. A lot of them had big families themselves, hence the experience. All of my family and friends were born at home. Lots of children died very young, one of the first things people did [if they could afford it] was take out an insurance policy which was usually a "One Penny Policy" for very young children.

Phones,
Most people did not have phones [I didn't know any] and in an emergency had to use the telephone boxes or a friendly shopkeeper. The other alternative was to use the "Police boxes" which were strategically positioned in large numbers throughout the city. [a vast network of 323 boxes at one time in Glasgow]. These were originally coloured red in Glasgow because they were maintained by the Post office but were changed to blue in the late 1960's. they looked like the ones in "Dr Who" TV series but I think they were definitely different inside !! The police constables used these boxes to phone through to their stations and when the station wanted to contact the constable a blue light would flash on and off on top of the police box. The boxes had a small flap/door on the outside which covered a mesh type grill. Members of the public cold open this flap/door and speak to a police station operator via this link. I'm also pretty certain that I saw a "break the glass" fire alarm outside a building in Crown st, I think it was the Bank of Scotland building Crown st/Rutherglen rd. The public could use this to report a fire in the vicinity.

Appendix,
My older brother told me that my Father was part of a three man Vickers machine gun team in WW1 but I thought he was a baker. ? I'm sure he told me he went to France with all the buns [sorry I couldn't resist that !!]

Overcrowding,
In the 1930's the population of Glasgow was more densely packed than any other city in Europe, one of the reasons being an expansion of industry which attracted immigrants from Ireland and the Highlands. Plans had been in place I believe since the 1930's to ease this but with the exception of Pollok which was started in the1930's and finished in 1951, the other 3 peripheral housing estates didn't start until the 1950's including

[1]Drumchapel 1951.
[2]Castlemilk 1954.
[3]Easterhouse 1955.

Each was designed to accommodate 50,000 each.

Overspill,
Glasgow council also had an "overspill"plan and people were moved away from Glasgow to designated areas outside the city. Cumbernauld was designated a new town and was built in 1955, others were East Kilbride, Irvine, Glenrothes and Livingstone.

Sweet rationing ended in February 1953 and sugar rationing ended in September that year.

The final end of all rationing did not come until 1954 with the end of it on meat and bacon.

Rationing stopped on 4th July 1954.

From **Alex Neil**.

Epilogue

So folks my book of "The streets of Gorbals past" is over, leaving behind that era of the tenements, but what happened next. ?

Well we had the ["new hooses" the "newbuilds" the "multi storeys"] which changed the face of the Gorbals that people of my generation grew up with. Of course there was trouble with lots of the "new builds" and lots of them in turn were demolished because of dampness and a multitude of other complaints.

Some of these only lasted 30 years or less and again were replaced with "newer new hooses", looking at the Gorbals now is almost totally unrecognizable from the 1940's and 50's, I like the bright coloured brick built houses that were built but not the darker coloured brick built flats. [my view].

Hardly any shops [well a few] but of course we must take into consideration that lots of people have cars and do shopping at the supermarkets whereas my generation done daily shopping [the messages] and there are online delivery services to peoples flats.

Yes I'm glad that people nowadays have inside toilets/bathrooms and some with a bit of a garden too, but to me its not the "streets of Gorbals past" although I do realise that time marches on and life changes in many ways.

What will happen to the Gorbals in the future ?, will the "old builds" that are still standing be demolished and replaced with what?. Look at the area at Laurieston [as I write in 2020] will those buildings be replaced with hotels, Picture hoose complexes, supermarkets etc ?. Will the "Star bar" tenement be left standing, will the railway tracks that used to go into St Enoch's station be demolished or built on. Will Cumberland st railway station be opened up as a Gorbals museum ?

Only time will tell my friends and I wish the very best of luck to everyone who lives to see all the changes that will happen with the advent of time. Again going back to an old saying when you talk about the Gorbals it all depends on what year you're talking about, or what decade you're talking about or even what century you're talking about. I can honestly say that I was truly glad that I lived I and was brought up in the late 1940's - 50's and 60's, again others may opt for a later era its entirely up to the readers choice.

On a personal note,
I am 72 years old now and it gives me great pleasure to write my books [mainly covering Laurieston, Gorbals, Hutchesontown and Oatlands] and donating the money to two very worthwhile causes, its just my way of saying thanks to the Soo-side for the brilliant memories. I feel I have a few more books still in me to be written but my health is not the best, and now my eyesight is deteriorating. Still I may astound the medical profession [and myself!!] and live till I'm 80.

I have put money aside for my three daughters to bring my ashes back from London and scattered outside of St Francis's in Cumberland st and Danny boy after being away for so long will be back hame at last.

Thank you for taking the time to read my book.

God bless all. x

Printed in Great Britain
by Amazon